Workshop on Continuous Vector Space Models and their Compositionality 2013

Sofia, Bulgaria
9 August 2013

ISBN: 978-1-62993-006-0

Printed from e-media with permission by:

Curran Associates, Inc.
57 Morehouse Lane
Red Hook, NY 12571

Some format issues inherent in the e-media version may also appear in this print version.

Printed by Curran Associates, Inc. (2013)

For permission requests, please contact the Association for Computational Linguistics at the address below.

Association for Computational Linguistics
209 N. Eighth Street
Stroudsburg, Pennsylvania 18360

Phone: 1-570-476-8006
Fax: 1-570-476-0860

acl@aclweb.org

Additional copies of this publication are available from:

Curran Associates, Inc.
57 Morehouse Lane
Red Hook, NY 12571 USA
Phone: 845-758-0400
Fax: 845-758-2634
Email: curran@proceedings.com
Web: www.proceedings.com

ACL 2013

51st Annual Meeting of the Association for Computational Linguistics

Proceedings of the Workshop on Continuous Vector Space Models and their Compositionality

August 9, 2013
Sofia, Bulgaria

Introduction

In recent years, there has been a growing interest in algorithms that learn a continuous representation for words, phrases, or documents. For instance, one can see latent semantic analysis (Landauer and Dumais, 1997) and latent Dirichlet allocation (Blei et al. 2003) as a mapping of documents or words into a continuous lower dimensional topic-space. Another example, continuous word vector-space models (Sahlgren 2006, Reisinger 2012, Turian et al., 2010, Huang et al., 2012) represent word meanings with vectors that capture semantic and syntactic information. These representations can be used to induce similarity measures by computing distances between the vectors, leading to many useful applications, such as information retrieval (Schuetze 1992, Manning et al., 2008), search query expansions (Jones et al., 2006), document classification (Sebastiani, 2002) and question answering (Tellex et al., 2003).

On the fundamental task of language modeling, many hard clustering approaches have been proposed such as Brown clustering (Brown et al.,1992) or exchange clustering (Martin et al.,1998). These algorithms can provide desparsification and can be seen as examples of unsupervised pre-training. However, they have not been shown to consistently outperform models based on Kneser-Ney smoothed language models which have at their core discrete n-gram representations. On the contrary, one influential proposal that uses the idea of continuous vector spaces for language modeling is that of neural language models (Bengio et al., 2003, Mikolov 2012). In these approaches, n-gram probabilities are estimated using a continuous representation of words in lieu of standard discrete representations, using a neural network that performs both the projection and the probability estimate. They report state of the art performance on several well studied language modeling datasets.

Other neural network based models that use continuous vector representations achieve state of the art performance in speech recognition applications (Schwenk, 2007, Dahl et al. 2011), multitask learning, NER and POS tagging (Collobert et al., 2011) or sentiment analysis (Socher et al. 2011). Moreover, in (Le et al., 2012), a continuous space translation model was introduced and its use in a large scale machine translation system yielded promising results in the last WMT evaluation.

Despite the success of single word vector space models, they are severely limited since they do not capture compositionality, the important quality of natural language that allows speakers to determine the meaning of a longer expression based on the meanings of its words and the rules used to combine them (Frege, 1892). This prevents them from gaining a deeper understanding of the semantics of longer phrases or sentences. Recently, there has been much progress in capturing compositionality in vector spaces, e.g., (Pado and Lapata 2007; Erk and Pado 2008; Mitchell and Lapata, 2010; Baroni and Zamparelli, 2010; Zanzotto et al., 2010; Yessenalina and Cardie, 2011; Grefenstette and Sadrzadeh 2011). The work of Socher et al. 2012 compares several of these approaches on supervised tasks and for phrases of arbitrary type and length.

Another different trend of research belongs to the family of spectral methods. The motivation in that context is that working in a continuous space allows for the design of algorithms that are not plagued with the local minima issues that discrete latent space models (e.g. HMM trained with EM) tend to suffer from (Hsu et al. 2008). In fact, this motivation strikes with the conventional justification behind vector space models from the neural network literature, which are usually motivated as a way of tackling data sparsity issues. This apparent dichotomy is interesting and has not been investigated yet. Finally, spectral methods have recently been developed for word representation learning (Dhillon et al. 2011), dependency parsing (Dhillon et al. 2012) and probabilistic context-free grammars (Cohen et al. 2012).

In this workshop, we bring together researchers who are interested in how to learn continuous vector space models, their compositionality and how to use this new kind of representation in NLP applications. The goal is to review the recent progress and propositions, to discuss the challenges, to identify promising future research directions and the next challenges for the NLP community.

Organizers:

Alexandre Allauzen, LIMSI-CNRS/Université Paris-Sud
Hugo Larochelle, Université de de Sherbrooke
Richard Socher, Stanford University
Christopher Manning, Stanford University

Program Committee:

Yoshua Bengio, Université de Montréal
Antoine Bordes, Université Technologique de Compiègne
Léon Bottou, Microsoft Research
Xavier Carreras, Universitat Politècnica de Catalunya
Shay Cohen, Columbia University
Michael Collins, Columbia University
Ronan Collobert, IDIAP Research Institute
Kevin Duh, Nara Institute of Science and Technology
Dean Foster, University of Pennsylvania
Percy Liang, Stanford University
Andriy Mnih, Gatsby Computational Neuroscience Unit
John Platt, Microsoft Research
Holger Schwenk, Université du Maine
Jason Weston, Google
Guillaume Wisniewski, LIMSI-CNRS/Université

Invited Speaker:

Xavier Carreras, Universitat Politècnica de Catalunya
Mirella Lapata, University of Edinburgh

Table of Contents

Conference Program

(9:00) Oral session 1

9:00 Opening

9:05 INVITED TALK: Structured Prediction with Low-Rank Bilinear Models by Xavier Carreras

10:00 *Vector Space Semantic Parsing: A Framework for Compositional Vector Space Models*
Jayant Krishnamurthy and Tom Mitchell

10:20 *Learning from errors: Using vector-based compositional semantics for parse reranking*
Phong Le, Willem Zuidema and Remko Scha

10:40 Coffee Break

(11:00) Poster session

A Structured Distributional Semantic Model : Integrating Structure with Semantics
Kartik Goyal, Sujay Kumar Jauhar, Huiying Li, Mrinmaya Sachan, Shashank Srivastava and Eduard Hovy

Letter N-Gram-based Input Encoding for Continuous Space Language Models
Henning Sperr, Jan Niehues and Alex Waibel

Transducing Sentences to Syntactic Feature Vectors: an Alternative Way to "Parse"?
Fabio Massimo Zanzotto and Lorenzo Dell'Arciprete

General estimation and evaluation of compositional distributional semantic models
Georgiana Dinu, Nghia The Pham and Marco Baroni

Applicative structure in vector space models
Marton Makrai, David Mark Nemeskey and Andras Kornai

Determining Compositionality of Expresssions Using Various Word Space Models and Methods
Lubomír Krčmář, Karel Ježek and Pavel Pecina

"Not not bad" is not "bad": A distributional account of negation
Karl Moritz Hermann, Edward Grefenstette and Phil Blunsom

Poster session (continued)

	Towards Dynamic Word Sense Discrimination with Random Indexing Hans Moen, Erwin Marsi and Björn Gambäck
12:30	Lunch Break
	(14:00) Oral session 2
14:00	INVITED TALK: Learning to Ground Meaning in the Visual World by Mirella Lapata
15:00	*A Generative Model of Vector Space Semantics* Jacob Andreas and Zoubin Ghahramani
15:20	*Aggregating Continuous Word Embeddings for Information Retrieval* Stephane Clinchant and Florent Perronnin
15:40	Coffee Break
16:00	*Answer Extraction by Recursive Parse Tree Descent* Christopher Malon and Bing Bai
16:20	*Recurrent Convolutional Neural Networks for Discourse Compositionality* Nal Kalchbrenner and Phil Blunsom
	(16:40) Panel Discussion

Vector Space Semantic Parsing: A Framework for Compositional Vector Space Models

Jayant Krishnamurthy
Carnegie Mellon University
5000 Forbes Avenue
Pittsburgh, PA 15213
jayantk@cs.cmu.edu

Tom M. Mitchell
Carnegie Mellon University
5000 Forbes Avenue
Pittsburgh, PA 15213
tom.mitchell@cmu.edu

Abstract

We present *vector space semantic parsing* (VSSP), a framework for learning compositional models of vector space semantics. Our framework uses Combinatory Categorial Grammar (CCG) to define a correspondence between syntactic categories and semantic representations, which are vectors and functions on vectors. The complete correspondence is a direct consequence of minimal assumptions about the semantic representations of basic syntactic categories (e.g., nouns are vectors), and CCG's tight coupling of syntax and semantics. Furthermore, this correspondence permits nonuniform semantic representations and more expressive composition operations than previous work. VSSP builds a CCG semantic parser respecting this correspondence; this semantic parser parses text into lambda calculus formulas that evaluate to vector space representations. In these formulas, the meanings of words are represented by parameters that can be trained in a task-specific fashion. We present experiments using noun-verb-noun and adverb-adjective-noun phrases which demonstrate that VSSP can learn composition operations that RNN (Socher et al., 2011) and MV-RNN (Socher et al., 2012) cannot.

1 Introduction

Vector space models represent the semantics of natural language using vectors and operations on vectors (Turney and Pantel, 2010). These models are most commonly used for individual words and short phrases, where vectors are created using distributional information from a corpus. Such models achieve impressive performance on standardized tests (Turney, 2006; Rapp, 2003), correlate well with human similarity judgments (Griffiths et al., 2007), and have been successfully applied to a number of natural language tasks (Collobert et al., 2011).

While vector space representations for individual words are well-understood, there remains much uncertainty about how to compose vector space representations for phrases out of their component words. Recent work in this area raises many important theoretical questions. For example, should all syntactic categories of words be represented as vectors, or are some categories, such as adjectives, different? Using distinct semantic representations for distinct syntactic categories has the advantage of representing the operational nature of modifier words, but the disadvantage of more complex parameter estimation (Baroni and Zamparelli, 2010). Also, does semantic composition factorize according to a constituency parse tree (Socher et al., 2011; Socher et al., 2012)? A binarized constituency parse cannot directly represent many intuitive intra-sentence dependencies, such as the dependence between a verb's subject and its object. What is needed to resolve these questions is a comprehensive theoretical framework for compositional vector space models.

In this paper, we observe that we *already have such a framework*: Combinatory Categorial Grammar (CCG) (Steedman, 1996). CCG provides a tight mapping between syntactic categories and semantic types. If we assume that nouns, sentences, and other basic syntactic categories are represented by vectors, this mapping prescribes semantic types for all other syntactic categories.[1] For example, we get that adjectives are functions from noun vectors to noun vectors, and that prepo-

[1] It is not necessary to assume that sentences are vectors. However, this assumption simplifies presentation and seems like a reasonable first step. CCG can be used similarly to explore alternative representations.

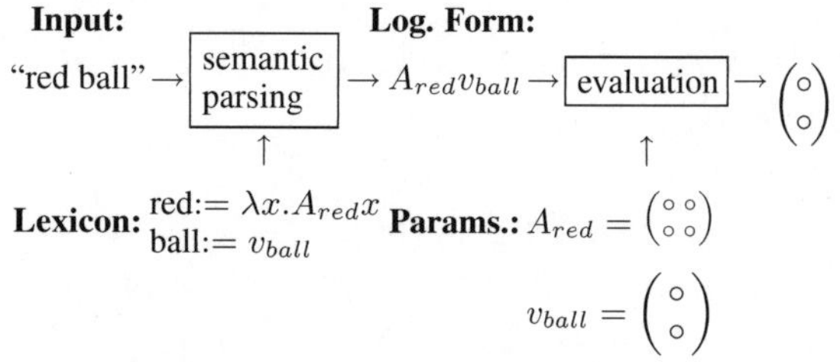

Figure 1: Overview of vector space semantic parsing (VSSP). A semantic parser first translates natural language into a logical form, which is then evaluated to produce a vector.

sitions are functions from a pair of noun vectors to a noun vector. These semantic type specifications permit a variety of different composition operations, many of which cannot be represented in previously-proposed frameworks. Parsing in CCG applies these functions to each other, naturally deriving a vector space representation for an entire phrase.

The CCG framework provides function type specifications for each word's semantics, given its syntactic category. Instantiating this framework amounts to selecting particular functions for each word. *Vector space semantic parsing* (VSSP) produces these per-word functions in a two-step process. The first step chooses a parametric functional form for each syntactic category, which contains as-yet unknown per-word and global parameters. The second step estimates these parameters using a concrete task of interest, such as predicting the corpus statistics of adjective-noun compounds. We present a stochastic gradient algorithm for this step which resembles training a neural network with backpropagation. These parameters may also be estimated in an unsupervised fashion, for example, using distributional statistics.

Figure 1 presents an overview of VSSP. The input to VSSP is a natural language phrase and a *lexicon*, which contains the parametrized functional forms for each word. These per-word representations are combined by CCG semantic parsing to produce a logical form, which is a symbolic mathematical formula for producing the vector for a phrase – for example, $A_{red}v_{ball}$ is a formula that performs matrix-vector multiplication. This formula is evaluated using learned per-word and global parameters (values for A_{red} and v_{ball}) to produce the language's vector space representation.

The contributions of this paper are threefold. First, we demonstrate how CCG provides a theoretical basis for vector space models. Second, we describe VSSP, which is a method for concretely instantiating this theoretical framework. Finally, we perform experiments comparing VSSP against other compositional vector space models. We perform two case studies of composition using noun-verb-noun and adverb-adjective-noun phrases, finding that VSSP can learn composition operations that existing models cannot. We also find that VSSP produces intuitively reasonable parameters.

2 Combinatory Categorial Grammar for Vector Space Models

Combinatory Categorial Grammar (CCG) (Steedman, 1996) is a lexicalized grammar formalism that has been used for both broad coverage syntactic parsing and semantic parsing. Like other lexicalized formalisms, CCG has a rich set of syntactic categories, which are combined using a small set of parsing operations. These syntactic categories are tightly coupled to semantic representations, and parsing in CCG simultaneously derives both a syntactic parse tree and a semantic representation for each node in the parse tree. This coupling between syntax and semantics motivates CCG's use in semantic parsing (Zettlemoyer and Collins, 2005), and provides a framework for building compositional vector space models.

2.1 Syntax

The intuition embodied in CCG is that, syntactically, words and phrases behave like functions. For example, an adjective like "red" can combine with a noun like "ball" to produce another noun, "red ball." Therefore, adjectives are naturally viewed as functions that apply to nouns and return nouns. CCG generalizes this idea by defining most parts of speech in terms of such functions.

Parts of speech in CCG are called *syntactic categories*. CCG has two kinds of syntactic categories: atomic categories and functional categories. Atomic categories are used to represent phrases that do not accept arguments. These categories include N for noun, NP for noun phrase, S for sentence, and PP for prepositional phrase. All other parts of speech are represented using functional categories. Functional categories are written as X/Y or $X\backslash Y$, where both X and Y are syn-

Part of speech	Syntactic category	Example usage	Semantic type	Example log. form
Noun	N	**person** : N	$\mathbb{R}^d$	v_{person}
Adjective	N/N_x	**good** person : N	$\langle\mathbb{R}^d, \mathbb{R}^d\rangle$	$\lambda x.A_{good}x$
Determiner	NP/N_x	**the** person : NP	$\langle\mathbb{R}^d, \mathbb{R}^d\rangle$	$\lambda x.x$
Intrans. Verb	$S\backslash NP_x$	the person **ran** : S	$\langle\mathbb{R}^d, \mathbb{R}^d\rangle$	$\lambda x.A_{ran}x + b_{ran}$
Trans. Verb	$S\backslash NP_y/NP_x$	the person **ran** home : S	$\langle\mathbb{R}^d, \langle\mathbb{R}^d, \mathbb{R}^d\rangle\rangle$	$\lambda x.\lambda y.(\mathcal{T}_{ran}x)y$
Adverb	$(S\backslash NP)\backslash(S\backslash NP)$	ran **lazily** : $S\backslash NP$	$\langle\langle\mathbb{R}^d, \mathbb{R}^d\rangle, \langle\mathbb{R}^d, \mathbb{R}^d\rangle\rangle$	$[\lambda y.Ay \rightarrow \lambda y.(\mathcal{T}_{lazy}A)y]$
	$(S\backslash NP)/(S\backslash NP)$	**lazily** ran : $S\backslash NP$	$\langle\langle\mathbb{R}^d, \mathbb{R}^d\rangle, \langle\mathbb{R}^d, \mathbb{R}^d\rangle\rangle$	$[\lambda y.Ay \rightarrow \lambda y.(\mathcal{T}_{lazy}A)y]$
	$(N/N)/(N/N)$	**very** good person : N	$\langle\langle\mathbb{R}^d, \mathbb{R}^d\rangle, \langle\mathbb{R}^d, \mathbb{R}^d\rangle\rangle$	$[\lambda y.Ay \rightarrow \lambda y.(\mathcal{T}_{very}A)y]$
Preposition	$(N\backslash N_y)/N_x$	person **in** France : N	$\langle\mathbb{R}^d, \langle\mathbb{R}^d, \mathbb{R}^d\rangle\rangle$	$\lambda x.\lambda y.(\mathcal{T}_{in}x)y$
	$(S\backslash NP_y)\backslash(S\backslash NP)_f/NP_x$	ran **in** France : $S\backslash NP$	$\langle\mathbb{R}^d, \langle\langle\mathbb{R}^d, \mathbb{R}^d\rangle, \langle\mathbb{R}^d, \mathbb{R}^d\rangle\rangle\rangle$	$\lambda x.\lambda f.\lambda y.(\mathcal{T}_{in}x)(f(y))$

Table 1: Common syntactic categories in CCG, paired with their semantic types and example logical forms. The example usage column shows phrases paired with the syntactic category that results from using the exemplified syntactic category for the bolded word. For ease of reference, each argument to a syntactic category on the left is subscripted with its corresponding semantic variable in the example logical form on the right. The variables x, y, b, v denote vectors, f denotes a function, A denotes a matrix, and $\mathcal{T}$ denotes a tensor. Subscripted variables (A_{red}) denote parameters. Functions in logical forms are specified using lambda calculus; for example $\lambda x.Ax$ is the function that accepts a (vector) argument x and returns the vector Ax. The notation $[f \rightarrow g]$ denotes the higher-order function that, given input function f, outputs function g.

tactic categories. These categories represent functions that accept an argument of category Y and return a phrase of category X. The direction of the slash defines the expected location of the argument: X/Y expects an argument on the right, and $X\backslash Y$ expects an argument on the left.[2] For example, adjectives are represented by the category N/N – a function that accepts a noun on the right and returns a noun.

The left part of Table 1 shows examples of common syntactic categories, along with example uses. Note that some intuitive parts of speech, such as prepositions, are represented by multiple syntactic categories. Each of these categories captures a different use of a preposition, in this case the noun-modifying and verb-modifying uses.

2.2 Semantics

Semantics in CCG are given by first associating a semantic type with each syntactic category. Each word in a syntactic category is then assigned a semantic representation of the corresponding semantic type. These semantic representations are known as *logical forms*. In our case, a logical form is a fragment of a formula for computing a vector space representation, containing word-specific parameters and specifying composition operations.

In order to construct a vector space model, we associate all of the atomic syntactic categories, N, NP, S, and PP, with the type $\mathbb{R}^d$. Then, the logical form for a noun like "ball" is a vector $v_{ball} \in \mathbb{R}^d$. The functional categories X/Y and $X\backslash Y$ are associated with functions from the semantic type of X to the semantic type of Y. For example, the semantic type of N/N is $\langle\mathbb{R}^d, \mathbb{R}^d\rangle$, representing the set of functions from $\mathbb{R}^d$ to $\mathbb{R}^d$.[3] This semantic type captures the same intuition as adjective-noun composition models: semantically, adjectives are functions from noun vectors to noun vectors.

The right portion of Table 1 shows semantic types for several syntactic categories, along with example logical forms. All of these mappings are a direct consequence of the assumption that all atomic categories are semantically represented by vectors. Interestingly, many of these semantic types contain functions that cannot be represented in other frameworks. For example, adverbs have type $\langle\langle\mathbb{R}^d, \mathbb{R}^d\rangle, \langle\mathbb{R}^d, \mathbb{R}^d\rangle\rangle$, representing functions that accept an adjective argument and return an adjective. In Table 1, the example logical form applies a 4-mode tensor to the adjective's matrix. Another powerful semantic type is $\langle\mathbb{R}^d, \langle\mathbb{R}^d, \mathbb{R}^d\rangle\rangle$, which corresponds to transitive verbs and prepo-

[2] As a memory aid, note that the top of the slash points in the direction of the expected argument.

[3] The notation $\langle A, B\rangle$ represents the set of functions whose domain is A and whose range is B. Somewhat confusingly, the bracketing in this notation is backward relative to the syntactic categories – the syntactic category $(N\backslash N)/N$ has semantic type $\langle\mathbb{R}^d, \langle\mathbb{R}^d, \mathbb{R}^d\rangle\rangle$, where the inner $\langle\mathbb{R}^d, \mathbb{R}^d\rangle$ corresponds to the left $(N\backslash N)$.

the	red	ball	on	the	table
NP/N	N/N	N	$(NP\backslash NP)/NP$	NP/N	N
$\lambda x.x$	$\lambda x.A_{red}x$	v_{ball}	$\lambda x.\lambda y.A_{on}x + B_{on}y$	$\lambda x.x$	v_{table}

$$N : A_{red}v_{ball} \qquad NP : v_{table}$$

$$NP : A_{red}v_{ball} \qquad NP\backslash NP : \lambda y.A_{on}v_{table} + B_{on}y$$

$$NP : A_{on}v_{table} + B_{on}A_{red}v_{ball}$$

Figure 2: Syntactic CCG parse and corresponding vector space semantic derivation.

sitions. This type represents functions from two argument vectors to an output vector, which have been curried to accept one argument vector at a time. The example logical form for this type uses a 3-mode tensor to capture interactions between the two arguments.

Note that this semantic correspondence permits a wide range of logical forms for each syntactic category. Each logical form can have an arbitrary functional form, as long as it has the correct semantic type. This flexibility permits experimentation with different composition operations. For example, adjectives can be represented nonlinearly by using a logical form such as $\lambda x.\tanh(Ax)$. Or, adjectives can be represented nonparametrically by using kernel regression to learn the appropriate function from vectors to vectors. We can also introduce simplifying assumptions, as demonstrated by the last entry in Table 1. CCG treats prepositions as modifying intransitive verbs (the category $S\backslash N$). In the example logical form, the verb's semantics are represented by the function f, the verb's subject noun is represented by y, and $f(y)$ represents the sentence vector created by composing the verb with its argument. By only operating on $f(y)$, this logical form assumes that the action of a preposition is conditionally independent of the verb f and noun y, given the sentence $f(y)$.

2.3 Lexicon

The main input to a CCG parser is a *lexicon*, which is a mapping from words to syntactic categories and logical forms. A lexicon contains entries such as:

ball := $N : v_{ball}$

red := $N/N : \lambda x.A_{red}x$

red := $N : v_{red}$

flies := $((S\backslash NP)/NP) : \lambda x.\lambda y.(T_{flies}x)y$

Each entry of the lexicon associates a word (ball) with a syntactic category (N) and a logical form (v_{ball}) giving its vector space representation. Note that a word may appear multiple times in the lexicon with distinct syntactic categories and logical forms. Such repeated entries capture words with multiple possible uses; parsing must determine the correct use in the context of a sentence.

2.4 Parsing

Parsing in CCG has two stages. First, a category for each word in the input is retrieved from the lexicon. Second, adjacent categories are iteratively combined by applying one of a small number of combinators. The most common combinator is function application:

$$X/Y : f \quad Y : g \implies X : f(g)$$
$$Y : g \quad X\backslash Y : f \implies X : f(g)$$

The function application rule states that a category of the form X/Y behaves like a function that accepts an input category Y and returns category X. The rule also derives a logical form for the result by applying the function f (the logical form for X/Y) to g (the logical form for Y). Figure 2 shows how repeatedly applying this rule produces a syntactic parse tree and logical form for a phrase. The top row of the parse represents retrieving a lexicon entry for each word in the input. Each following line represents a use of the function application combinator to syntactically and semantically combine a pair of adjacent categories. The order of these operations is ambiguous, and different orderings may result in different parses – a CCG parser's job is to find a correct ordering. The result of parsing is a syntactic category for the entire phrase, coupled with a logical form giving the phrase's vector space representation.

3 Vector Space Semantic Parsing

Vector space semantic parsing (VSSP) is an approach for constructing compositional vector space models based on the theoretical framework of the previous section. VSSP concretely instantiates CCG's syntactic/semantic correspondence by adding appropriately-typed logical forms to a syntactic CCG parser's lexicon. Parsing a sentence with this lexicon and evaluating the resulting logi-

Semantic type	Example syntactic categories	Logical form template
$\mathbb{R}^d$	N, NP, PP, S	v_w
$\langle \mathbb{R}^d, \mathbb{R}^d \rangle$	N/N, NP/N, S/S, $S\backslash NP$	$\lambda x.\sigma(A_w x)$
$\langle \mathbb{R}^d, \langle \mathbb{R}^d, \mathbb{R}^d \rangle \rangle$	$(S\backslash NP)/NP$, $(NP\backslash NP)/NP$	$\lambda x.\lambda y.\sigma((\mathcal{T}_w x)y)$
$\langle \langle \mathbb{R}^d, \mathbb{R}^d \rangle, \langle \mathbb{R}^d, \mathbb{R}^d \rangle \rangle$	$(N/N)/(N/N)$	$[\lambda y.\sigma(Ay) \rightarrow \lambda y.\sigma((\mathcal{T}_w A)y)]$

Table 2: Lexicon templates used in this paper to produce a CCG semantic parser. σ represents the sigmoid function, $\sigma(x) = \frac{e^x}{1+e^x}$.

cal form produces the sentence's vector space representation.

While it is relatively easy to devise vector space representations for individual nouns, it is more challenging to do so for the fairly complex function types licensed by CCG. VSSP defines these functions in two phases. First, we create a lexicon mapping words to parametrized logical forms. This lexicon specifies a functional form for each word, but leaves free some per-word parameters. Parsing with this lexicon produces logical forms that are essentially functions from these per-word parameters to vector space representations. Next, we train these parameters to produce good vector space representations in a task-specific fashion. Training performs stochastic gradient descent, backpropagating gradient information through the logical forms.

3.1 Producing the Parametrized Lexicon

We create a lexicon using a set of manually-constructed templates that associate each syntactic category with a parametrized logical form. Each template contains variables that are instantiated to define per-word parameters. The output of this step is a CCG lexicon which can be used in a broad coverage syntactic CCG parser (Clark and Curran, 2007) to produce logical forms for input language.[4]

Table 2 shows some templates used to create logical forms for syntactic categories. To reduce annotation effort, we define one template per semantic type, covering all syntactic categories with that type. These templates are instantiated by replacing the variable w in each logical form with the current word. For example, instantiating the second template for "red" produces the logical form $\lambda x.\sigma(A_{red}x)$, where A_{red} is a matrix of parameters.

[4]In order to use the lexicon in an existing parser, the generated syntactic categories must match the parser's syntactic categories. Then, to produce a logical form for a sentence, simply syntactically parse the sentence, generate logical forms for each input word, and retrace the syntactic derivation while applying the corresponding semantic operations to the logical forms.

Note that Table 2 is a only starting point – devising appropriate functional forms for each syntactic category is an empirical question that requires further research. We use these templates in our experiments (Section 4), suggesting that they are a reasonable first step. More complex data sets will require more complex logical forms. For example, to use high-dimensional vectors, all matrices and tensors will have to be made low rank. Another possible improvement is to tie the parameters for a single word across related syntactic categories (such as the transitive and intransitive forms of a verb).

3.2 Training the Logical Form Parameters

The training problem in VSSP is to optimize the logical form parameters to best perform a given task. Our task formulation subsumes both classification and regression: we assume the input is a logical form, and the output is a vector. Given a data set of this form, training can be performed using stochastic gradient descent in a fashion similar to backpropagation in a neural network.

The data set for training consists of tuples, $\{(\ell^i, y^i)\}_{i=1}^n$, where ℓ is a logical form and y is a label vector representing the expected task output. Each logical form ℓ is treated as a function from parameter vectors θ to vectors in $\mathbb{R}^d$. For example, the logical form $A_{red}v_{ball}$ is a function from A_{red} and v_{ball} to a vector. We use θ to denote the set of all parameters; for example, $\theta = \{A_{red}, v_{ball}\}$. We further assume a loss function $\mathcal{L}$ defined over pairs of label vectors. The training problem is therefore to minimize the objective:

$$O(\theta) = \sum_{i=1}^{n} \mathcal{L}(y^i, g(\ell^i(\theta)) + \frac{\lambda}{2}||\theta||^2$$

Above, g represents a global postprocessing function which is applied to the output of VSSP to make a task-specific prediction. This function may also be parametrized, but we suppress these parameters for simplicity. As a concrete example, consider a classification task (as in our evaluation). In this case, y represents a target distribution over labels, $\mathcal{L}$ is the KL divergence between the predicted and target distributions, and g represents a softmax classifier.

We optimize the objective O by running stochastic gradient descent. The gradients of the parameters θ can be computed by iteratively applying the chain rule to ℓ, which procedurally resembles performing backpropagation in a neural network (Rumelhart et al., 1988; Goller and Küchler, 1996).

4 Comparing Models of Semantic Composition

This section compares the expressive power of VSSP to previous work. An advantage of VSSP is its ability to assign complex logical forms to categories like adverbs and transitive verbs. This section examines cases where such complex logical forms are necessary, using synthetic data sets. Specifically, we create simple data sets mimicking expected forms of composition in noun-verb-noun and adverb-adjective-noun phrases. VSSP is able to learn the correct composition operations for these data sets, but previously proposed models cannot.

We compare VSSP against RNN (Socher et al., 2011) and MV-RNN (Socher et al., 2012), two recursive neural network models which factorize composition according to a binarized constituency parse tree. The RNN model represents the semantics of each parse tree node using a single vector, while the MV-RNN represents each node using both a matrix and a vector. These representations seem sufficient for adjectives and nouns, but it is unclear how they generalize to other natural language constructions.

In these experiments, each model is used to map an input phrase to a vector, which is used to train a softmax classifier that predicts the task output. For VSSP, we use the lexicon templates from Table 2. All nouns are represented as two-dimensional vectors, and all matrices and tensors are full rank. The parameters of each model (i.e., the per-word vectors, matrices and tensors) and the softmax classifier are trained as described in Section 3.2.

4.1 Propositional Logic

The propositional logic experiment examines the impact of VSSP's representation of transitive verbs. VSSP directly represents these verbs as two-argument functions, allowing it to learn operations with complex interactions between both

false and false	0,1	false or false	0,1	false xor false	0,1
true and false	0,1	true or false	1,0	true xor false	1,0
false and true	0,1	false or true	1,0	false xor true	1,0
true and true	1,0	true or true	1,0	true xor true	0,1

Table 3: Data for propositional logic experiment.

Composition Formula	KL divergence
RNN	0.44
MV-RNN	0.12
VSSP	0.01

Table 4: Training error on the propositional logic data set. VSSP achieves zero error because its verb representation can learn arbitrary logical operations.

arguments. In contrast, the RNN and MV-RNN models learn a set of global weights which are used to combine the verb with its arguments. The functional forms of these models limit the kinds of interactions that can be captured by verbs.

We evaluated the learnability of argument interactions using the simple data set shown in Table 3. In this data set, the words "and," "or," and "xor" are treated as transitive verbs, while "true" and "false" are nouns. The goal is to predict the listed truth values, which are represented as two-dimensional distributions over true and false.

Table 4 shows the training error of each model on this data set, measured in terms of KL divergence between the model's predictions and the true values. VSSP achieves essentially zero training error because its 3-mode tensor representation of transitive verbs is trivially able to learn arbitrary logical operations. RNN and MV-RNN can learn each logical operation independently, but cannot learn all three at the same time – this phenomenon occurs because XOR requires different global weight matrices than AND/OR. As a result, these models learn both AND and OR, but fail to learn XOR. This result suggests that much of the learning in these models occurs in the global weight matrices, while the verb representations can have only limited influence.

Although this data set is synthetic, the interaction given by XOR seems necessary to represent real verbs. To learn AND and OR, the arguments need not interact – it is sufficient to detect a set of appropriate subject and object arguments, then threshold the number of such arguments. This information is essentially type constraints for the subject and object of a verb. However, type constraints are insufficient for real verbs. For example, consider the verb "eats." All animals eat and

very big elephant	1,0	very big mouse	0.3,0.7
pretty big elephant	0.9,0.1	pretty big mouse	0.2,0.8
pretty small elephant	0.8,0.2	pretty small mouse	0.1,0.9
very small elephant	0.7,0.3	very small mouse	0,1

Table 5: Data for adverb-adjective-noun composition experiment. Higher first dimension values represent larger objects.

Composition Model	KL divergence
RNN	0.10
MV-RNN	0.10
VSSP	0.00

Table 6: Training error of each composition model on the adverb-adjective-noun experiment.

can be eaten, but not all animals eat all other animals; whether or not "X eats Y" is true depends on an interaction between X and Y.

4.2 Adverb-Adjective-Noun Composition

Adverbs can enhance or attenuate the properties of adjectives, which in turn can enhance or attenuate the properties of nouns. The adverb-adjective-noun experiment compares each model's ability to learn these effects using a synthetic object size data set, shown in Table 5. The task is to predict the size of each described object, which is represented as a two-dimensional distribution over big and small. The challenge of this data set is that an adverb's impact on size depends on the adjective being modified – a very big elephant is *bigger* than a big elephant, but a very small elephant is *smaller* than a small elephant. Note that this task is more difficult than adverb-adjective composition (Socher et al., 2012), since in this task the adverb has to enhance/attenuate the enhancing/attenuating properties of an adjective.

Table 6 shows the training error of each model on this data set. VSSP achieves zero training error because its higher-order treatment of adverbs allows it to accurately represent their enhancing and attenuating effects. However, none of the other models are capable of representing these effects. This result is unsurprising, considering that the RNN and MV-RNN models essentially *add* the adverb and adjective parameters using a learned linear operator (followed by a nonlinearity). Such additive combination forces adverbs to have a consistent direction of effect on the size of the noun, which is incompatible with the desired enhancing and attenuating behavior.

Examining VSSP's learned parameters clearly demonstrates its ability to learn enhancing and

"elephant" $\begin{pmatrix} 1.6 \\ -0.1 \end{pmatrix}$ "mouse" $\begin{pmatrix} -0.1 \\ 1.6 \end{pmatrix}$

"small" $\begin{pmatrix} 0.22 & 0 \\ 0 & 1.7 \end{pmatrix}$ "big" $\begin{pmatrix} 1.7 & -1.1 \\ 0 & 0.22 \end{pmatrix}$

"very small" $\begin{pmatrix} 0.25 & -.12 \\ -1.34 & 2.3 \end{pmatrix}$ "very big" $\begin{pmatrix} 2.3 & -1.34 \\ -0.12 & 0.25 \end{pmatrix}$

Figure 3: Parameters for nouns, adjectives and adjective phrases learned by VSSP. When the adverb "very" is applied to "small" and "big," it enhances their effect on a modified noun.

attenuating phenomena. Figure 3 demonstrates VSSP's learned treatment of "very." In the figure, a high first dimension value represents a large object, while a high second dimension value represents a small object; hence the vectors for elephant and mouse show that, by default, elephants are larger than mice. Similarly, the matrices for big and small scale up the appropriate dimension while shrinking the other dimension. Finally, we show the computed matrices for "very big" and "very small" – this operation is possible because these phrases have an adjective's syntactic category, N/N. These matrices have the same direction of effect as their unenhanced versions, but produce a larger scaling in that direction.

5 Related Work

Several models for compositionality in vector spaces have been proposed in recent years. Much work has focused on evaluating composition operations for word pairs (Mitchell and Lapata, 2010; Widdows, 2008). Many operations have been proposed, including various combinations of addition, multiplication, and linear operations (Mitchell and Lapata, 2008), holographic reduced representations (Plate, 1991) and others (Kintsch, 2001). Other work has used regression to train models for adjectives in adjective-noun phrases (Baroni and Zamparelli, 2010; Guevara, 2010). All of this work is complementary to ours, as these composition operations can be used within VSSP by appropriately choosing the logical forms in the lexicon.

A few comprehensive frameworks for composition have also been proposed. One approach is to take tensor outer products of word vectors, following syntactic structure (Clark and Pulman, 2007). However, this approach results in differently-shaped tensors for different grammatical structures. An improvement of this framework uses a categorial grammar to ensure that similarly-typed objects lie in the same vector space (Clark et al., 2008; Coecke et al., 2010; Grefenstette and Sadrzadeh, 2011). VSSP generalizes this work by allowing nonlinear composition operations and considering supervised parameter estimation. Several recent neural network models implicitly use a framework which assumes that composition factorizes according to a binarized constituency parse, and that words and phrases have uniform semantic representations (Socher et al., 2011; Socher et al., 2012). Notably, Hermann and Blunsom (2013) instantiate such a framework using CCG. VSSP generalizes these approaches, as they can be implemented within VSSP by choosing appropriate logical forms. Furthermore, our experiments demonstrate that VSSP can learn composition operations that cannot be learned by these approaches.

The VSSP framework uses semantic parsing to define a compositional vector space model. Semantic parsers typically map sentences to logical semantic representations (Zelle and Mooney, 1996; Kate and Mooney, 2006), with many systems using CCG as the parsing formalism (Zettlemoyer and Collins, 2005; Kwiatkowski et al., 2011; Krishnamurthy and Mitchell, 2012). Although previous work has focused on logical semantics, it has demonstrated that semantic parsing is an elegant technique for specifying models of compositional semantics. In this paper, we show how to use semantic parsing to produce compositional models of vector space semantics.

6 Discussion and Future Work

We present vector space semantic parsing (VSSP), a general framework for building compositional models of vector space semantics. Our framework is based on Combinatory Categorial Grammar (CCG), which defines a correspondence between syntactic categories and semantic types representing vectors and functions on vectors. A model in VSSP instantiates this mapping in a CCG semantic parser. This semantic parser parses natural language into logical forms, which are in turn evaluated to produce vector space representations. We further propose a method for constructing such a semantic parser using a small number of logical form templates and task-driven estimation of per-word parameters. Synthetic data experiments show that VSSP's treatment of adverbs and transitive verbs can learn more functions than prior work.

An interesting aspect of VSSP is that it highlights cases where propositional semantics seem superior to vector space semantics. For example, compare "the ball that I threw" and "I threw the ball." We expect the semantics of these phrases to be closely related, differing only in that one phrase refers to the ball, while the other refers to the throwing event. Therefore, our goal is to define a logical form for "that" which appropriately relates the semantics of the above expressions. It is easy to devise such a logical form in propositional semantics, but difficult in vector space semantics. Producing vector space solutions to such problems is an area for future work.

Another direction for future work is joint training of both the semantic parser and vector space representations. Our proposed approach of adding logical forms to a broad CCG coverage parser has the advantage of allowing VSSP to be applied to general natural language. However, using the syntactic parses from this parser may not result in the best possible factorization of semantic composition. Jointly training the semantic parser and the vector space representations may lead to better models of semantic composition.

We also plan to apply VSSP to real data sets. We have made some progress applying VSSP to SemEval Task 8, learning to extract relations between nominals (Hendrickx et al., 2010). Although our work thus far is preliminary, we have found that the generality of VSSP makes it easy to experiment with different models of composition. To swap between models, we simply modify the CCG lexicon templates – all of the remaining infrastructure is unchanged. Such preliminary results suggest the power of VSSP as a general framework for learning vector space models.

Acknowledgments

This research has been supported in part by DARPA under award FA8750-13-2-0005, and in part by a gift from Google. We thank Matt Gardner, Justin Betteridge, Brian Murphy, Partha Talukdar, Alona Fyshe and the anonymous reviewers for their helpful comments.

References

Marco Baroni and Roberto Zamparelli. 2010. Nouns are vectors, adjectives are matrices: representing adjective-noun constructions in semantic space. In

Proceedings of the 2010 Conference on Empirical Methods in Natural Language Processing.

Stephen Clark and James R. Curran. 2007. Wide-coverage efficient statistical parsing with CCG and log-linear models. *Computational Linguistics*, 33(4):493–552.

Stephen Clark and Stephen Pulman. 2007. Combining symbolic and distributional models of meaning. In *Proceedings of AAAI Spring Symposium on Quantum Interaction*.

Stephen Clark, Bob Coecke, and Mehrnoosh Sadrzadeh. 2008. A compositional distributional model of meaning. *Proceedings of the Second Symposium on Quantum Interaction*.

Bob Coecke, Mehrnoosh Sadrzadeh, and Stephen Clark. 2010. Mathematical Foundations for a Compositional Distributed Model of Meaning. *Lambek Festschirft, Linguistic Analysis*, 36.

Ronan Collobert, Jason Weston, Léon Bottou, Michael Karlen, Koray Kavukcuoglu, and Pavel Kuksa. 2011. Natural language processing (almost) from scratch. *Journal of Machine Learning Research*, 12:2493–2537, November.

Christoph Goller and Andreas Küchler. 1996. Learning task-dependent distributed representations by backpropagation through structure. In *Proceedings of the International Conference on Neural Networks (ICNN-96)*, pages 347–352. IEEE.

Edward Grefenstette and Mehrnoosh Sadrzadeh. 2011. Experimental support for a categorical compositional distributional model of meaning. In *Proceedings of the Conference on Empirical Methods in Natural Language Processing*.

Thomas L. Griffiths, Joshua B. Tenenbaum, and Mark Steyvers. 2007. Topics in semantic representation. *Psychological Review 114*.

Emiliano Guevara. 2010. A regression model of adjective-noun compositionality in distributional semantics. In *Proceedings of the 2010 Workshop on Geometrical Models of Natural Language Semantics*.

Iris Hendrickx, Su Nam Kim, Zornitsa Kozareva, Preslav Nakov, Diarmuid Ó. Séaghdha, Sebastian Padó, Marco Pennacchiotti, Lorenza Romano, and Stan Szpakowicz. 2010. Semeval-2010 task 8: Multi-way classification of semantic relations between pairs of nominals. In *Proceedings of the 5th International Workshop on Semantic Evaluation*.

Karl Moritz Hermann and Phil Blunsom. 2013. The Role of Syntax in Vector Space Models of Compositional Semantics. In *Proceedings of the 51st Annual Meeting of the Association for Computational Linguistics*.

Rohit J. Kate and Raymond J. Mooney. 2006. Using string-kernels for learning semantic parsers. In *21st International Conference on Computational Linguistics and 44th Annual Meeting of the Association for Computational Linguistics, Proceedings of the Conference*.

Walter Kintsch. 2001. Predication. *Cognitive Science*, 25(2).

Jayant Krishnamurthy and Tom M. Mitchell. 2012. Weakly supervised training of semantic parsers. In *Proceedings of the 2012 Joint Conference on Empirical Methods in Natural Language Processing and Computational Natural Language Learning*.

Tom Kwiatkowski, Luke Zettlemoyer, Sharon Goldwater, and Mark Steedman. 2011. Lexical generalization in ccg grammar induction for semantic parsing. In *Proceedings of the Conference on Empirical Methods in Natural Language Processing*.

Jeff Mitchell and Mirella Lapata. 2008. Vector-based models of semantic composition. In *Proceedings of ACL-08: HLT*.

Jeff Mitchell and Mirella Lapata. 2010. Composition in Distributional Models of Semantics. *Cognitive Science*, 34(8):1388–1429.

Tony Plate. 1991. Holographic reduced representations: convolution algebra for compositional distributed representations. In *Proceedings of the 12th International Joint Conference on Artificial Intelligence - Volume 1*.

Reinhard Rapp. 2003. Word sense discovery based on sense descriptor dissimilarity. In *Proceedings of the Ninth Machine Translation Summit*.

David E. Rumelhart, Geoffrey E. Hinton, and Ronald J. Williams. 1988. Neurocomputing: foundations of research. chapter Learning internal representations by error propagation.

Richard Socher, Jeffrey Pennington, Eric H. Huang, Andrew Y. Ng, and Christopher D. Manning. 2011. Semi-Supervised Recursive Autoencoders for Predicting Sentiment Distributions. In *Proceedings of the 2011 Conference on Empirical Methods in Natural Language Processing (EMNLP)*.

Richard Socher, Brody Huval, Christopher D. Manning, and Andrew Y. Ng. 2012. Semantic Compositionality Through Recursive Matrix-Vector Spaces. In *Proceedings of the 2012 Conference on Empirical Methods in Natural Language Processing (EMNLP)*.

Mark Steedman. 1996. *Surface Structure and Interpretation*. The MIT Press.

Peter D. Turney and Patrick Pantel. 2010. From frequency to meaning: vector space models of semantics. *Journal of Artificial Intelligence Research*, 37(1), January.

Peter D. Turney. 2006. Similarity of semantic relations. *Computational Linguistics*, 32(3), September.

Dominic Widdows. 2008. Semantic vector products: Some initial investigations. In *Proceedings of the Second AAAI Symposium on Quantum Interaction*.

John M. Zelle and Raymond J. Mooney. 1996. Learning to parse database queries using inductive logic programming. In *Proceedings of the thirteenth national conference on Artificial Intelligence*.

Luke S. Zettlemoyer and Michael Collins. 2005. Learning to map sentences to logical form: structured classification with probabilistic categorial grammars. In *UAI '05, Proceedings of the 21st Conference in Uncertainty in Artificial Intelligence*.

Learning from errors: Using vector-based compositional semantics for parse reranking

Phong Le, Willem Zuidema, Remko Scha
Institute for Logic, Language, and Computation
University of Amsterdam, the Netherlands
{p.le,zuidema,scha}@uva.nl

Abstract

In this paper, we address the problem of how to use semantics to improve syntactic parsing, by using a hybrid reranking method: a k-best list generated by a symbolic parser is reranked based on parse-correctness scores given by a compositional, connectionist classifier. This classifier uses a recursive neural network to construct vector representations for phrases in a candidate parse tree in order to classify it as syntactically correct or not. Tested on the WSJ23, our method achieved a statistically significant improvement of 0.20% on F-score (2% error reduction) and 0.95% on exact match, compared with the state-of-the-art Berkeley parser. This result shows that vector-based compositional semantics can be usefully applied in syntactic parsing, and demonstrates the benefits of combining the symbolic and connectionist approaches.

1 Introduction

Following the idea of compositionality in formal semantics, compositionality in vector-based semantics is also based on the *principle of compositionality*, which says that "The meaning of a whole is a function of the meanings of the parts and of the way they are syntactically combined" (Partee, 1995). According to this principle, composing the meaning of a phrase or sentence requires a syntactic parse tree, which is, in most current systems, given by a statistical parser. This parser, in turn, is trained on syntactically annotated corpora.

However, there are good reasons to also consider information flowing in the opposite direction: from semantics to syntactic parsing. Performance of parsers trained and evaluated on the Penn WSJ treebank has reached a plateau, as many ambiguities cannot be resolved by syntactic information alone. Further improvements in parsing may depend on the use of additional sources of information, including semantics. In this paper, we study the use of semantics for syntactic parsing.

The currently dominant approach to syntactic parsing is based on extracting symbolic grammars from a treebank and defining appropriate probability distributions over the parse trees that they license (Charniak, 2000; Collins, 2003; Klein and Manning, 2003; Petrov et al., 2006; Bod et al., 2003; Sangati and Zuidema, 2011; van Cranenburgh et al., 2011). An alternative approach, with promising recent developments (Socher et al., 2010; Collobert, 2011), is based on using neural networks. In the present paper, we combine the 'symbolic' and 'connectionist' approaches through reranking: a symbolic parser is used to generate a k-best list which is then reranked based on parse-correctness scores given by a connectionist compositional-semantics-based classifier.

The idea of reranking is motivated by analyses of the results of state-of-the-art symbolic parsers such as the Brown and Berkeley parsers, which have shown that there is still considerable room for improvement: oracle results on 50-best lists display a dramatic improvement in accuracy (96.08% vs. 90.12% on F-score and 65.56% vs. 37.22% on exact match with the Berkeley parser). This suggests that parsers that rely on syntactic corpus-statistics, though not sufficient by themselves, may very well serve as a basis for systems that integrate other sources of information by means of reranking.

One important complementary source of information is the semantic plausibility of the constituents of the syntactically viable parses. The exploitation of that kind of information is the topic of the research we report here. In this work, we follow up on a proposal by Mark Steedman

(1999), who suggested that the realm of semantics lacks the clearcut hierarchical structures that characterise syntax, and that semantic information may therefore be profitably treated by the classificatory mechanisms of neural nets—while the treatment of syntactic structures is best left to symbolic parsers. We thus developed a hybrid system, which parses its input sentences on the basis of a symbolic probabilistic grammar, and reranks the candidate parses based on scores given by a neural network.

Our work is inspired by the work of Socher and colleagues (2010; 2011). They proposed a parser using a recursive neural network (RNN) for encoding parse trees, representing phrases in a vector space, and scoring them. Their experimental result (only 1.92% lower than the Stanford parser on unlabelled bracket F-score for sentences up to a length of 15 words) shows that an RNN is expressive enough for syntactic parsing. Additionally, their qualitative analysis indicates that the learnt phrase features capture some aspects of phrasal semantics, which could be useful to resolve semantic ambiguity that syntactical information alone can not. Our work in this paper differs from their work in that we replace the parsing task by a reranking task, and thus reduce the object space significantly to a set of parses generated by a symbolic parser rather than the space of all parse trees. As a result, we can apply our method to sentences which are much longer than 15 words.

Reranking a k-best list is not a new idea. Collins (2000), Charniak and Johnson (2005), and Johnson and Ural (2010) have built reranking systems with performances that are state-of-the-art. In order to achieve such high F-scores, those rerankers rely on a very large number of features selected on the basis of expert knowledge. Unlike them, our feature set is selected automatically, yet the reranker achieved a statistically significant improvement on both F-score and exact match.

Closest to our work is Menchetti et al. (2005) and Socher et al. (2013): both also rely on symbolic parsers to reduce the search space and use RNNs to score candidate parses. However, our work differs in the way the feature set for reranking is selected. In their methods, only the score at the tree root is considered whereas in our method the scores at all internal nodes are taken into account. Selecting the feature set like that gives us a flexible way to deal with errors accumulated from the leaves to the root.

Figure 1 shows a diagram of our method. First, a parser (in this paper: the Berkeley parser) is used to generate k-best lists of the Wall Street Journal (WSJ) sections 02-21. Then, all parse trees in these lists and the WSJ02-21 are preprocessed by marking head words, binarising, and performing error-annotation (Section 2). After that, we use the annotated trees to train our parse-correctness classifier (Section 3). Finally, those trees and the classifier are used to train the reranker (Section 4).

2 Experimental Setup

The experiments presented in this paper have the following setting. We use the WSJ corpus with the standard splits: sections 2-21 for training, section 22 for development, and section 23 for testing. The latest implementation (version 1.7) of the Berkeley parser[1] (Petrov et al., 2006) is used for generating 50-best lists. We mark head words and binarise all trees in the WSJ and the 50-best lists as in Subsection 2.1, and annotate them as in Subsection 2.2 (see Figure 2).

2.1 Preprocessing Trees

We preprocess trees by marking head words and binarising the trees. For head word marking, we used the head finding rules of Collins (1999) which are implemented in the Stanford parser. To binarise a k-ary branching, e.g. $P \rightarrow C_1 \ldots H \ldots C_k$ where H is the top label of the head constituent, we use the following method. If H is not the left-most child, then

$$P \rightarrow C_1\ @P\ ;\ @P \rightarrow C_2 \ldots H \ldots C_k$$

otherwise,

$$P \rightarrow @P\ C_k\ ;\ @P \rightarrow H \ldots C_{k-1}$$

where $@P$, which is called extra-P, now is the head of P. We then apply this transformation again on the children until we reach terminal nodes. In this way, we ensure that every internal node has one head word.

2.2 Error Annotation

We annotate nodes (as *correct* or *incorrect*) as follows. Given a parse tree T in a 50-best list and a corresponding gold-standard tree G in the WSJ,

[1] https://code.google.com/p/berkeleyparser

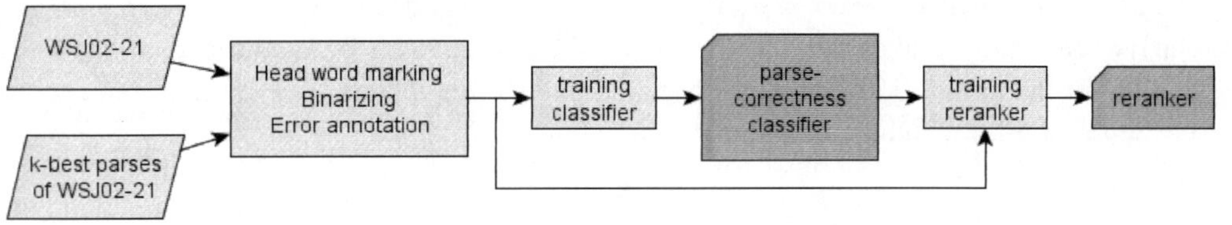

Figure 1: An overview of our method.

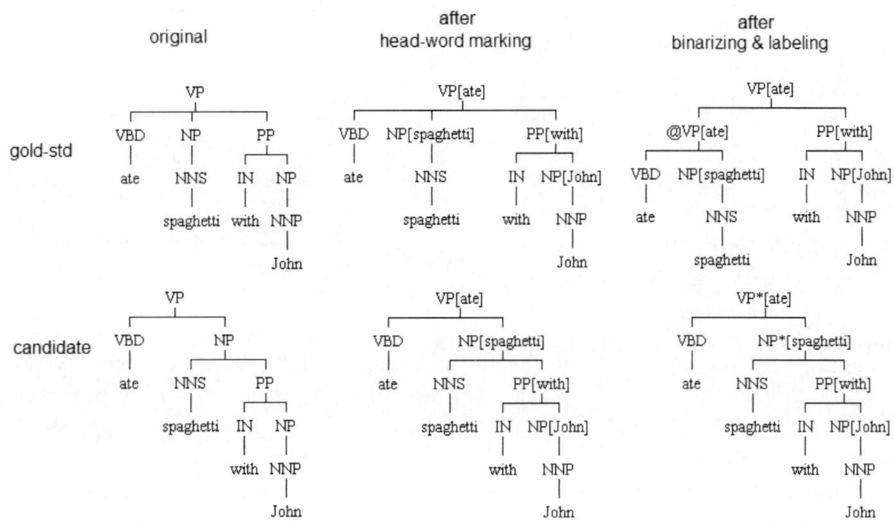

Figure 2: Example for preprocessing trees. Nodes marked with (*) are labelled *incorrect* whereas the other nodes are labelled *correct*.

we first attempt to align their terminal nodes according to the following criterion: a terminal node t is aligned to a terminal node g if they are at the same position counting from-left-to-right and they have the same label. Then, a non-terminal node $P[w_h]$ with children $C_1, ..., C_k$ is aligned to a gold-standard non-terminal node $P^*[w_h^*]$ with children $C_1^*, ..., C_l^*$ ($1 \leq k, l \leq 2$ in our case) if they have the same word head, the same syntactical category, and their children are all aligned in the right order. In other words, the following conditions have to be satisfied

$$P = P^* \; ; \; w_h = w_h^* \; ; \; k = l$$
$$C_i \textit{ is aligned to } C_i^*, \text{ for all } i = 1..k$$

Aligned nodes are annotated as *correct* whereas the other nodes are annotated as *incorrect*.

3 Parse-Correctness Classification

This section describes how a neural network is used to construct vector representations for phrases given parse trees and to identify if those trees are syntactically correct or not. In order to encode tree structures, we use an RNN[2] (see Figure 3 and Figure 4) which is similar to the one proposed by Socher and colleagues (2010). However, unlike their RNN, our RNN can handle unary branchings, and also takes head words and syntactic tags as input. It is worth noting that, although we can use some transformation to remove unary branchings, handling them is helpful in our case because the system avoids dealing with so many syntactic tags that would result from the transfor-

[2]The first neural-network approach attempting to operate and represent compositional, recursive structure is the Recursive Auto-Associative Memory network (RAAM), which was proposed by Pollack (1988). In order to encode a binary tree, the RAAM network contains three layers: an input layer for two daughter nodes, a hidden layer for their parent node, and an output layer for their reconstruction. Training the network is to minimise the reconstruction error such that we can decode the information captured in the hidden layer to the original tree form. Our RNN differs from the RAAM network in that its output layer is not for reconstruction but for classification.

mation. In addition, using a new set of weight matrices for unary branchings makes our RNN more expressive without facing the problem of sparsity thanks to a large number of unary branchings in the treebank.

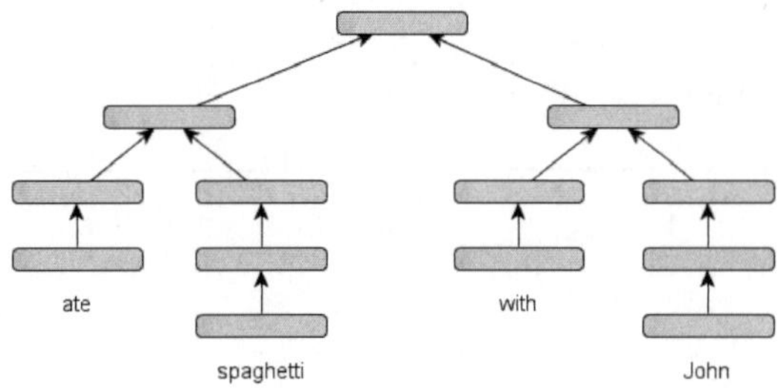

Figure 3: An RNN attached to the parse tree shown in the top-right of Figure 2. All unary branchings share a set of weight matrices, and all binary branchings share another set of weight matrices (see Figure 4).

An RNN processes a tree structure by repeatedly applying itself at each internal node. Thus, walking bottom-up from the leaves of the tree to the root, we compute for every node a vector based on the vectors of its children. Because of this process, those vectors have to have the same dimension. It is worth noting that, because information at leaves, i.e. lexical semantics, is composed according to a given syntactic parse, what a vector at each internal node captures is some aspects of compositional semantics of the corresponding phrase. In the remainder of this subsection, we describe in more detail how to construct compositional vector-based semantics geared towards the parse-correctness classification task.

Similar to Socher et al. (2010), and Collobert (2011), given a string of words $(w_1, ..., w_l)$, we first compute a string of vectors $(x_1, ..., x_l)$ representing those words by using a look-up table (i.e., word embeddings) $L \in \mathbb{R}^{n \times |V|}$, where $|V|$ is the size of the vocabulary and n is the dimensionality of the vectors. This look-up table L could be seen as a storage of lexical semantics where each column is a vector representation of a word. Hence, let b_i be the binary representation of word w_i (i.e., all of the entries of b_i are zero except the one corresponding to the index of the word in the dictionary), then

$$x_i = Lb_i \in \mathbb{R}^n \quad (1)$$

We also encode syntactic tags by binary vectors but put an extra bit at the end of each vector to mark if the corresponding tag is extra or not (i.e., $@P$ or P).

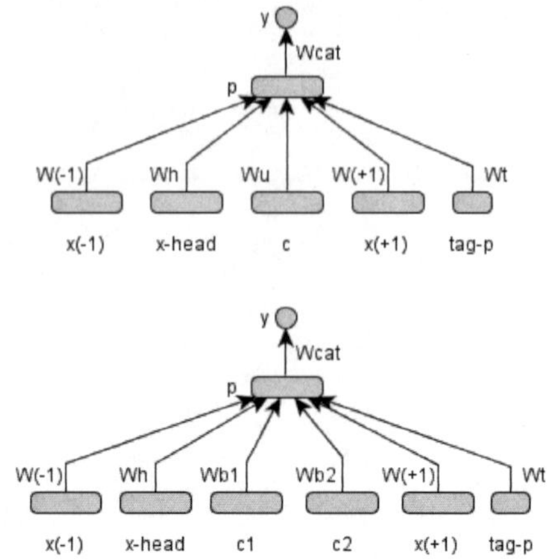

Figure 4: Details about our RNN for a unary branching (top) and a binary branching (bottom). The bias is not shown for the simplicity.

Then, given a unary branching $P[w_h] \to C$, we can compute the vector at the node P by (see Figure 4-top)

$$p = f\big(W_u c + W_h x_h + W_{-1} x_{-1} + W_{+1} x_{+1} + W_t t_p + b_u\big)$$

where c, x_h are vectors representing the child C and the head word, x_{-1}, x_{+1} are the left and right neighbouring words of P, t_p encodes the syntactic tag of P, $W_u, W_h, W_{-1}, W_{+1} \in \mathbb{R}^{n \times n}$, $W_t \in \mathbb{R}^{n \times (|T|+1)}$, $|T|$ is the size of the set of syntactic tags, $b_u \in \mathbb{R}^n$, and f can be any activation function ($tanh$ is used in this case). With a binary branching $P[w_h] \to C_1\ C_2$, we simply change the way the children's vectors added (see Figure 4-bottom)

$$p = f\big(W_{b1} c_1 + W_{b2} c_2 + W_h x_h + W_{-1} x_{-1} + W_{+1} x_{+1} + W_t t_p + b_b\big)$$

Finally, we put a sigmoid neural unit on the top of each internal node (except pre-terminal nodes because we are not concerned with POS-tagging) to detect the correctness of the subparse tree rooted at that node

$$y = sigmoid(W_{cat} p + b_{cat}) \quad (2)$$

where $W_{cat} \in \mathbb{R}^{1 \times n}, b_{cat} \in \mathbb{R}$.

3.1 Learning

The error on a parse tree is computed as the sum of classification errors of all subparses. Hence, the learning is to minimise the objective

$$J(\theta) = \frac{1}{N}\sum_{T}\sum_{(y(\theta),t)\in T}\frac{1}{2}(t - y(\theta))^2 + \lambda\|\theta\|^2 \quad (3)$$

where θ are the model parameters, N is the number of trees, λ is a regularisation hyperparameter, T is a parse tree, $y(\theta)$ is given by Equation 2, and t is the class of the corresponding subparse ($t = 1$ means *correct*). The gradient $\frac{\partial J}{\partial \theta}$ is computed efficiently thanks to backpropagation through the structure (Goller and Kuchler, 1996). L-BFGS (Liu and Nocedal, 1989) is used to minimise the objective function.

3.2 Experiments

We implemented our classifier in Torch7[3] (Collobert et al., 2011a), which is a powerful Matlab-like environment for machine learning. In order to save time, we only trained the classifier on 10-best parses of WSJ02-21. The training phase took six days on a computer with 16 800MHz CPU-cores and 256GB RAM. The word embeddings given by Collobert et al. (2011b)[4] were used as L in Equation 1. Note that these embeddings, which are the result of training a language model neural network on the English Wikipedia and Reuters, have been shown to capture many interesting semantic similarities between words.

We tested the classifier on the development set WSJ22, which contains $1,700$ sentences, and measured the performance in positive rate and negative rate

$$\text{pos-rate} = \frac{\#\text{true\_pos}}{\#\text{true\_pos} + \#\text{false\_neg}}$$

$$\text{neg-rate} = \frac{\#\text{true\_neg}}{\#\text{true\_neg} + \#\text{false\_pos}}$$

The positive/negative rate tells us the rate at which positive/negative examples are correctly labelled *positive/negative*. In order to achieve high performance in the reranking task, the classifier must have a high positive rate as well as a high negative rate. In addition, percentage of positive examples is also interesting because it shows the unbalancedness of the data. Because the accuracy is not a reliable measurement when the dataset is highly unbalanced, we do not show it here. Table 1, Figure 5, and Figure 6 show the classification results.

	pos-rate (%)	neg-rate (%)	%-Pos
gold-std	75.31	-	1
1-best	90.58	64.05	71.61
10-best	93.68	71.24	61.32
50-best	95.00	73.76	56.43

Table 1: Classification results on the WSJ22 and the k-best lists.

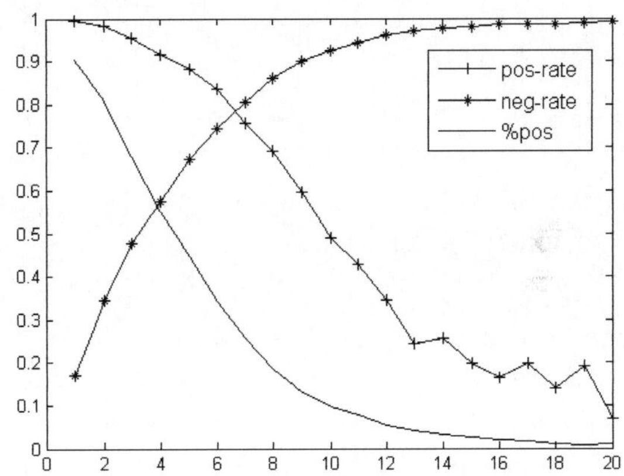

Figure 5: Positive rate, negative rate, and percentage of positive examples w.r.t. subtree depth.

3.3 Discussion

Table 1 shows the classification results on the gold-standard, 1-best, 10-best, and 50-best lists. The positive rate on the gold-standard parses, 75.31%, gives us the upper bound of %-pos when this classifier is used to yield 1-best lists. On the 1-best data, the classifier missed less than one tenth positive subtrees and correctly found nearly two third of the negative ones. That is, our classifier might be useful for avoiding many of the mistakes made by the Berkeley parser, whilst not introducing too many new mistakes of its own. This fact gave us hope to improve parsing performance when using this classifier for reranking.

Figure 5 shows positive rate, negative rate, and percentage of positive examples w.r.t. subtree depth on the 50-best data. We can see that the positive rate is inversely proportional to the subtree depth, unlike the negative rate. That is because the

[3]http://www.torch.ch/

[4]http://ronan.collobert.com/senna/

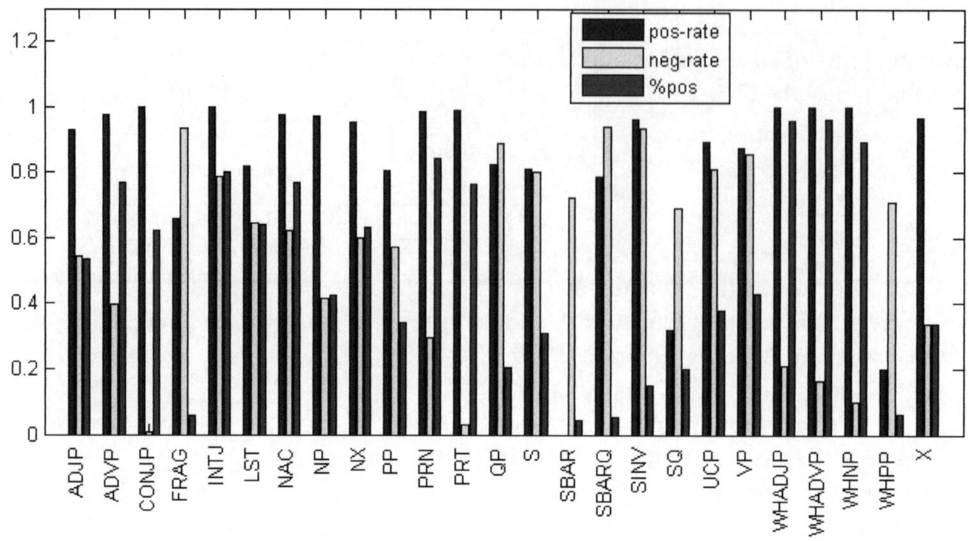

Figure 6: Positive rate, negative rate, and percentage of positive samples w.r.t. syntactic categories (excluding POS tags).

deeper a subtree is, the lower the a priori likelihood that the subtree is positive (we can see this in the percentage-of-positive-example curve). In addition, deep subtrees are difficult to classify because uncertainty is accumulated when propagating from bottom to top.

4 Reranking

In this section, we describe how we use the above classifier for the reranking task. First, we need to represent trees in one vector space, i.e., $\mu(T) = \big(\mu_1(T), ..., \mu_v(T)\big)$ for an arbitrary parse tree T. Collins (2000), Charniak and Johnson (2005), and Johnson and Ural (2010) set the first entry to the model score and the other entries to the number of occurrences of specific discrete hand-chosen properties (e.g., how many times the word *pizza* comes after the word *eat*) of trees. We here do the same with a trick to discretize results from the classifier: we use a 2D histogram to store predicted scores w.r.t. subtree depth. This gives us a flexible way to penalise low score subtrees and reward high score subtrees w.r.t. the performance of the classifier at different depths (see Subsection 3.3). However, unlike the approaches just mentioned, we do not use any expert knowledge for feature selection; instead, this process is fully automatic.

Formally speaking, a vector feature $\mu(T)$ is computed as following. $\mu_1(T)$ is the model score (i.e., max-rule-sum score) given by the parser, $\big(\mu_2(T), ..., \mu_v(T)\big)$ is the histogram of a set of (y, h) where y is given by Equation 2 and h is the depth of the corresponding subtree. The domain of y (i.e., $[0, 1]$) is split into γ_y equal bins whereas the domain of h (i.e., $\{1, 2, 3, ...\}$) is split into γ_h bins such that the i-th ($i < \gamma_h$) bin corresponds to subtrees of depth i and the γ_h-th bin corresponds to subtrees of depth equal or greater than γ_h. The parameters γ_y and γ_h are then estimated on the development set.

After extracting feature vectors for parse trees, we then find a linear ranking function

$$f(T) = w^\top \mu(T)$$

such that

$$f(T_1) > f(T_2) \text{ iff } \textit{fscore}(T_1) > \textit{fscore}(T_2)$$

where $\textit{fscore}(.)$ is the function giving F-score, and $w \in \mathbb{R}^v$ is a weight vector, which is efficiently estimated by SVM ranking (Yu and Kim, 2012). SVM was initially used for binary classification. Its goal is to find the hyperplane which has the largest margin to best separate two example sets. It was then proved to be efficient in solving the ranking task in information retrieval, and in syntactic parsing (Shen and Joshi, 2003; Titov and Henderson, 2006). In our experiments, we used SVM-

Rank[5] (Joachims, 2006), which runs extremely fast (less than two minutes with about $38,000$ 10-best lists).

4.1 Experiments

Using the classifier in Section 3, we implemented the reranker in Torch7, trained it on WSJ02-21. We used WSJ22 to estimate the parameters γ_y and γ_h by the grid search and found that $\gamma_y = 9$ and $\gamma_h = 4$ yielded the best F-score.

Table 2 shows the results of our reranker on 50-best WSJ23 given by the Berkeley parser, using the standard evalb. Our method improves 0.20% on F-score for sentences with all length, and 0.22% for sentences with $\leq$ 40 words. These differences are statistically significant[6] with *p-value* < 0.003. Our method also improves exact match (0.95% for all sentences as well as for sentences with ≤ 40 words).

Parser	LR	LP	LF	EX
all				
Berkeley parser	89.98	90.25	90.12	37.22
This paper	90.10	90.54	90.32	38.17
Oracle	95.94	96.21	96.08	65.56
$\leq$ 40 words				
Berkeley parser	90.43	90.70	90.56	39.65
This paper	90.57	91.01	90.78	40.50
Oracle	96.47	96.73	96.60	68.51

Table 2: Reranking results on 50-best lists on WSJ23 (LR is labelled recall, LP is labelled precision, LF is labelled F-score, and EX is exact match.)

Table 3 shows the comparison of the three parsers that use the same hybrid reranking approach. On F-score, our method performed 0.1% lower than Socher et al. (2013), and 1.5% better than Menchetti et al. (2005). However, our method achieved the least improvement on F-score over its corresponding baseline. That could be because our baseline parser (i.e., the Berkeley parser) performs much better than the other two baseline parsers; and hence, detecting errors it makes on candidate parse trees is more difficult.

Parser	LF (all)	K-best parser
Menchetti et al. (2005)	88.8 (0.6)	Collins (1999)
Socher et al. (2013)	90.4 (3.8)	PCFG Stanford parser
This paper	90.3 (0.2)	Berkeley parser

Table 3: Comparison of parsers using the same hybrid reranking approach. The numbers in the blankets indicate the improvements on F-score over the corresponding baselines (i.e., the k-best parsers).

5 Conclusions

This paper described a new reranking method which uses semantics in syntactic parsing: a symbolic parser is used to generate a k-best list which is later reranked thanks to parse-correctness scores given by a connectionist compositional-semantics-based classifier. Our classifier uses a recursive neural network, like Socher et al., (2010; 2011), to not only represent phrases in a vector space given parse trees, but also identify if these parse trees are grammatically correct or not.

Tested on WSJ23, our method achieved a statistically significant improvement on F-score (0.20%) as well as on exact match (0.95%). This result, although not comparable to the results reported by Collins (2000), Charniak and Johnson (2005), and Johnson and Ural (2010), shows an advantage of using vector-based compositional semantics to support available state-of-the-art parsers.

One of the limitations of the current paper is the lack of a qualitative analysis of how learnt vector-based semantics has affected the reranking results. Therefore, the need for "compositional semantics" in syntactical parsing may still be doubted. In future work, we will use vector-based semantics together with non-semantic features (e.g., the ones of Charniak and Johnson (2005)) to find out whether the semantic features are truly helpful or they just resemble non-semantic features.

Acknowledgments

We thank two anonymous reviewers for helpful comments.

[5] www.cs.cornell.edu/people/tj/svm_light/svm_rank.html

[6] We used the "Significance testing for evaluation statistics" software (http://www.nlpado.de/ sebastian/software/sigf.shtml) given by Padó (2006).

References

Rens Bod, Remko Scha, and Khalil Sima'an. 2003. *Data-Oriented Parsing*. CSLI Publications, Stanford, CA.

Eugene Charniak and Mark Johnson. 2005. Coarse-to-fine n-best parsing and MaxEnt discriminative reranking. In *Proceedings of the 43rd Annual Meeting on Association for Computational Linguistics*, pages 173–180. Association for Computational Linguistics.

Eugene Charniak. 2000. A maximum-entropy-inspired parser. In *Proceedings of the 1st North American chapter of the Association for Computational Linguistics*, pages 132–139. Association for Computational Linguistics.

Michael Collins. 1999. *Head-Driven Statistical Models for Natural Language Parsing*. Ph.D. thesis, University of Pennsylvania.

Michael Collins. 2000. Discriminative reranking for natural language parsing. In *Proceedings of the International Workshop on Machine Learning (then Conference)*, pages 175–182.

Michael Collins. 2003. Head-driven statistical models for natural language parsing. *Computational linguistics*, 29(4):589–637.

Ronan Collobert, Koray Kavukcuoglu, and Clément Farabet. 2011a. Torch7: A matlab-like environment for machine learning. In *BigLearn, NIPS Workshop*.

Ronan Collobert, Jason Weston, Léon Bottou, Michael Karlen, Koray Kavukcuoglu, and Pavel Kuksa. 2011b. Natural language processing (almost) from scratch. *The Journal of Machine Learning Research*, 12:2493–2537.

Ronan Collobert. 2011. Deep learning for efficient discriminative parsing. In *International Conference on Artificial Intelligence and Statistics (AISTATS)*.

Christoph Goller and Andreas Kuchler. 1996. Learning task-dependent distributed representations by backpropagation through structure. In *IEEE International Conference on Neural Networks*, volume 1, pages 347–352. IEEE.

Thorsten Joachims. 2006. Training linear SVMs in linear time. In *Proceedings of the 12th ACM SIGKDD international conference on Knowledge discovery and data mining*, pages 217–226. ACM.

Mark Johnson and Ahmet Engin Ural. 2010. Reranking the Berkeley and Brown parsers. In *Human Language Technologies: The 2010 Annual Conference of the North American Chapter of the Association for Computational Linguistics*, pages 665–668. Association for Computational Linguistics.

Dan Klein and Christopher D Manning. 2003. Accurate unlexicalized parsing. In *Proceedings of the 41st Annual Meeting on Association for Computational Linguistics, Volume 1*, pages 423–430. Association for Computational Linguistics.

Dong C Liu and Jorge Nocedal. 1989. On the limited memory BFGS method for large scale optimization. *Mathematical programming*, 45(1-3):503–528.

Sauro Menchetti, Fabrizio Costa, Paolo Frasconi, and Massimiliano Pontil. 2005. Wide coverage natural language processing using kernel methods and neural networks for structured data. *Pattern Recogn. Lett.*, 26(12):1896–1906, September.

Sebastian Padó, 2006. *User's guide to* `sigf`*: Significance testing by approximate randomisation.*

Barbara Partee. 1995. Lexical semantics and compositionality. In L. R. Gleitman and M. Liberman, editors, *Language. An Invitation to Cognitive Science*, volume 1, pages 311–360. MIT Press, Cambridge, MA.

Slav Petrov, Leon Barrett, Romain Thibaux, and Dan Klein. 2006. Learning accurate, compact, and interpretable tree annotation. In *Proceedings of the 21st International Conference on Computational Linguistics and the 44th annual meeting of the Association for Computational Linguistics*, pages 433–440. Association for Computational Linguistics.

Jordan B Pollack. 1988. Recursive auto-associative memory. *Neural Networks*, 1:122.

Federico Sangati and Willem Zuidema. 2011. Accurate parsing with compact tree-substitution grammars: Double-DOP. In *Proceedings of the Conference on Empirical Methods in Natural Language Processing*, pages 84–95. Association for Computational Linguistics.

Libin Shen and Aravind K Joshi. 2003. An SVM based voting algorithm with application to parse reranking. In *Proceedings of the seventh conference on Natural language learning at HLT-NAACL 2003-Volume 4*, pages 9–16. Association for Computational Linguistics.

Richard Socher, Christopher D Manning, and Andrew Y Ng. 2010. Learning continuous phrase representations and syntactic parsing with recursive neural networks. In *Proceedings of the NIPS-2010 Deep Learning and Unsupervised Feature Learning Workshop*.

Richard Socher, Cliff C Lin, Andrew Y Ng, and Christopher D Manning. 2011. Parsing natural scenes and natural language with recursive neural networks. In *Proceedings of the 26th International Conference on Machine Learning (ICML)*, volume 2.

Richard Socher, John Bauer, Christopher D. Manning, and Andrew Y. Ng. 2013. Parsing With Compositional Vector Grammars. In *Proceedings of the ACL conference (to appear)*.

Mark Steedman. 1999. Connectionist sentence processing in perspective. *Cognitive Science*, 23(4):615–634.

Ivan Titov and James Henderson. 2006. Loss minimization in parse reranking. In *Proceedings of the 2006 Conference on Empirical Methods in Natural Language Processing*, pages 560–567. Association for Computational Linguistics.

Andreas van Cranenburgh, Remko Scha, and Federico Sangati. 2011. Discontinuous Data-Oriented Parsing: A mildly context-sensitive all-fragments grammar. In *Proceedings of the Second Workshop on Statistical Parsing of Morphologically Rich Languages*, pages 34–44. Association for Computational Linguistics.

Hwanjo Yu and Sungchul Kim. 2012. SVM tutorial: Classification, regression, and ranking. In Grzegorz Rozenberg, Thomas Bäck, and Joost N. Kok, editors, *Handbook of Natural Computing*, volume 1, pages 479–506. Springer.

A Structured Distributional Semantic Model : Integrating Structure with Semantics

Kartik Goyal* **Sujay Kumar Jauhar*** **Huiying Li***
Mrinmaya Sachan* **Shashank Srivastava*** **Eduard Hovy**
Language Technologies Institute
School of Computer Science
Carnegie Mellon University
{kartikgo,sjauhar,huiyingl,mrinmays,shashans,hovy}@cs.cmu.edu

Abstract

In this paper we present a novel approach (SDSM) that incorporates structure in distributional semantics. SDSM represents meaning as relation specific distributions over syntactic neighborhoods. We empirically show that the model can effectively represent the semantics of single words and provides significant advantages when dealing with phrasal units that involve word composition. In particular, we demonstrate that our model outperforms both state-of-the-art window-based word embeddings as well as simple approaches for composing distributional semantic representations on an artificial task of verb sense disambiguation and a real-world application of judging event coreference.

1 Introduction

With the advent of statistical methods for NLP, Distributional Semantic Models (DSMs) have emerged as powerful method for representing word semantics. In particular, the distributional vector formalism, which represents meaning by a distribution over neighboring words, has gained the most popularity.

DSMs are widely used in information retrieval (Manning et al., 2008), question answering (Tellex et al., 2003), semantic similarity computation (Wong and Raghavan, 1984; McCarthy and Carroll, 2003), automated dictionary building (Curran, 2003), automated essay grading (Landauer and Dutnais, 1997), word-sense discrimination and disambiguation (McCarthy et al., 2004; Schütze, 1998), selectional preference modeling (Erk, 2007) and identification of translation equivalents (Hjelm, 2007).

Systems that use DSMs implicitly make a bag of words assumption: that the meaning of a phrase can be reasonably estimated from the meaning of its constituents. However, semantics in natural language is a compositional phenomenon, encompassing interactions between syntactic structures, and the meaning of lexical constituents. It follows that the DSM formalism lends itself poorly to composition since it implicitly disregards syntactic structure. For instance, the distributions for "Lincoln", "Booth", and "killed" when merged produce the same result regardless of whether the input is "Booth killed Lincoln" or "Lincoln killed Booth". As suggested by Pantel and Lin (2000) and others, modeling the distribution over preferential attachments for each syntactic relation separately can yield greater expressive power.

Attempts have been made to model linguistic composition of individual word vectors (Mitchell and Lapata, 2009), as well as remedy the inherent failings of the standard distributional approach (Erk and Padó, 2008). The results show varying degrees of efficacy, but have largely failed to model deeper lexical semantics or compositional expectations of words and word combinations.

In this paper we propose an extension to the traditional DSM model that explicitly preserves structural information and permits the approximation of distributional expectation over dependency relations. We extend the generic DSM model by representing a word as distributions over relation-specific syntactic neighborhoods. One can think of the Structured DSM (SDSM) representation of a word/phrase as several vectors defined over the same vocabulary, each vector representing the

*Equally contributing authors

word's selectional preferences for a different syntactic argument. We argue that this representation captures individual word semantics effectively, and is better able to express the semantics of composed units.

The overarching theme of our framework of evaluation is to explore the semantic space of the SDSM. We do this by measuring its ability to discriminate between varying surface forms of the same underlying concept. We perform the following set of experiments to evaluate its expressive power, and conclude the following:

1. Experiments with single words on similarity scoring and substitute selection: SDSM performs at par with window-based distributional vectors.

2. Experiments with phrasal units on two-word composition: state-of-the-art results are produced on the dataset from Mitchell and Lapata (2008) in terms of correlation with human judgment.

3. Experiments with larger structures on the task of judging event coreferentiality: SDSM shows superior performance over state-of-the-art window-based word embeddings, and simple models for composing distributional semantic representations.

2 Related Work

Distributional Semantic Models are based on the intuition that "a word is characterized by the company it keeps" (Firth, 1957). While DSMs have been very successful on a variety of NLP tasks, they are generally considered inappropriate for deeper semantics because they lack the ability to model composition, modifiers or negation.

Recently, there has been a surge in studies to model a stronger form of semantics by phrasing the problem of DSM compositionality as one of vector composition. These techniques derive the meaning of the combination of two words a and b by a single vector $c = f(a, b)$. Mitchell and Lapata (2008) propose a framework to define the composition $c = f(a, b, r, K)$ where r is the relation between a and b, and K is the additional knowledge used to define composition.

While the framework is quite general, most models in the literature tend to disregard K and r and are generally restricted to component-wise addition and multiplication on the vectors to be composed, with slight variations. Dinu and Lapata (2010) and Séaghdha and Korhonen (2011) introduced a probabilistic model to represent word meanings by a latent variable model. Subsequently, other high-dimensional extensions by Rudolph and Giesbrecht (2010), Baroni and Zamparelli (2010) and Grefenstette et al. (2011), regression models by Guevara (2010), and recursive neural network based solutions by Socher et al. (2012) and Collobert et al. (2011) have been proposed.

Pantel and Lin (2000) and Erk and Padó (2008) attempted to include syntactic context in distributional models. However, their approaches do not explicitly construct phrase-level meaning from words which limits their applicability to real world problems. A quasi-compositional approach was also attempted in Thater et al. (2010) by a systematic combination of first and second order context vectors. To the best of our knowledge the formulation of composition we propose is the first to account for K and r within the general framework of composition $c = f(a, b, r, K)$.

3 Structured Distributional Semantics

In this section, we describe our Structured Distributional Semantic framework in detail. We first build a large knowledge base from sample english texts and use it to represent basic lexical units. Next, we describe a technique to obtain the representation for larger units by composing their constituents.

3.1 The PropStore

To build a lexicon of SDSM representations for a given vocabulary we construct a proposition knowledge base (the PropStore) by processing the text of Simple English Wikipedia through a dependency parser. Dependency arcs are stored as 3-tuples of the form $\langle w_1, r, w_2 \rangle$, denoting occurrences of words w_1 and word w_2 related by the syntactic dependency r. We also store sentence identifiers for each triple for reasons described later. In addition to the words' surface-forms, the PropStore also stores their POS tags, lemmas, and Wordnet supersenses.

The PropStore can be used to query for preferred expectations of words, supersenses, relations, etc., around a given word. In the example in Figure 1, the query (SST(W_1)

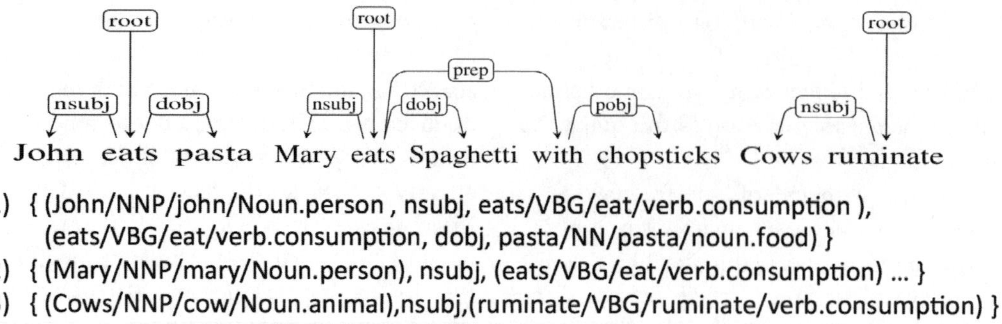

Figure 1: Sample sentences & triples

= verb.consumption, ?, dobj) i.e., "what is consumed", might return expectations [pasta:1, spaghetti:1, mice:1 . . .]. In our implementation, the relations and POS tags are obtained using the Fanseparser (Tratz and Hovy, 2011), supersense tags using sst-light (Ciaramita and Altun, 2006), and lemmas are obtained from Wordnet (Miller, 1995).

3.2 Building the Representation

Next, we describe a method to represent lexical entries as structured distributional matrices using the PropStore.

The canonical form of a concept C (word, phrase etc.) in the SDSM framework is a matrix M^C, whose entry M^C_{ij} is a list of sentence identifiers obtained by querying the PropStore for contexts in which C appears in the syntactic neighborhood of the word j linked by the dependency relation i. As with other distributional models in the literature, the content of a cell is the frequency of co-occurrence of its concept and word under the given relational constraint.

This canonical matrix form can be interpreted in several different ways. Each interpretation is based on a different normalization scheme.

1. **Row Norm**: Each row of the matrix is interpreted as a distribution over words that attach to the target concept with the given dependency relation.

$$M^C_{ij} = \frac{M_{ij}}{\Sigma_j M_{ij}} \qquad \forall i$$

2. **Full Norm**: The entire matrix is interpreted as a distribution over the word-relation pairs which can attach to the target concept.

$$M^C_{ij} = \frac{M_{ij}}{\Sigma_{i,j} M_{ij}} \qquad \forall i,j$$

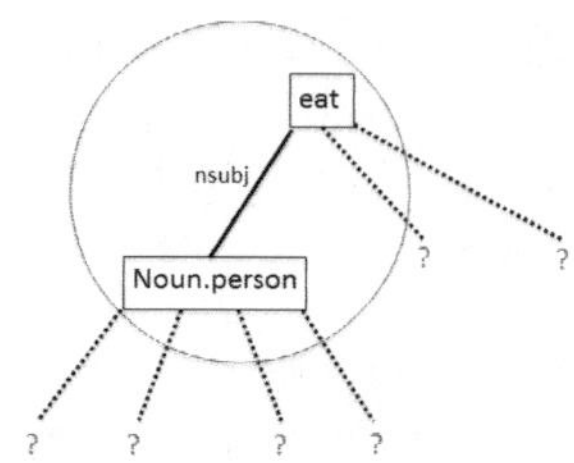

Figure 2: Mimicking composition of two words

3. **Collapsed Vector Norm**: The columns of the matrix are collapsed to form a standard normalized distributional vector trained on dependency relations rather than sliding windows.

$$M^C_j = \frac{\Sigma_i M_{ij}}{\Sigma_{i,j} M_{ij}} \qquad \forall j$$

3.3 Mimicking Compositionality

For representing intermediate multi-word phrases, we extend the above word-relation matrix symbolism in a bottom-up fashion. The combination hinges on the intuition that when lexical units combine to form a larger syntactically connected phrase, the representation of the phrase is given by its own distributional neighborhood within the embedded parse tree. The distributional neighborhood of the net phrase can be computed using the PropStore given syntactic relations anchored on its parts. For the example in Figure 1, we can compose SST(w_1) = Noun.person and Lemma(W_1) = eat with relation 'nsubj' to obtain expectations around "people eat" yielding [pasta:1, spaghetti:1 . . .] for the *object* relation ([dining room:2, restaurant:1 . . .] for the *location* relation, etc.) (See Figure 2). Larger phrasal queries can be built to answer questions like "What do people in China eat with?", "What do cows do?", etc. All of this helps us to account for both relation r and knowledge K obtained from the PropStore within the compositional framework $c = f(a, b, r, K)$.

The general outline to obtain a composition of two words is given in Algorithm 1. Here, we first determine the sentence indices where the two words w_1 and w_2 occur with relation r. Then, we return the expectations around the two words within these sentences. Note that the entire algorithm can conveniently be written in the form of database queries to our PropStore.

Algorithm 1 ComposePair(w_1, r, w_2)

```
M1 ← queryMatrix(w1)
M2 ← queryMatrix(w2)
SentIDs ← M1(r) ∩ M2(r)
return ((M1∩ SentIDs) ∪ (M2∩ SentIDs))
```

Similar to the two-word composition process, given a parse subtree T of a phrase, we obtain its matrix representation of empirical counts over word-relation contexts. This procedure is described in Algorithm 2. Let the $E = \{e_1 \dots e_n\}$ be the set of edges in T, $e_i = (w_{i1}, r_i, w_{i2}) \forall i = 1 \dots n$.

Algorithm 2 ComposePhrase(T)

```
SentIDs ← All Sentences in corpus
for i = 1 → n do
    Mi1 ← queryMatrix(wi1)
    Mi2 ← queryMatrix(wi2)
    SentIDs ← SentIDs ∩(M1(ri) ∩ M2(ri))
end for
return ((M11∩ SentIDs) ∪ (M12∩ SentIDs)
 ··· ∪ (Mn1∩ SentIDs) ∪ (Mn2∩ SentIDs))
```

3.4 Tackling Sparsity

The SDSM model reflects syntactic properties of language through preferential filler constraints. But by distributing counts over a set of relations the resultant SDSM representation is comparatively much sparser than the DSM representation for the same word. In this section we present some ways to address this problem.

3.4.1 Sparse Back-off

The first technique to tackle sparsity is to back off to progressively more general levels of linguistic granularity when sparse matrix representations for words or compositional units are encountered or when the word or unit is not in the lexicon. For example, the composition "Balthazar eats" cannot be directly computed if the named entity "Balthazar" does not occur in the PropStore's knowledge base. In this case, a query for a supersense substitute – "Noun.person eat" – can be issued instead. When supersenses themselves fail to provide numerically significant distributions for words or word combinations, a second back-off step involves querying for POS tags. With coarser levels of linguistic representation, the expressive power of the distributions becomes diluted. But this is often necessary to handle rare words. Note that this is an issue with DSMs too.

3.4.2 Densification

In addition to the back-off method, we also propose a secondary method for "densifying" distributions. A concept's distribution is modified by using words encountered in its syntactic neighborhood to infer counts for other semantically similar words. In other terms, given the matrix representation of a concept, densification seeks to populate its null columns (which each represent a word-dimension in the structured distributional context) with values weighted by their scaled similarities to words (or effectively word-dimensions) that actually occur in the syntactic neighborhood.

For example, suppose the word "play" had an "nsubj" preferential vector that contained the following counts: [cat:4 ; Jane:2]. One might then populate the column for "dog" in this vector with a count proportional to its similarity to the word cat (say 0.8), thus resulting in the vector [cat:4 ; Jane:2 ; dog:3.2]. These counts could just as well be probability values or PMI associations (suitably normalized). In this manner, the k most similar word-dimensions can be densified for each word that actually occurs in a syntactic context. As with sparse back-off, there is an inherent trade-off between the degree of densification k and the expressive power of the resulting representation.

3.4.3 Dimensionality Reduction

The final method tackles the problem of sparsity by reducing the representation to a dense low-dimensional word embedding using singular value decomposition (SVD). In a typical term-document matrix, SVD finds a low-dimensional approximation of the original matrix where columns become latent concepts while similarity structure between rows are preserved. The PropStore, as described in Section 3.1, is an order-3 tensor with w_1, w_2 and

rel as its three axes. We explore the following two possibilities to perform dimensionality reduction using SVD.

Word-word matrix SVD. In this experiment, we preserve the axes w_1 and w_2 and ignore the relational information. Following the SVD regime ($W = U\Sigma V^T$) where Σ is a square diagonal matrix of k largest singular values, and U and V are $m \times k$ and $n \times k$ matrices respectively. We adopt matrix U as the compacted concept representation.

Tensor SVD. To remedy the relation-agnostic nature of the word-word SVD matrix representation, we use tensor SVD (Vasilescu and Terzopoulos, 2002) to preserve the structural information. The mode-n vectors of an order-N tensor $\mathcal{A}\in\mathbb{R}^{I_1 \times I_2 \times \ldots \times I_N}$ are the I_n-dimensional vectors obtained from $\mathcal{A}$ by varying index i_n while keeping other indices fixed. The matrix formed by all the mode-n vectors is a mode-n flattening of the tensor. To obtain the compact representations of concepts we thus first apply mode w_1 flattening and then perform SVD on the resulting tensor.

4 Single Word Evaluation

In this section we describe experiments and results for judging the expressive power of the structured distributional representation for individual words. We use a similarity scoring task and a lexical substitute selection task for the purpose of this evaluation. We compare the SDSM representation to standard window-based distributional vectors trained on the same corpus (Simple English Wikipedia). We also experiment with different normalization techniques outlined in Section 3.2, which effectively lead to structured distributional representations with distinct interpretations.

We experimented with various similarity metrics and found that the normalized cityblock distance metric provides the most stable results.

$$
\begin{aligned}
CityBlock(X,Y) &= \frac{ArcTan(d(X,Y))}{d(X,Y)} \\
d(X,Y) &= \frac{1}{|R|}\sum_{r\in R} d(X_r,Y_r)
\end{aligned}
$$

Results in the rest of this section are thus reported using the normalized cityblock metric. We also report experimental results for the two methods of alleviating sparsity discussed in Section 3.4, namely, densification and SVD.

4.1 Similarity Scoring

On this task, the different semantic representations were used to compute similarity scores between two (out of context) words. We used a dataset from Finkelstein et al. (2002) for our experiments. It consists of 353 pairs of words along with an averaged similarity score on a scale of 1.0 to 10.0 obtained from 13–16 human judges.

4.2 Lexical Substitute Selection

In the second task, the same set of semantic representations was used to produce a similarity ranking on the Turney (2002) ESL dataset. This dataset comprises 50 words that appear in a context (we discarded the context in this experiment), along with 4 candidate lexical substitutions. We evaluate the semantic representations on the basis of their ability to discriminate the top-ranked candidate.[1]

4.3 Results and Discussion

Table 1 summarizes the results for the window-based baseline and each of the structured distributional representations on both tasks. It shows that our representations for single words are competitive with window based distributional vectors. Densification in certain conditions improves our results, but no consistent pattern is discernible. This can be attributed to the trade-off between the gain from generalization and the noise introduced by semantic drift.

Hence we resort to dimensionality reduction as an additional method of reducing sparsity. Table 2 gives correlation scores on the Finkelstein et al. (2002) dataset when SVD is performed on the representations, as described in Section 3.4.3. We give results when 100 and 500 principal components are preserved for both SVD techniques.

These experiments suggest that though afflicted by sparsity, the proposed structured distributional paradigm is competitive with window-based distributional vectors. In the following sections we show that that the framework provides considerably greater power for modeling composition when dealing with units consisting of more than one word.

[1]While we are aware of the standard lexical substitution corpus from McCarthy and Navigli (2007) we chose the one mentioned above for its basic vocabulary, lower dependence on context, and simpler evaluation framework.

Model	Finklestein (Corr.)	ESL (% Acc.)
DSM	**0.283**	0.247
Collapsed	0.260	0.178
FullNorm	0.282	0.192
RowNorm	0.236	0.264
Densified RowNorm	0.259	**0.267**

Table 1: Single Word Evaluation

Model	Correlation
matSVD100	0.207
matSVD500	0.221
tenSVD100	0.267
tenSVD500	**0.315**

Table 2: Finklestein: Correlation using SVD

5 Verb Sense Disambiguation using Composition

In this section, we examine how well our model performs composition on a pair of words. We derive the compositional semantic representations for word pairs from the M&L dataset (Mitchell and Lapata, 2008) and compare our performance with M&L's additive and multiplicative models of composition.

5.1 Dataset

The M&L dataset consists of polysemous intransitive verb and subject pairs that co-occur at least 50 times in the BNC corpus. Additionally two landmark words are given for every polysemous verb, each corresponding to one of its senses. The subject nouns provide contextual disambiguation for the senses of the verb. For each [subject, verb, landmark] tuple, a human assigned score on a 7-point scale is provided, indicating the compatibility of the landmark with the reference verb-subj pair. For example, for the pair "gun bomb", landmark "thunder" is more similar to the verb than landmark "prosper". The corpus contains 120 tuples and altogether 3600 human judgments. Reliability of the human ratings is examined by calculating inter-annotator Spearman's ρ correlation coefficient.

5.2 Experiment procedure

For each tuple in the dataset, we derive the composed word-pair matrix for the reference *verb-subj* pair based on the algorithm described in Section 3.3 and query the single-word matrix for the landmark word. A few modifications are made to adjust the algorithm for the current task:

1. In our formulation, the dependency relation needs to be specified in order to compose a pair of words. Hence, we determine the five most frequent relations between w_1 and w_2 by querying the PropStore. We then use the algorithm in Section 3.3 to compose the verb-subj word pair using these relations, resulting in five composed representations.
2. The word pairs in M&L corpus are extracted from a parsed version of the BNC corpus, while our PropStore is built on Simple Wikipedia texts, whose vocabulary is significantly different from that of the BNC corpus. This causes *null* returns in our PropStore queries, in which case we back-off to retrieving results for super-sense tags of both the words. Finally, the composed matrix and the landmark matrix are compared against each other by different matrix distance measures, which results in a similarity score. For a [subject, verb, landmark] tuple, we average the similarity scores yielded by the relations obtained in 1.

The Spearman Correlation ρ between our similarity ratings and the ones assigned by human judges is computed over all the tuples. Following M&L's experiments, the inter-annotator agreement correlation coefficient serves an upper bound on the task.

5.3 Results and Discussion

As in Section 4, we choose the cityblock measure as the similarity metric of choice. Table 3 shows the evaluation results for two word composition. Except for row normalization, both forms of normalization in the structured distributional paradigm show significant improvement over the results reported by M&L. The results are statistically significant at p-value = 0.004 and 0.001 for Full Norm and Collapsed Vector Norm, respectively.

Model	ρ
M&L combined	0.19
Row Norm	0.134
Full Norm	0.289
Collapsed Vector Norm	0.259
UpperBound	0.40

Table 3: Two Word Composition Evaluation

These results validate our hypothesis that the integration of structure into distributional semantics as well as our framing of word composition together outperform window-based representations under simplistic models of composition such as addition and multiplication. This finding is further re-enforced in the following experiments on event coreferentiality judgment.

6 Event Coreference Judgment

Given the SDSM formulation and assuming no sparsity constraints, it is possible to calculate SDSM matrices for composed concepts. However, are these correct? Intuitively, if they truly capture semantics, the two SDSM matrix representations for “Booth assassinated Lincoln” and “Booth shot Lincoln with a gun" should be (almost) the same. To test this hypothesis we turn to the task of predicting whether two event mentions are coreferent or not, even if their surface forms differ.

While automated resolution of entity coreference has been an actively researched area (Haghighi and Klein, 2009; Stoyanov et al., 2009; Raghunathan et al., 2010), there has been relatively little work on event coreference resolution. Lee et al. (2012) perform joint cross-document entity and event coreference resolution using the two-way feedback between events and their arguments.

In this paper, however, we only consider coreferentiality between pairs of events. Formally, two event mentions generally refer to the same event when their respective actions, agents, patients, locations, and times are (almost) the same. Given the non-compositional nature of determining equality of locations and times, we represent each event mention by a triple $\mathbf{E} = (e, a, p)$ for the event, agent, and patient.

While linguistic theory of argument realization is a debated research area (Levin and Rappaport Hovav, 2005; Goldberg, 2005), it is commonly believed that event structure (Moens and Steedman, 1988) centralizes on the predicate, which governs and selects its role arguments (Jackendoff, 1987). In the corpora we use for our experiments, most event mentions are verbs. However, when nominalized events are encountered, we replace them by their verbal forms. We use SRL Collobert et al. (2011) to determine the agent and patient arguments of an event mention. When SRL fails to determine either role, its empirical substitutes are obtained by querying the PropStore for the most likely word expectations for the role. The triple (e, a, p) is thus the composition of the triples (a, rel_{agent}, e) and $(p, rel_{patient}, e)$, and hence a complex object. To determine equality of this complex composed representation we generate three levels of progressively simplified event constituents for comparison:

Level 1: Full Composition:
$M_{full} = \mathit{ComposePhrase}(e, a, p)$.
Level 2: Partial Composition:
$M_{part:EA} = \mathit{ComposePair}(e, r, a)$
$M_{part:EP} = \mathit{ComposePair}(e, r, p)$.
Level 3: No Composition:
$M_E = queryMatrix(e)$
$M_A = queryMatrix(a)$
$M_P = queryMatrix(p)$.

To judge coreference between events **E1** and **E2**, we compute pairwise similarities $\text{Sim}(M1_{full}, M2_{full})$, $\text{Sim}(M1_{part:EA}, M2_{part:EA})$, etc., for each level of the composed triple representation. Furthermore, we vary the computation of similarity by considering different levels of granularity (lemma, SST), various choices of distance metric (Euclidean, Cityblock, Cosine), and score normalization techniques (Row-wise, Full, Column collapsed). This results in 159 similarity-based features for every pair of events, which are used to train a classifier to make a binary decision for coreferentiality.

6.1 Datasets

We evaluate our method on two datasets and compare it against four baselines, two of which use window based distributional vectors and two that employ weaker forms of composition.

IC Event Coreference Corpus: The dataset (citation suppressed), drawn from 100 news articles about violent events, contains manually created annotations for 2214 pairs of co-referent and non-coreferent events each. Where available, events' semantic role-fillers for *agent* and *patient* are annotated as well. When missing, empirical substitutes were obtained by querying the PropStore for the preferred word attachments.

EventCorefBank (ECB) corpus: This corpus (Bejan and Harabagiu, 2010) of 482 documents from Google News is clustered into 45 topics, with event coreference chains annotated over each topic. The event mentions are enriched with semantic roles to obtain the canonical event structure described above. Positive instances are ob-

	IC Corpus				ECB Corpus			
	Prec	Rec	F-1	Acc	Prec	Rec	F-1	Acc
SDSM	**0.916**	0.929	**0.922**	**0.906**	0.901	0.401	**0.564**	**0.843**
Senna	0.850	0.881	0.865	0.835	0.616	**0.408**	0.505	0.791
DSM	0.743	0.843	0.790	0.740	0.854	0.378	0.524	0.830
MVC	0.756	**0.961**	0.846	0.787	**0.914**	0.353	0.510	0.831
AVC	0.753	0.941	0.837	0.777	0.901	0.373	0.528	0.834

Table 4: Cross-validation Performance on IC and ECB dataset

tained by taking pairwise event mentions within each chain, and negative instances are generated from pairwise event mentions across chains, but within the same topic. This results in 11039 positive instances and 33459 negative instances.

6.2 Baselines:

To establish the efficacy of our model, we compare SDSM against a purely window-based baseline (DSM) trained on the same corpus. In our experiments we set a window size of three words to either side of the target. We also compare SDSM against the window-based embeddings trained using a recursive neural network (SENNA) (Collobert et al., 2011) on both datsets. SENNA embeddings are state-of-the-art for many NLP tasks. The second baseline uses SENNA to generate level 3 similarity features for events' individual words (agent, patient and action). As our final set of baselines, we extend two simple techniques proposed by Mitchell and Lapata (2008) that use element-wise addition and multiplication operators to perform composition. The two baselines thus obtained are AVC (element wise addition) and MVC (element-wise multiplication).

6.3 Results and Discussion:

We experimented with a number of common classifiers, and selected decision-trees (J48) as they give the best classification accuracy. Table 4 summarizes our results on both datasets.

The results reveal that the SDSM model consistently outperforms DSM, SENNA embeddings, and the MVC and AVC models, both in terms of F-1 score and accuracy. The IC corpus comprises of domain specific texts, resulting in high lexical overlap between event mentions. Hence, the scores on the IC corpus are consistently higher than those on the ECB corpus.

The improvements over DSM and SENNA embeddings, support our hypothesis that syntax lends greater expressive power to distributional semantics in compositional configurations. Furthermore, the increase in predictive accuracy over MVC and AVC shows that our formulation of composition of two words based on the relation binding them yields a stronger form of composition than simple additive and multiplicative models.

Next, we perform an ablation study to determine the most predictive features for the task of determining event coreferentiality. The forward selection procedure reveals that the most informative attributes are the level 2 compositional features involving the agent and the action, as well as their individual level 3 features. This corresponds to the intuition that the agent and the action are the principal determiners for identifying events. Features involving the patient and level 1 features are least useful. The latter involves full composition, resulting in sparse representations and hence have low predictive power.

7 Conclusion and Future Work

In this paper we outlined an approach that introduces structure into distributional semantics. We presented a method to compose distributional representations of individual units into larger composed structures. We tested the efficacy of our model on several evaluation tasks. Our model's performance is competitive for tasks dealing with semantic similarity of individual words, even though it suffers from the problem of sparsity. Additionally, it outperforms window-based approaches on tasks involving semantic composition. In future work we hope to extend this formalism to other semantic tasks like paraphrase detection and recognizing textual entailment.

Acknowledgments

The authors would like to thank the anonymous reviewers for their valuable comments and suggestions to improve the quality of the paper. This work was supported in part by the following grants: NSF grant IIS-1143703, NSF award IIS-1147810, DARPA grant FA87501220342.

References

Marco Baroni and Roberto Zamparelli. 2010. Nouns are vectors, adjectives are matrices: representing adjective-noun constructions in semantic space. In *Proceedings of the 2010 Conference on Empirical Methods in Natural Language Processing*, EMNLP '10, pages 1183–1193, Stroudsburg, PA, USA. Association for Computational Linguistics.

Cosmin Adrian Bejan and Sanda Harabagiu. 2010. Unsupervised event coreference resolution with rich linguistic features. In *Proceedings of the 48th Annual Meeting of the Association for Computational Linguistics*, ACL '10, pages 1412–1422, Stroudsburg, PA, USA. Association for Computational Linguistics.

Massimiliano Ciaramita and Yasemin Altun. 2006. Broad-coverage sense disambiguation and information extraction with a supersense sequence tagger. In *Proceedings of the 2006 Conference on Empirical Methods in Natural Language Processing*, EMNLP '06, pages 594–602, Stroudsburg, PA, USA. Association for Computational Linguistics.

Ronan Collobert, Jason Weston, Léon Bottou, Michael Karlen, Koray Kavukcuoglu, and Pavel Kuksa. 2011. Natural language processing (almost) from scratch. *J. Mach. Learn. Res.*, 999888:2493–2537, November.

James Richard Curran. 2003. From distributional to semantic similarity. Technical report.

Georgiana Dinu and Mirella Lapata. 2010. Measuring distributional similarity in context. In *Proceedings of the 2010 Conference on Empirical Methods in Natural Language Processing*, EMNLP '10, pages 1162–1172, Stroudsburg, PA, USA. Association for Computational Linguistics.

Katrin Erk and Sebastian Padó. 2008. A structured vector space model for word meaning in context. In *Proceedings of the Conference on Empirical Methods in Natural Language Processing*, EMNLP '08, pages 897–906, Stroudsburg, PA, USA. Association for Computational Linguistics.

Katrin Erk. 2007. A simple, similarity-based model for selectional preferences.

Lev Finkelstein, Evgeniy Gabrilovich, Yossi Matias, Ehud Rivlin, Zach Solan, Gadi Wolfman, and Eytan Ruppin. 2002. Placing search in context: The concept revisited. In *ACM Transactions on Information Systems*, volume 20, pages 116–131, January.

John R. Firth. 1957. A Synopsis of Linguistic Theory, 1930-1955. *Studies in Linguistic Analysis*, pages 1–32.

Adele E. Goldberg. 2005. *Argument Realization: Cognitive Grouping and Theoretical Extensions.*

Edward Grefenstette, Mehrnoosh Sadrzadeh, Stephen Clark, Bob Coecke, and Stephen Pulman. 2011. Concrete sentence spaces for compositional distributional models of meaning. In *Proceedings of the Ninth International Conference on Computational Semantics*, IWCS '11, pages 125–134, Stroudsburg, PA, USA. Association for Computational Linguistics.

Emiliano Guevara. 2010. A regression model of adjective-noun compositionality in distributional semantics. In *Proceedings of the 2010 Workshop on GEometrical Models of Natural Language Semantics*, GEMS '10, pages 33–37, Stroudsburg, PA, USA. Association for Computational Linguistics.

Aria Haghighi and Dan Klein. 2009. Simple coreference resolution with rich syntactic and semantic features. In *Proceedings of the 2009 Conference on Empirical Methods in Natural Language Processing: Volume 3 - Volume 3*, EMNLP '09, pages 1152–1161, Stroudsburg, PA, USA. Association for Computational Linguistics.

Hans Hjelm. 2007. Identifying cross language term equivalents using statistical machine translation and distributional association measures. In *Proceedings of NODALIDA*, pages 97–104. Citeseer.

Ray Jackendoff. 1987. The status of thematic roles in linguistic theory. *Linguistic Inquiry*, 18(3):369–411.

Thomas K Landauer and Susan T. Dutnais. 1997. A solution to plato's problem: The latent semantic analysis theory of acquisition, induction, and representation of knowledge. *Psychological review*, pages 211–240.

Heeyoung Lee, Marta Recasens, Angel Chang, Mihai Surdeanu, and Dan Jurafsky. 2012. Joint entity and event coreference resolution across documents. In *Proceedings of the 2012 Joint Conference on Empirical Methods in Natural Language Processing and Computational Natural Language Learning*, EMNLP-CoNLL '12, pages 489–500, Stroudsburg, PA, USA. Association for Computational Linguistics.

Beth Levin and Malka Rappaport Hovav. 2005. *Argument Realization.* Cambridge University Press.

Christopher D. Manning, Prabhakar Raghavan, and Hinrich Schütze. 2008. *Introduction to Information Retrieval.* Cambridge University Press, New York, NY, USA.

Diana McCarthy and John Carroll. 2003. Disambiguating nouns, verbs, and adjectives using automatically acquired selectional preferences. *Comput. Linguist.*, 29(4):639–654, December.

Diana McCarthy and Roberto Navigli. 2007. Semeval-2007 task 10: English lexical substitution task. In *Proceedings of the 4th International Workshop on Semantic Evaluations (SemEval-2007), Prague, Czech Republic*, pages 48–53.

Diana McCarthy, Rob Koeling, Julie Weeds, and John Carroll. 2004. Finding predominant word senses in untagged text. In *Proceedings of the 42nd Annual Meeting on Association for Computational Linguistics*, ACL '04, Stroudsburg, PA, USA. Association for Computational Linguistics.

George A. Miller. 1995. Wordnet: a lexical database for english. *Commun. ACM*, 38(11):39–41, November.

Jeff Mitchell and Mirella Lapata. 2008. Vector-based models of semantic composition. In *In Proceedings of ACL-08: HLT*, pages 236–244.

Jeff Mitchell and Mirella Lapata. 2009. Language models based on semantic composition. In *Proceedings of the 2009 Conference on Empirical Methods in Natural Language Processing: Volume 1 - Volume 1*, EMNLP '09, pages 430–439, Stroudsburg, PA, USA. Association for Computational Linguistics.

Marc Moens and Mark Steedman. 1988. Temporal ontology and temporal reference. *Computational linguistics*, 14(2):15–28.

Patrick Pantel and Dekang Lin. 2000. Word-for-word glossing with contextually similar words. In *Proceedings of the 1st North American chapter of the Association for Computational Linguistics conference*, NAACL 2000, pages 78–85, Stroudsburg, PA, USA. Association for Computational Linguistics.

Karthik Raghunathan, Heeyoung Lee, Sudarshan Rangarajan, Nathanael Chambers, Mihai Surdeanu, Dan Jurafsky, and Christopher Manning. 2010. A multi-pass sieve for coreference resolution. In *Proceedings of the 2010 Conference on Empirical Methods in Natural Language Processing*, EMNLP '10, pages 492–501, Stroudsburg, PA, USA. Association for Computational Linguistics.

Sebastian Rudolph and Eugenie Giesbrecht. 2010. Compositional matrix-space models of language. In *Proceedings of the 48th Annual Meeting of the Association for Computational Linguistics*, ACL '10, pages 907–916, Stroudsburg, PA, USA. Association for Computational Linguistics.

Hinrich Schütze. 1998. Automatic word sense discrimination. *Comput. Linguist.*, 24(1):97–123.

Diarmuid Ó Séaghdha and Anna Korhonen. 2011. Probabilistic models of similarity in syntactic context. In *Proceedings of the Conference on Empirical Methods in Natural Language Processing*, EMNLP '11, pages 1047–1057, Stroudsburg, PA, USA. Association for Computational Linguistics.

Richard Socher, Brody Huval, Christopher D. Manning, and Andrew Y. Ng. 2012. Semantic compositionality through recursive matrix-vector spaces. In *Proceedings of the 2012 Joint Conference on Empirical Methods in Natural Language Processing and Computational Natural Language Learning*, EMNLP-CoNLL '12, pages 1201–1211, Stroudsburg, PA, USA. Association for Computational Linguistics.

Veselin Stoyanov, Nathan Gilbert, Claire Cardie, and Ellen Riloff. 2009. Conundrums in noun phrase coreference resolution: making sense of the state-of-the-art. In *Proceedings of the Joint Conference of the 47th Annual Meeting of the ACL and the 4th International Joint Conference on Natural Language Processing of the AFNLP: Volume 2 - Volume 2*, ACL '09, pages 656–664, Stroudsburg, PA, USA. Association for Computational Linguistics.

Stefanie Tellex, Boris Katz, Jimmy J. Lin, Aaron Fernandes, and Gregory Marton. 2003. Quantitative evaluation of passage retrieval algorithms for question answering. In *SIGIR*, pages 41–47.

Stefan Thater, Hagen Fürstenau, and Manfred Pinkal. 2010. Contextualizing semantic representations using syntactically enriched vector models. In *Proceedings of the 48th Annual Meeting of the Association for Computational Linguistics*, ACL '10, pages 948–957, Stroudsburg, PA, USA. Association for Computational Linguistics.

Stephen Tratz and Eduard Hovy. 2011. A fast, accurate, non-projective, semantically-enriched parser. In *Proceedings of the Conference on Empirical Methods in Natural Language Processing*, EMNLP '11, pages 1257–1268, Stroudsburg, PA, USA. Association for Computational Linguistics.

Peter D. Turney. 2002. Mining the web for synonyms: Pmi-ir versus lsa on toefl. *CoRR*.

M. Alex O. Vasilescu and Demetri Terzopoulos. 2002. Multilinear analysis of image ensembles: Tensorfaces. In *In Proceedings of the European Conference on Computer Vision*, pages 447–460.

S. K. M. Wong and Vijay V. Raghavan. 1984. Vector space model of information retrieval: a reevaluation. In *Proceedings of the 7th annual international ACM SIGIR conference on Research and development in information retrieval*, SIGIR '84, pages 167–185, Swinton, UK. British Computer Society.

Letter N-Gram-based Input Encoding for Continuous Space Language Models

Henning Sperr[†], **Jan Niehues**[⋆] **and Alexander Waibel**[⋆]
Institute of Anthropomatics
KIT - Karlsruhe Institute of Technology
Karlsruhe, Germany
[⋆] firstname.lastname@kit.edu
[†] henning.sperr@student.kit.edu

Abstract

We present a letter-based encoding for words in continuous space language models. We represent the words completely by letter n-grams instead of using the word index. This way, similar words will automatically have a similar representation. With this we hope to better generalize to unknown or rare words and to also capture morphological information. We show their influence in the task of machine translation using continuous space language models based on restricted Boltzmann machines. We evaluate the translation quality as well as the training time on a German-to-English translation task of TED and university lectures as well as on the news translation task translating from English to German. Using our new approach a gain in BLEU score by up to 0.4 points can be achieved.

1 Introduction

Language models play an important role in natural language processing. The most commonly used approach is n-gram-based language models (Chen and Goodman, 1999).

In recent years Continuous Space Language Models (CSLMs) have gained a lot of attention. Compared to standard n-gram-based language models they promise better generalization to unknown histories or n-grams with only few occurrences. Since the words are projected into a continuous space, true interpolation can be performed when an unseen sample appears. The standard input layer for CSLMs is a so called 1-of-n coding where a word is represented as a vector with a single neuron turned on and the rest turned off. In the standard approach it is problematic to infer probabilities for words that are not inside the vocabulary. Sometimes an extra unknown neuron is used in the input layer to represent these words (Niehues and Waibel, 2012). Since all unseen words get mapped to the same neuron, no real discrimination between those words can be done. Furthermore, rare words are also hard to model, since there is too few training data available to estimate their associated parameters.

We try to overcome these shortcomings by using subword features to cluster similar words closer together and generalize better over unseen words. We hope that words containing similar letter n-grams will yield a good indicator for words that have the same function inside the sentence. Introducing a method for subword units also has the advantage that the input layer can be smaller, while still representing nearly the same vocabulary with unique feature vectors. By using a smaller input layer, less weights need to be trained and the training is faster. In this work we present the letter n-gram approach to represent words in an CSLM, and compare it to the word-based CSLM presented in Niehues and Waibel (2012).

The rest of this paper is structured as follows: First we will give an overview of related work. After that we give a brief overview of restricted Boltzmann machines which are the basis of the letter-based CSLM presented in Section 4. Then we will present the results of the experiments and conclude our work.

2 Related Work

First research on neural networks to predict word categories has been done in Nakamura et al. (1990) where neural networks were used to predict word categories. Xu and Rudnicky (2000) proposed a language model that has an input consisting of one word and no hidden units. This network was limited to infer unigram and bigram statistics. There has been research on feed forward neural network language models where they achieved a decrease in perplexity compared to standard n-gram language models (Bengio et al., 2003). In Schwenk and Gauvain (2005) and later in Schwenk (2007) research was performed on training large scale neural network language models on millions of words resulting in a decrease of the word error rate for continuous speech recognition. In Schwenk et al. (2006) they use the CSLM framework to rescore n-best lists of a machine translation system during tuning and testing steps. Usually these networks use short lists to reduce the size of the output layer and to make calculation feasible. There have been approaches to optimize the output layer of such a network, so that vocabularies of arbitrary size can be used and there is no need to back off to a smaller n-gram model (Le et al., 2011). In this Structured Output Layer (SOUL) neural network language model a hierarchical output layer was chosen. Recurrent Neural Networks have also been used to try and improve language model perplexities in Mikolov et al. (2010), concluding that Recurrent Neural Networks potentially improve over classical n-gram language models with increasing data and a big enough hidden unit size of the model. In the work of Mnih and Hinton (2007) and Mnih (2010) training factored restricted Boltzmann machines yielded no gain compared to Kneser-Ney smoothed n-gram models. But it has been shown in Niehues and Waibel (2012), that using a restricted Boltzmann machine with a different layout during decoding can yield an increase in BLEU score. There has also been a lot of research in the field of using subword units for language modeling. In Shaik et al. (2011) linguistically motivated sub-lexical units were proposed to improve open vocabulary speech recognition for German. Research on morphology-based and subword language models on a Turkish speech recognition task has been done by Sak et al. (2010). The idea of Factored Language models in machine translation has been introduced by Kirchhoff and Yang (2005). Similar approaches to develop joint language models for morphologically rich languages in machine translation have been presented by Sarikaya and Deng (2007). In Emami et al. (2008) a factored neural network language model for Arabic was built. They used different features such as segmentation, part-of-speech and diacritics to enrich the information for each word.

3 Restricted Boltzmann Machine-based Language Model

In this section we will briefly review the continuous space language models using restricted Boltzmann machines (RBM). We will focus on the parts that are important for the implementation of the input layers described in the next section. A restricted Boltzmann machine is a generative stochastic neural network which consists of a visible and a hidden layer of neurons that have unidirectional connections between the layers but no inner layer connections as shown in Figure 1.

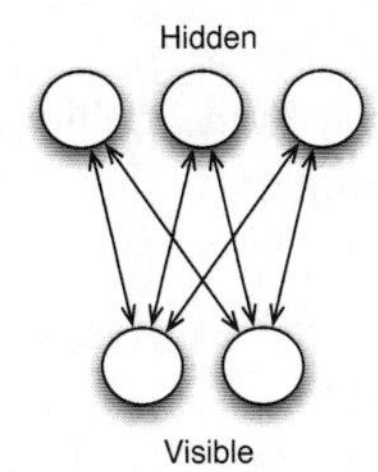

Figure 1: Restricted Boltzmann Machine.

The activation of the visible neurons will be determined by the input data. The standard input layer for neural network language models uses a 1-of-n coding to insert a word from the vocabulary into the network. This is a vector, where only the index of the word in the vocabulary is set to one and the rest to zero. Sometimes this is also referred to as a *softmax* layer of binary units. The activation of the hidden units is usually binary and will be inferred from the visible units by using sampling techniques. In Niehues and Waibel (2012) an n-gram Boltzmann machine language model is proposed using such a softmax layer for each context. In this work, we want to explore different ways of encoding the word observations in the input layer. Figure 2 is an example of the original model with three hidden units, two contexts and a vocabulary of two words. In this example the bigram *my house* is modeled.

To calculate the probability of a visible configuration v we will use the definition of the free energy in a restricted Boltzmann machine with binary stochastic hidden units, which is

$$F(v) = -\sum_i v_i a_i - \sum_j log(1 + e^{x_j}) \qquad (1)$$

where a_i is the bias of the ith visible neuron v_i and

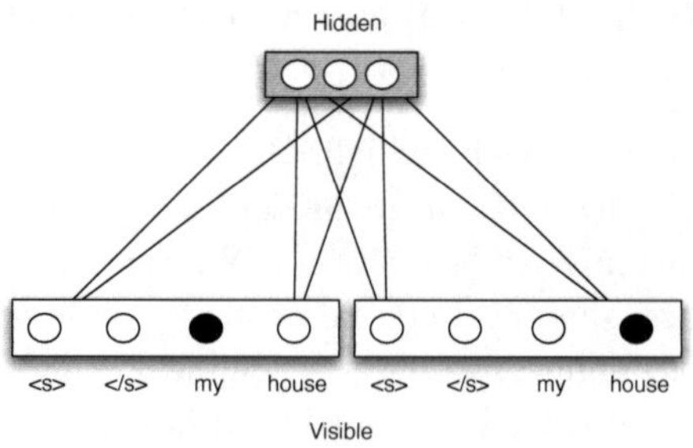

Figure 2: RBMLM with three hidden units and a vocabulary size of two words and two word contexts, where activated units are marked as black.

x_j is the activation of the jth hidden neuron. The activation x_j is defined as

$$x_j = b_j + \sum_i v_i w_{ij} \tag{2}$$

where b_j is the bias of the jth hidden neuron and w_{ij} is the weight between visible unit v_i and hidden unit x_j. Using these definitions, the probability of our visible configuration v is

$$p(v) = \frac{1}{Z} e^{-F(v)} \tag{3}$$

with the partition function $Z = \sum_v e^{-F(v)}$ being the normalization constant. Usually this normalization constant is not easy to compute since it is a sum over an exponential amount of values. We know that the free energy will be proportional to the true probability of our visible vector, this is the reason for using the free energy as a feature in our log-linear model instead of the true probability. In order to use it as a feature inside the decoder we actually need to be able to compute the probability for a whole sentence. As shown in Niehues and Waibel (2012) we can do this by summing over the free energy of all n-grams contained in the sentence.

3.1 Training

For training the restricted Boltzmann machine language model (RBMLM) we used the Contrastive Divergence (CD) algorithm as proposed in Hinton (2010). In order to do this, we need to calculate the derivation of the probability of the example given the weights

$$\frac{\delta \log p(v)}{\delta w_{ij}} = <v_i h_j>_{data} - <v_i h_j>_{model} \tag{4}$$

where $<v_i h_j>_{model}$ is the expected value of $v_i h_j$ given the distribution of the model. In other words we calculate the expectation of how often v_i and h_j are activated together, given the distribution of the data, minus the expectation of them being activated together given the distribution of the model, which will be calculated using Gibbs-Sampling techniques. Usually many steps of Gibbs-Sampling are necessary to get an unbiased sample from the distribution, but in the Contrastive Divergence algorithm only one step of sampling is performed (Hinton, 2002).

4 Letter-based Word Encoding

In this section we will describe the proposed input layers for the RBMLM. Compared to the word index-based representation explained above, we try to improve the capability to handle unknown words and morphology by splitting the word into subunits.

4.1 Motivation

In the example mentioned above, the word index model might be able to predict *my house* but it will fail on *my houses* if the word *houses* is not in the training vocabulary. In this case, a neuron that classifies all unknown tokens or some other techniques to handle such a case have to be utilized.

In contrast, a human will look at the single letters and see that these words are quite similar. He will most probably recognize that the appended *s* is used to mark the plural form, but both words refer to the same thing. So he will be able to infer the meaning although he has never seen it before.

Another example in English are be the words *happy* and *unhappy*. A human speaker who does not know the word *unhappy* will be able to know from the context what *unhappy* means and he can guess that both of the words are adjectives, that have to do with happiness, and that they can be used in the same way.

In other languages with a richer morphology, like German, this problem is even more important. The German word *schön* (engl. *beautiful*) can have 16 different word forms, depending on case, number and gender.

Humans are able to share information about words that are different only in some morphemes like *house* and *houses*. With our letter-based input encoding we want to generalize over the common word index model to capture morphological information about the words to make better predictions for unknown words.

4.2 Features

In order to model the aforementioned morphological word forms, we need to create features for every word that represent which letters are used in the word. If we look at the example of *house*, we need to model that the first letter is an *h*, the second is an *o* and so on.

If we want to encode a word this way, we have the problem that we do not have a fixed size of features, but the feature size depends on the length of the word. This is not possible in the framework of continuous space language models. Therefore, a different way to represent the word is needed.

An approach for having a fixed size of features is to just model which letters occur in the word. In this case, every input word is represented by a vector of dimension n, where n is the size of the alphabet in the text. Every symbol, that is used in the word is set to one and all the other features are zero. By using a sparse representation, which shows only the features that are activated, the word *house* would be represented by

$$w_1 = \text{e h o s u}$$

The main problem of this representation is that we lose all information about the order of the letters. It is no longer possible to see how the word ends and how the word starts. Furthermore, many words will be represented by the same feature vector. For example, in our case the words *house* and *houses* would be identical. In the case of *houses* and *house* this might not be bad, but the words *shortest* and *others* or *follow* and *wolf* will also map to the same input vector. These words have no real connection as they are different in meaning and part of speech.

Therefore, we need to improve this approach to find a better model for input words. N-grams of words or letters have been successfully used to model sequences of words or letters in language models. We extend our approach to model not only the letters that occur in the in the word, but the letter n-grams that occur in the word. This will of course increase the dimension of the feature space, but then we are able to model the order of the letters. In the example of *my house* the feature vector will look like

w_1 = my <w>m y</w>

w_2 = ho ou se us <w>h e</w>

We added markers for the beginning and end of the word because this additional information is important to distinguish words. Using the example of the word *houses*, modeling directly that the last letter is an *s* could serve as an indication of a plural form.

If we use higher order n-grams, this will increase the information about the order of the letters. But these letter n-grams will also occur more rarely and therefore, the weights of these features in the RBM can no longer be estimated as reliably. To overcome this, we did not only use the n-grams of order n, but all n-grams of order n and smaller. In the last example, we will not only use the bigrams, but also the unigrams.

This means *my house* is actually represented as

w_1 = m y my <w>m y</w>

w_2 = e h o s u ho ou se us <w>h e</w>

With this we hope to capture many morphological variants of the word *house*. Now the representations of the words *house* and *houses* differ only in the ending and in an additional bigram.

houses = ... es s</w>

house = ... se e</w>

The beginning letters of the two words will contribute to the same free energy only leaving the ending letter n-grams to contribute to the different usages of *houses* and *house*.

The actual layout of the model can be seen in Figure 3. For the sake of clarity we left out the unigram letters. In this representation we now do not use a softmax input layer, but a logistic input layer defined as

$$p(v_i = \text{on}) = \frac{1}{1 + \mathrm{e}^{-x_i}} \tag{5}$$

where v_i is the ith visible neuron and x_i is the input from the hidden units for the ith neuron defined as

$$x_i = a_i + \sum_j h_j w_{ij} \tag{6}$$

with a_i being the bias of the visible neuron v_i and w_{ij} being the weight between the hidden unit h_j and v_i.

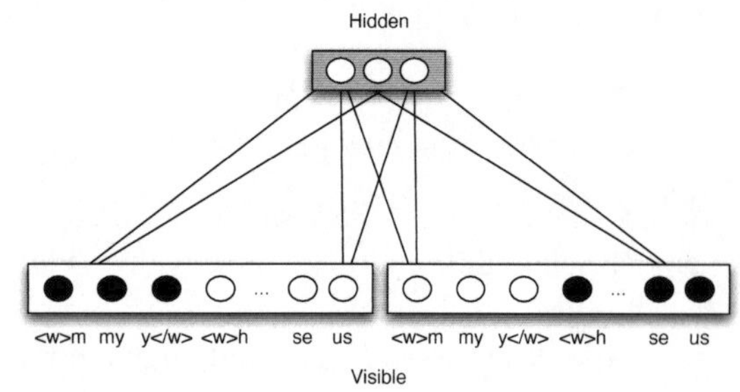

Figure 3: A bigram letter index RBMLM with three hidden units and two word contexts, where activated units are marked as black.

4.3 Additional Information

The letter index approach can be extended by several features to include additional information about the words. This could for example be part-of-speech tags or other morphological information. In this work we tried to include a neuron to capture capital letter information. To do this we included a neuron that will be turned on if the first letter was capitalized and another neuron that will be turned on if the word was written in all capital letters. The word itself will be lowercased after we extracted this information.

Using the example of *European Union*, the new input vector will look like this

w_1 =a e n o p r u an ea eu op pe ro ur
<w>e n</w><CAPS>
w_2 =u i n o un io ni on
<w>u n</w><CAPS>

This will lead to a smaller letter n-gram vocabulary since all the letter n-grams get lowercased. This also means there is more data for each of the letter n-gram neurons that were treated differently before. We also introduced an all caps feature which is turned on if the whole word was written in capital letters. We hope that this can help detect abbreviations which are usually written in all capital letters. For example *EU* will be represented as

w_1 = e u eu <w>e u</w><ALLCAPS>

5 Evaluation

We evaluated the RBM-based language model on different statistical machine translation (SMT) tasks. We will first analyze the letter-based word representation. Then we will give a brief description of our SMT system. Afterwards, we describe in detail our experiments on the German-to-English translation task. We will end with additional experiments on the task of translating English news documents into German.

5.1 Word Representation

In first experiments we analyzed whether the letter-based representation is able to distinguish between different words. In a vocabulary of 27,748 words, we compared for different letter n-gram sizes how many words are mapped to the same input feature vector.

Table 1 shows the different models, their input dimensions and the total number of unique clusters as well as the amount of input vectors containing one, two, three or four or more words that get mapped to this input vector. In the word index representation every word has its own feature vector. In this case the dimension of the input vector is 27,748 and each word has its own unique input vector.

If we use only letters, as done in the unigram model, only 62% of the words have a unique representation. Furthermore, there are 606 feature vectors representing 4 or more words. This type of encoding of the words is not sufficient for the task.

When using a bigram letter context nearly each of the 27,748 words has a unique input representation, although the input dimension is only 7% compared to the word index. With the three letter vocabulary context and higher there is no input vector that represents more than three words from the vocabulary. This is good since we want similar words to be close together but not have exactly the same input vector. The words that are still clustered to the same input are mostly numbers or typing mistakes like "YouTube" and "Youtube".

5.2 Translation System Description

The translation system for the German-to-English task was trained on the European Parliament corpus, News Commentary corpus, the BTEC corpus and TED talks[1]. The data was preprocessed and compound splitting was applied for German. Afterwards the discriminative word alignment approach as described in Niehues and Vogel (2008) was applied to generate the alignments between source and target words. The phrase table was

[1]http://www.ted.com

Model	Caps	VocSize	TotalVectors	#Vectors mapping to 1 Word	2 Words	3 Words	4+ Words
WordIndex	-	27,748	27,748	27,748	0	0	0
Letter 1-gram	No	107	21,216	17,319	2,559	732	606
Letter 2-gram	No	1,879	27,671	27,620	33	10	8
Letter 3-gram	No	12,139	27,720	27,701	10	9	0
Letter 3-gram	Yes	8,675	27,710	27,681	20	9	0
Letter 4-gram	No	43,903	27,737	27,727	9	1	0
Letter 4-gram	Yes	25,942	27,728	27,709	18	1	0

Table 1: Comparison of the vocabulary size and the possibility to have a unique representation of each word in the training corpus.

built using the scripts from the Moses package described in Koehn et al. (2007). A 4-gram language model was trained on the target side of the parallel data using the SRILM toolkit from Stolcke (2002). In addition, we used a bilingual language model as described in Niehues et al. (2011). Reordering was performed as a preprocessing step using part-of-speech (POS) information generated by the Tree-Tagger (Schmid, 1994). We used the reordering approach described in Rottmann and Vogel (2007) and the extensions presented in Niehues et al. (2009) to cover long-range reorderings, which are typical when translating between German and English. An in-house phrase-based decoder was used to generate the translation hypotheses and the optimization was performed using the MERT implementation as presented in Venugopal et al. (2005). All our evaluation scores are measured using the BLEU metric.

We trained the RBMLM models on 50K sentences from TED talks and optimized the weights of the log-linear model on a separate set of TED talks. For all experiments the RBMLMs have been trained with a context of four words. The development set consists of 1.7K segments containing 16K words. We used two different test sets to evaluate our models. The first test set contains TED talks with 3.5K segments containing 31K words. The second task was from an in-house computer science lecture corpus containing 2.1K segments and 47K words. For both tasks we used the weights optimized on TED.

For the task of translating English news texts into German we used a system developed for the Workshop on Machine Translation (WMT) evaluation. The continuous space language models were trained on a random subsample of 100K sentences from the monolingual training data used for this task. The out-of-vocabulary rates for the TED task are 1.06% while the computer science lectures have 2.73% and nearly 1% on WMT.

5.3 German-to-English TED Task

The results for the translation of German TED lectures into English are shown in Table 2. The baseline system uses a 4-gram Kneser-Ney smoothed language model trained on the target side parallel data. We then added a RBMLM, which was only trained on the English side of the TED corpus.

If the word index RBMLM trained for one iteration using 32 hidden units is added, an improvement of about 1 BLEU can be achieved. The letter bigram model performs about 0.4 BLEU points better than no additional model, but significantly worse then the word index model or the other letter n-gram models. The letter 3- to 5-gram-based models obtain similar BLEU scores, varying only by 0.1 BLEU point. They also achieve a 0.8 to 0.9 BLEU points improvement against the baseline system and a 0.2 to 0.1 BLEU points decrease than the word index-based encoding.

System	Dev	Test
Baseline	26.31	23.02
+WordIndex	**27.27**	**24.04**
+Letter 2-gram	26.67	23.44
+Letter 3-gram	26.80	23.84
+Letter 4-gram	26.79	23.93
+Letter 5-gram	26.64	23.82

Table 2: Results for German-to-English TED translation task

Using the word index model with the first baseline system increases the BLEU score nearly as much as adding a n-gram-based language model trained on the TED corpus as done in the baseline of the systems presented in Table 3. In these experiments all letter-based models outperformed the baseline system. The bigram-based language model performs worst and the 3- and 4-gram-based models perform only slightly worse than the word index-based model.

System	Dev	Test
Baseline+ngram	27.45	24.06
+WordIndex	**27.70**	**24.34**
+Letter 2-gram	27.45	24.15
+Letter 3-gram	27.52	24.25
+Letter 4-gram	27.60	24.30

Table 3: Results of German-to-English TED translations using an additional in-domain language model.

A third experiment is presented in Table 4. Here we also applied phrase table adaptation as described in Niehues et al. (2010). In this experiment the word index model improves the system by 0.4 BLEU points. In this case all letter-based models perform very similar. They are again performing slightly worse than the word index-based system, but better than the baseline system.

To summarize the results, we could always improve the performance of the system by adding the letter n-gram-based language model. Furthermore, in most cases, the bigram model performs worse than the higher order models. It seems to be important for this task to have more context information. The 3- and 4-gram-based models perform almost equal, but slightly worse than the word index-based model.

System	Dev	Test
BL+ngram+adaptpt	28.40	24.57
+WordIndex	**28.55**	**24.96**
+Letter 2-gram	28.31	24.80
+Letter 3-gram	28.31	24.71
+Letter 4-gram	28.46	24.65

Table 4: Results of German-to-English TED translations with additional in-domain language model and adapted phrase table.

5.3.1 Caps Feature

In addition, we evaluated the proposed caps feature compared to the non-caps letter n-gram model and the baseline systems. As we can see in Table 5, caps sometimes improves and sometimes decreases the BLEU score by about ±0.2 BLEU points. One reason for that might be that most English words are written lowercased, therefore we do not gain much information.

System	Dev	Test
Baseline	26.31	23.02
+Letter 3-gram	**26.80**	23.84
+Letter 3-gram+caps	26.67	**23.85**
Baseline+ngram	27.45	24.06
+Letter 3-gram	27.52	24.25
+Letter 3-gram+caps	**27.60**	**24.47**
BL+ngram+adaptpt	28.40	24.57
+Letter 3-gram	28.31	**24.71**
+Letter 3-gram+caps	**28.43**	24.66

Table 5: Difference between caps and non-caps letter n-gram models.

5.4 German-to-English CSL Task

After that, we evaluated the computer science lecture (CSL) test set. We used the same system as for the TED translation task. We did not perform a new optimization, since we wanted so see how well the models performed on a different task.

The results are summarized in Table 6. In this case the baseline is outperformed by the word index approach by approximately 1.1 BLEU points. Except for the 4-gram model the results are similar to the result for the TED task. All systems could again outperform the baseline.

System	Test
Baseline	23.60
+WordIndex	**24.76**
+Letter 2-gram	24.17
+Letter 3-gram	24.36
+Letter 4-gram	23.82

Table 6: Results the baseline of the German-to-English CSL task.

The system with the additional in-domain language model in Table 7 shows that both letter n-gram language models perform better than the baseline and the word index model, improving the baseline by about 0.8 to 1 BLEU. Whereas the word index model only achieved an improvement of 0.6 BLEU points.

The results of the system with the additional phrase table adaption can be seen in Table 8. The

System	Test
Baseline+ngram	23.81
+WordIndex	24.41
+Letter 2-gram	24.37
+Letter 3-gram	24.66
+Letter 4-gram	**24.85**

Table 7: Results on German-to-English CSL corpus with additional in-domain language model.

word index model improves the baseline by 0.25 BLEU points. The letter n-gram models improve the baseline by about 0.3 to 0.4 BLEU points also improving over the word index model. The letter bigram model in this case performs worse than the baseline.

System	Test
BL+ngram+adaptpt	25.00
+WordIndex	25.25
+Letter 2-gram	24.68
+Letter 3-gram	**25.43**
+Letter 4-gram	25.33

Table 8: Results on German-to-English CSL with additional in-domain language model and adapted phrase table.

In summary, again the 3- and 4-gram letter models perform mostly better than the bigram version. They both perform mostly equal. In contrast to the TED task, they were even able to outperform the word index model in some configurations by up to 0.4 BLEU points.

5.5 English-to-German News Task

When translating English-to-German news we could not improve the performance of the baseline by using a word index model. In contrast, the performance dropped by 0.1 BLEU points. If we use a letter bigram model, we could improve the translation quality by 0.1 BLEU points over the baseline system.

System	Dev	Test
Baseline	16.90	17.36
+WordIndex	16.79	17.29
+Letter 2-gram	**16.91**	**17.48**

Table 9: Results for WMT2013 task English-to-German.

5.6 Model Size and Training Times

In general the letter n-gram models perform almost as good as the word index model on English language tasks. The advantage of the models up to the letter 3-gram context model is that the training time is lower compared to the word index model. All the models were trained using 10 cores and a batch size of 10 samples per contrastive divergence update. As can be seen in Table 10 the letter 3-gram model needs less than 50% of the weights and takes around 75% of the training time of the word index model. The four letter n-gram model takes longer to train due to more parameters.

Model	#Weights	Time
WordIndex	3.55 M	20 h 10 min
Letter 2-gram	0.24 M	1h 24 min
Letter 3-gram	1.55 M	15 h 12 min
Letter 4-gram	5.62 M	38 h 59 min

Table 10: Training time and number of parameters of the RBMLM models.

6 Conclusions

In this work we presented the letter n-gram-based input layer for continuous space language models. The proposed input layer enables us to encode the similarity of unknown words directly in the input layer as well as to directly model some morphological word forms.

We evaluated the encoding on different translation tasks. The RBMLM using this encoding could always improve the translation quality and perform similar to a RBMLM based on word indices. Especially in the second configuration which had a higher OOV rate, the letter n-gram model performed better than the word index model. Moreover, the model based on letter 3-grams uses only half the parameters of the word index model. This reduced the training time of the continuous space language model by a quarter.

Acknowledgments

This work was partly achieved as part of the Quaero Programme, funded by OSEO, French State agency for innovation. The research leading to these results has received funding from the European Union Seventh Framework Programme (FP7/2007-2013) under grant agreement n° 287658.

References

Yoshua Bengio, Réjean Ducharme, Pascal Vincent, and Christian Jauvin. 2003. A Neural Probabilistic Language Model. *Journal of Machine Learning Research*, 3:1137–1155.

Stanley F. Chen and Joshua Goodman. 1999. An empirical study of smoothing techniques for language modeling. *Computer Speech & Language*, 13(4):359–393.

Ahmad Emami, Imed Zitouni, and Lidia Mangu. 2008. Rich morphology based n-gram language models for arabic. In *INTERSPEECH*, pages 829–832. ISCA.

Geoffrey E. Hinton. 2002. Training products of experts by minimizing contrastive divergence. *Neural Comput.*, 14(8):1771–1800, August.

Geoffrey Hinton. 2010. A Practical Guide to Training Restricted Boltzmann Machines. Technical report, University of Toronto.

Katrin Kirchhoff and Mei Yang. 2005. Improved Language Modeling for Statistical Machine Translation. In *Proceedings of the ACL Workshop on Building and Using Parallel Texts*, pages 125–128, Ann Arbor, Michigan, USA.

Philipp Koehn, Hieu Hoang, Alexandra Birch, Chris Callison-Burch, Marcello Federico, Nicola Bertoldi, Brooke Cowan, Wade Shen, Christine Moran, Richard Zens, Chris Dyer, Ondrej Bojar, Alexandra Constantin, and Evan Herbst. 2007. Moses: Open Source Toolkit for Statistical Machine Translation. In *ACL 2007, Demonstration Session*, Prague, Czech Republic.

Hai Son Le, Ilya Oparin, Abdelkhalek Messaoudi, Alexandre Allauzen, Jean-Luc Gauvain, and François Yvon. 2011. Large vocabulary soul neural network language models. In *INTERSPEECH 2011, 12th Annual Conference of the International Speech Communication Association, Florence, Italy.*

Tomas Mikolov, Martin Karafiát, Lukas Burget, Jan Cernocký, and Sanjeev Khudanpur. 2010. Recurrent neural network based language model. In *INTERSPEECH 2010, 11th Annual Conference of the International Speech Communication Association, Makuhari, Chiba, Japan.*

Andriy Mnih and Geoffrey Hinton. 2007. Three new graphical models for statistical language modelling. In *Proceedings of the 24th international conference on Machine Learning*, ICML '07, pages 641–648, New York, NY, USA. ACM.

Andriy Mnih. 2010. *Learning distributed representations for statistical language modelling and collaborative filtering*. Ph.D. thesis, University of Toronto, Toronto, Ont., Canada. AAINR73159.

Masami Nakamura, Katsuteru Maruyama, Takeshi Kawabata, and Kiyohiro Shikano. 1990. Neural network approach to word category prediction for english texts. In *Proceedings of the 13th conference on Computational linguistics - Volume 3*, COLING '90, pages 213–218, Stroudsburg, PA, USA.

Jan Niehues and Muntsin Kolss. 2009. A POS-Based Model for Long-Range Reorderings in SMT. In *Fourth Workshop on Statistical Machine Translation (WMT 2009)*, Athens, Greece.

Jan Niehues and Stephan Vogel. 2008. Discriminative Word Alignment via Alignment Matrix Modeling. In *Proceedings of the Third Workshop on Statistical Machine Translation*, StatMT '08, pages 18–25, Stroudsburg, PA, USA.

Jan Niehues and Alex Waibel. 2012. Continuous Space Language Models using Restricted Boltzmann Machines. In *Proceedings of the International Workshop for Spoken Language Translation (IWSLT 2012)*, Hong Kong.

Jan Niehues, Mohammed Mediani, Teresa Herrmann, Michael Heck, Christian Herff, and Alex Waibel. 2010. The KIT Translation system for IWSLT 2010. In *Proceedings of the Seventh International Workshop on Spoken Language Translation (IWSLT)*, Paris, France.

Jan Niehues, Teresa Herrmann, Stephan Vogel, and Alex Waibel. 2011. Wider Context by Using Bilingual Language Models in Machine Translation. In *Sixth Workshop on Statistical Machine Translation (WMT 2011)*, Edinburgh, UK.

Kay Rottmann and Stephan Vogel. 2007. Word Reordering in Statistical Machine Translation with a POS-Based Distortion Model. In *TMI*, Skövde, Sweden.

Hasim Sak, Murat Saraclar, and Tunga Gungor. 2010. Morphology-based and sub-word language modeling for Turkish speech recognition. In *2010 IEEE International Conference on Acoustics Speech and Signal Processing (ICASSP)*, pages 5402–5405.

Ruhi Sarikaya and Yonggang Deng. 2007. Joint Morphological-Lexical Language Modeling for Machine Translation. In *Human Language Technologies 2007: The Conference of the North American Chapter of the Association for Computational Linguistics; Companion Volume, Short Papers*, pages 145–148, Rochester, New York, USA.

Helmut Schmid. 1994. Probabilistic Part-of-Speech Tagging Using Decision Trees. In *International Conference on New Methods in Language Processing*, Manchester, UK.

Holger Schwenk and Jean-Luc Gauvain. 2005. Training neural network language models on very large corpora. In *Proceedings of the conference on Human Language Technology and Empirical Methods in Natural Language Processing*, HLT '05, pages 201–208, Stroudsburg, PA, USA.

Holger Schwenk, Daniel Dchelotte, and Jean-Luc Gauvain. 2006. Continuous Space Language mModels for Statistical Machine T ranslation. In *Proceedings of the COLING/ACL on Main conference poster sessions*, COLING-ACL '06, pages 723–730, Stroudsburg, PA, USA.

Holger Schwenk. 2007. Continuous Space Language Models. *Comput. Speech Lang.*, 21(3):492–518, July.

M. Ali Basha Shaik, Amr El-Desoky Mousa, Ralf Schlüter, and Hermann Ney. 2011. Hybrid language models using mixed types of sub-lexical units for open vocabulary german lvcsr. In *INTERSPEECH 2011, 12th Annual Conference of the International Speech Communication Association, Florence, Italy.*

Andreas Stolcke. 2002. SRILM - an extensible language modeling toolkit. In *7th International Conference on Spoken Language Processing, ICSLP2002/INTERSPEECH 2002, Denver, Colorado, USA.*

Ashish Venugopal, Andreas Zollman, and Alex Waibel. 2005. Training and Evaluation Error Minimization Rules for Statistical Machine Translation. In *Workshop on Data-driven Machine Translation and Beyond (WPT-05)*, Ann Arbor, MI, USA.

Wei Xu and Alex Rudnicky. 2000. Can artificial neural networks learn language models? In *Sixth International Conference on Spoken Language Processing, ICSLP 2000 / INTERSPEECH 2000, Beijing, China*, pages 202–205. ISCA.

Transducing Sentences to Syntactic Feature Vectors: an Alternative Way to *"Parse"*?

Fabio Massimo Zanzotto
University of Rome "Tor Vergata"
Via del Politecnico 1
00133 Roma, Italy
fabio.massimo.zanzotto@uniroma2.it

Lorenzo Dell'Arciprete
University of Rome "Tor Vergata"
Via del Politecnico 1
00133 Roma, Italy
lorenzo.dellarciprete@gmail.com

Abstract

Classification and learning algorithms use syntactic structures as *proxies* between source sentences and feature vectors. In this paper, we explore an alternative path to use syntax in feature spaces: the *Distributed Representation "Parsers"* (DRP). The core of the idea is straightforward: DRPs directly obtain syntactic feature vectors from sentences without explicitly producing symbolic syntactic interpretations. Results show that DRPs produce feature spaces significantly better than those obtained by existing methods in the same conditions and competitive with those obtained by existing methods with lexical information.

1 Introduction

Syntactic processing is widely considered an important activity in natural language understanding (Chomsky, 1957). Research in natural language processing (NLP) exploits this hypothesis in models and systems. Syntactic features improve performance in high level tasks such as question answering (Zhang and Lee, 2003), semantic role labeling (Gildea and Jurafsky, 2002; Pradhan et al., 2005; Moschitti et al., 2008; Collobert et al., 2011), paraphrase detection (Socher et al., 2011), and textual entailment recognition (MacCartney et al., 2006; Wang and Neumann, 2007; Zanzotto et al., 2009).

Classification and learning algorithms are key components in the above models and in current NLP systems, but these algorithms cannot directly use syntactic structures. The relevant parts of phrase structure trees or dependency graphs are explicitly or implicitly stored in feature vectors.

To fully exploit syntax in learning classifiers, kernel machines (Cristianini and Shawe-Taylor, 2000) use graph similarity algorithms (e.g., (Collins and Duffy, 2002) for trees) as structural kernels (Gärtner, 2003). These structural kernels allow to exploit high-dimensional spaces of syntactic tree fragments by concealing their complexity. These feature spaces, although hidden, still exist. Then, even in kernel machines, symbolic syntactic structures act only as *proxies* between the source sentences and the syntactic feature vectors.

In this paper, we explore an alternative way to use syntax in feature spaces: the *Distributed Representation Parsers* (DRP). The core of the idea is straightforward: DRPs directly bridge the gap between sentences and syntactic feature spaces. DRPs act as syntactic parsers and feature extractors at the same time. We leverage on the *distributed trees* recently introduced by Zanzotto&Dell'Arciprete (2012) and on multiple linear regression models. *Distributed trees* are small vectors that encode the large vectors of the syntactic tree fragments underlying the tree kernels (Collins and Duffy, 2002). These vectors effectively represent the original vectors and lead to performances in NLP tasks similar to tree kernels. Multiple linear regression allows to learn linear DRPs from training data. We experiment with the Penn Treebank data set (Marcus et al., 1993). Results show that DRPs produce distributed trees significantly better than those obtained by existing methods, in the same non-lexicalized conditions, and competitive with those obtained by existing methods with lexical information. Finally, DRPs are extremely faster than existing methods.

The rest of the paper is organized as follows. First, we present the background of our idea (Sec. 2). Second, we fully describe our model (Sec. 3). Then, we report on the experiments (Sec. 4). Finally, we draw some conclusions and outline future work (Sec. 5)

2 Background

Classification and learning algorithms for NLP tasks treat syntactic structures t as vectors in feature spaces $\vec{t} \in \mathbb{R}^m$. Each feature generally represents a substructure τ_i. In simple weighting schemes, feature values are 1 if τ_i is a substructure of t and 0 otherwise. Different weighting schemes are used and possible. Then, learning algorithms exploit these feature vectors in different ways. Decision tree learners (Quinlan, 1993) elect the most representative feature at each iteration, whereas kernel machines (Cristianini and Shawe-Taylor, 2000) exploit similarity between pairs of instances, $s(t_1, t_2)$. This similarity is generally measured as the dot product between the two vectors, i.e. $s(t_1, t_2) = \vec{t_1} \cdot \vec{t_2}$.

The use of syntactic features changed when tree kernels (Collins and Duffy, 2002) appeared. Tree kernels gave the possibility to fully exploit feature spaces of tree fragments. Until then, learning algorithms could not treat these huge spaces. It is infeasible to explicitly represent that kind of feature vectors and to directly compute similarities through dot products. Tree kernels (Collins and Duffy, 2002), by computing similarities between two trees with tree comparison algorithms, exactly determine dot products of vectors in these target spaces. After their introduction, different tree kernels have been proposed (e.g., (Vishwanathan and Smola, 2002; Culotta and Sorensen, 2004; Moschitti, 2006)). Their use spread in many NLP tasks (e.g., (Zhou et al., 2007; Wang and Neumann, 2007; Moschitti et al., 2008; Zanzotto et al., 2009; Zhang and Li, 2009)) and in other areas like biology (Vert, 2002; Hashimoto et al., 2008) and computer security (Düssel et al., 2008; Rieck and Laskov, 2007; Bockermann et al., 2009).

Tree kernels have played a very important role in promoting the use of syntactic information in learning classifiers, but this method obfuscated the fact that syntactic trees are ultimately used as vectors in learning algorithms. To work with the idea of directly obtaining rich syntactic feature vectors from sentences, we need some techniques to make these high-dimensional vectors again explicit, through smaller but expressive vectors.

A solution to the above problem stems from the recently revitalized research in Distributed Representations (DR) (Hinton et al., 1986; Bengio, 2009; Collobert et al., 2011; Socher et al., 2011; Zanzotto and Dell'Arciprete, 2012). Distributed Representations, studied in opposition to symbolic representations (Rumelhart and Mcclelland, 1986), are methods for encoding data structures such as trees into vectors, matrices, or high-order tensors. The targets of these representations are generally propositions, i.e., flat tree structures. The Holographic Reduced Representations (HRR), proposed by Plate (1994), produce nearly orthogonal vectors for different structures by combining circular convolution and randomly generated vectors for basic components (as in (Anderson, 1973; Murdock, 1983)).

Building on HRRs, Distributed Trees (DT) have been proposed to encode deeper trees in low dimensional vectors (Zanzotto and Dell'Arciprete, 2012). DTs approximate the feature space of tree fragments defined for the tree kernels (Collins and Duffy, 2002) and guarantee similar performances of classifiers in NLP tasks such as question classification and textual entailment recognition. Thus, Distributed Trees are good representations of syntactic trees, that we can use in our definition of distributed representation parsers (DRPs).

3 Distributed Representation Parsers

In this section, first, we sketch the idea of Distributed Representation "Parsers" (DRPs). Then, we review the *distributed trees* as a way to represent trees in low dimensional vectors. Finally, we describe how to build DRPs by mixing a function that encodes sentences in vectors and a linear regressor that can be induced from training data.

3.1 The Idea

The approach to using syntax in learning algorithms generally follows two steps: first, parse sentences s with a symbolic parser (e.g., (Collins, 2003; Charniak, 2000; Nivre et al., 2007)) and produce symbolic trees t; second, use an encoder to build syntactic feature vectors. Figure 1 sketches this idea when the final vectors are the *distributed trees* $\overset{\rightsquigarrow}{t} \in R^d$ (Zanzotto and Dell'Arciprete, 2012)[1]. In this case, the last step

[1]To represent a distributed tree for a tree t, we use the notation $\overset{\rightsquigarrow}{t}$ to stress that this small vector is an approximation of the original high-dimensional vector $\vec{t}$ in the space of tree

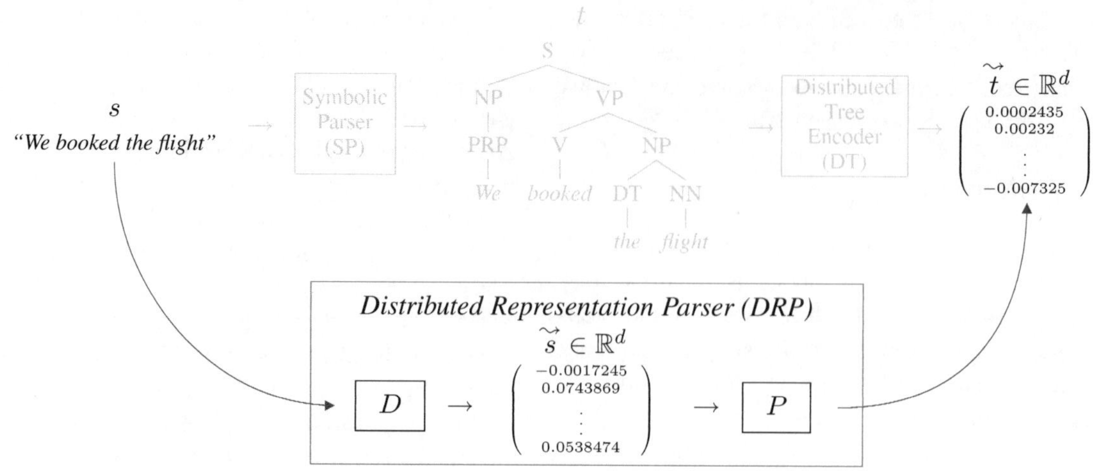

Figure 1: "Parsing" with distributed structures in perspective

is the Distributed Tree Encoder (DT).

Our proposal is to build a Distributed Representation "Parser" (DRP) that directly maps sentences s into the final vectors. We choose the distributed trees $\vec{t}$ as these reduced vectors fully represent the syntactic trees. A DRP acts as follows (see Figure 1): first, a function D encodes sentence s into a distributed vector $\vec{s} \in R^d$; second, a function P transforms the input vector $\vec{s}$ into a distributed tree $\vec{t}$. This second step is a vector to vector transformation and, in a wide sense, "parses" the input sentence.

Given an input sentence s, a DRP is then a function defined as follows:

$$\vec{t} = DRP(s) = P(D(s)) \tag{1}$$

In this paper, we design some functions D and we propose a linear function P, designed to be a regressor that can be induced from training data. In this study, we use a space with d dimensions for both sentences $\vec{s}$ and *distributed trees* $\vec{t}$, but, in general, these spaces can be of different size.

3.2 Syntactic Trees as Distributed Vectors

We here report on the *distributed trees*[2] (Zanzotto and Dell'Arciprete, 2012) to describe how these vectors represent syntactic trees and how the dot product between two distributed trees approximates the tree kernel defined by Collins and Duffy (2002).

Given a tree t, the corresponding distributed tree $\vec{t}$ is defined as follows:

$$DT(t) = \sum_{\tau_i \in S(t)} \omega_i \vec{\tau}_i \tag{2}$$

where $S(t)$ is the set of the subtrees τ_i of t, $\vec{\tau}_i$ is the small vector corresponding to tree fragment τ_i and ω_i is the weight of subtree τ_i in the final feature space. As in (Collins and Duffy, 2002), the set $S(t)$ contains tree fragments τ such that the root of τ is any non-terminal node in t and, if τ contains node n, it must contain all the siblings of n in t (see, for example, $S_{lex}(t)$ in Figure 2). The weight ω_i is defined as:

$$\omega_i = \begin{cases} \sqrt{\lambda^{|\tau_i|-1}} & \text{if } |\tau_i| > 1 \text{ and } \lambda \neq 0 \\ 1 & \text{if } |\tau_i| = 1 \\ 0 & \text{if } \lambda = 0 \end{cases} \tag{3}$$

where $|\tau_i|$ is the number of non-terminal nodes of tree fragment τ_i and λ is the traditional parameter used to penalize large subtrees. For $\lambda = 0$, ω_i has a value 1 for productions and 0 otherwise. If different tree fragments are associated to nearly orthonormal vectors, the dot product $\vec{t}_1 \cdot \vec{t}_2$ approximates the tree kernel (Zanzotto and Dell'Arciprete, 2012).

A key feature of the distributed tree fragments $\vec{\tau}$ is that these vectors are built compositionally from a set $\mathcal{N}$ of *nearly orthonormal random vectors* $\vec{n}$, associated to node labels n. Given a subtree τ, the related vector is obtained as:

$$\vec{\tau} = \vec{n}_1 \boxtimes \vec{n}_2 \boxtimes \ldots \boxtimes \vec{n}_k$$

fragments.

[2]For the experiments, we used the implementation of the distributed tree encoder available at http://code.google.com/p/distributed-tree-kernels/

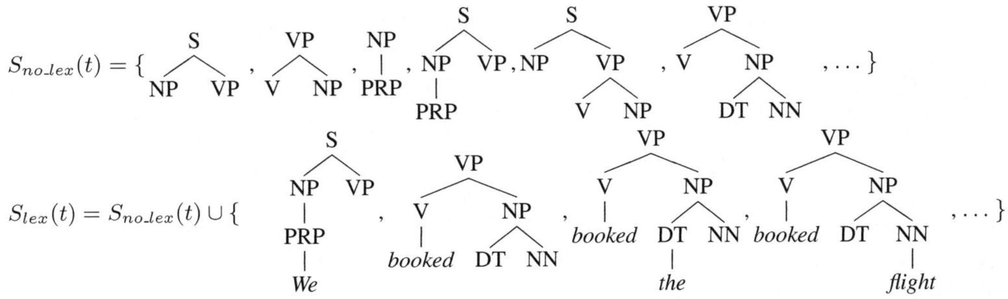

Figure 2: Subtrees of the tree t in Figure 1

where node vectors $\vec{n}_i$ are ordered according to a depth-first visit of subtree τ and $\boxtimes$ is a vector composition operation, specifically the *shuffled circular convolution*[3]. This function guarantees that two different subtrees have nearly orthonormal vectors (see (Zanzotto and Dell'Arciprete, 2012) for more details). For example, the fifth tree τ_5 of set $S_{no\_lex}(t)$ in Figure 2 is:

$$\vec{\tau}_5 = \vec{S} \boxtimes (\vec{NP} \boxtimes (\vec{VP} \boxtimes (\vec{V} \boxtimes \vec{NP})))$$

We experiment with two tree fragment sets: the non-lexicalized set $S_{no\_lex}(t)$, where tree fragments do not contain words, and the lexicalized set $S_{lex}(t)$, including all the tree fragments. An example is given in Figure 2.

3.3 The Model

To build a DRP, we need to define the encoder D and the transformer P. In the following, we present a non-lexicalized and a lexicalized model for the encoder D and we describe how we can learn the transformer P by means of a linear regression model.

3.3.1 Sentence Encoders

Establishing good models to encode input sentences into vectors is the most difficult challenge. The models should consider the kind of information that can lead to a correct syntactic interpretation. Only in this way, the distributed representation parser can act as a vector transforming module. Unlike in models such as (Socher et al., 2011), we want our encoder to represent the whole sentence as a fixed size vector. We propose a non-lexicalized model and a lexicalized model.

[3] The *shuffled circular convolution* $\boxtimes$ is defined as $\vec{a} \boxtimes \vec{b} = s_1(\vec{a}) \otimes s_2(\vec{b})$ where $\otimes$ is the circular convolution and s_1 and s_2 are two different random permutations of vector elements.

Non-lexicalized model The non-lexicalized model relies only on the pos-tags of the sentences s: $s = p_1 \dots p_n$ where p_i is the pos-tag associated with the i-th token of the sentence. In the following we discuss how to encode this information in a $\mathbb{R}^d$ space. The basic model $D_1(s)$ is the one that considers the bag-of-postags, that is:

$$D_1(s) = \sum_i \vec{p}_i \tag{4}$$

where $\vec{p}_i \in \mathcal{N}$ is the vector for label p_i, taken from the set of nearly orthonomal random vectors $\mathcal{N}$. It is basically in line with the bag-of-word model used in random indexing (Sahlgren, 2005). Due to the commutative property of the sum and since vectors in $\mathcal{N}$ are nearly orthonormal: (1) two sentences with the same set of pos-tags have the same vector; and, (2) the dot product between two vectors, $D_1(s_1)$ and $D_1(s_2)$, representing sentences s_1 and s_2, approximately counts how many pos-tags the two sentences have in common. The vector for the sentence in Figure 1 is then:

$$D_1(s) = \vec{PRP} + \vec{V} + \vec{DT} + \vec{NN}$$

The general non-lexicalized model that takes into account all n-grams of pos-tags, up to length j, is then the following:

$$D_j(s) = D_{j-1}(s) + \sum_i \vec{p}_i \boxtimes \dots \boxtimes \vec{p}_{i+j-1}$$

where $\boxtimes$ is again the *shuffled circular convolution*. An n-gram $p_i \dots p_{i+j-1}$ of pos-tags is represented as $\vec{p}_i \boxtimes \dots \boxtimes \vec{p}_{i+j-1}$. Given the properties of the *shuffled circular convolution*, an n-gram of pos-tags is associated to a versor, as it composes j versors, and two different n-grams have nearly orthogonal vectors. For example, vector $D_3(s)$ for the sentence in Figure 1 is:

$$
\begin{aligned}
D_3(s) \;=\; & \vec{PRP} + \vec{V} + \vec{DT} + \vec{NN} + \\
& \vec{PRP} \boxtimes \vec{V} + \vec{V} \boxtimes \vec{DT} + \vec{DT} \boxtimes \vec{NN} + \\
& \vec{PRP} \boxtimes \vec{V} \boxtimes \vec{DT} + \vec{V} \boxtimes \vec{DT} \boxtimes \vec{NN}
\end{aligned}
$$

Lexicalized model Including lexical information is the hardest part of the overall model, as it makes vectors denser in information. Here we propose an initial model that is basically as the non-lexicalized model, but includes a vector representing the words in the unigrams. The equation representing sentences as unigrams is:

$$D_1^{lex}(s) = \sum_i \vec{p}_i \boxtimes \vec{w}_i$$

Vector $\vec{w}_i$ represents word w_i and is taken from the set $\mathcal{N}$ of nearly orthonormal random vectors. This guarantees that $D_1^{lex}(s)$ is not lossy. Given a pair word-postag (w, p), it is possible to know if the sentence contains this pair, as $D_1^{lex}(s) \times \vec{p} \boxtimes \vec{w} \approx 1$ if (w, p) is in sentence s and $D_1^{lex}(s) \times \vec{p} \boxtimes \vec{w} \approx 0$ otherwise. Other vectors for representing words, e.g., distributional vectors or those obtained as look-up tables in deep learning architectures (Col lobert and Weston, 2008), do not guarantee this possibility.

The general equation for the lexicalized version of the sentence encoder follows:

$$D_j^{lex}(s) = D_{j-1}^{lex}(s) + \sum_i \vec{p}_i \boxtimes \ldots \boxtimes \vec{p}_{i+j-1}$$

This model is only an initial proposal in order to take into account lexical information.

3.3.2 Learning Transformers with Linear Regression

The transformer P of the DRP (see Equation 1) can be seen as a linear regressor:

$$\vec{t} = \mathbf{P}\vec{s} \tag{5}$$

where $\mathbf{P}$ is a square matrix. This latter can be estimated having training sets $(\mathbf{T}, \mathbf{S})$ of *oracle vectors* and sentence input vectors $(\vec{t}_i, \vec{s}_i)$ for sentences s_i. Interpreting these sets as matrices, we need to solve a linear set of equations, i.e.: $\mathbf{T} = \mathbf{PS}$.

An approximate solution can be computed using Principal Component Analysis and Partial Least Square Regression[4]. This method relies on *Moore-Penrose pseudo-inversion* (Penrose, 1955). Pseudo-inverse matrices $\mathbf{S}^+$ are obtained using singular value decomposition (SVD). Matrices have the property $\mathbf{SS}^+ = \mathbf{I}$. Using the iterative method for computing SVD (Golub and Kahan, 1965), we can obtain different approximations $\mathbf{S}^+_{(k)}$ of $\mathbf{S}^+$ considering k singular values. Final approximations of DRPs are then: $\mathbf{P}_{(k)} = \mathbf{TS}^+_{(k)}$.

Matrices $\mathbf{P}$ are estimated by pseudo-inverting matrices representing input vectors for sentences $\mathbf{S}$. Given the different input representations for sentences, we can then estimate different DRPs: $DRP_1 = \mathbf{TS}_1^+$, $DRP_2 = \mathbf{TS}_2^+$, and so on. We need to estimate the best k in a separate parameter estimation set.

4 Experiments

We evaluated three issues for assessing DRP models: the performance of DRPs in reproducing oracle distributed trees (Sec. 4.2); the quality of the topology of the vector spaces of distributed trees induced by DRPs (Sec. 4.3); and the computation run time of DRPs (Sec. 4.4). Section 4.1 describes the experimental set-up.

4.1 Experimental Set-up

Data We derived the data sets from the Wall Street Journal (WSJ) portion of the English Penn Treebank data set (Marcus et al., 1993), using a standard data split for training (sections 2-21 PT_{train} with 39,832 trees) and for testing (section 23 PT_{23} with 2,416 trees). We used section 24 PT_{24} with 1,346 trees for parameter estimation.

We produced the final data sets of *distributed trees* with three different λ values: λ=0, λ=0.2, and λ=0.4. For each λ, we have two versions of the data sets: a non-lexicalized version (no_lex), where syntactic trees are considered without words, and a lexicalized version (lex), where words are considered. Oracle trees t are transformed into oracle distributed trees $\vec{o}$ using the Distributed Tree Encoder DT (see Figure 1). We experimented with two sizes of the distributed trees space $\mathbb{R}^d$: 4096 and 8192.

We have designed the data sets to determine how DRPs behave with λ values relevant for syntax-sensitive NLP tasks. Both tree kernels and distributed tree kernels have the best performances in tasks such as question classification, semantic role labeling, or textual entailment recognition

[4]An implementation of this method is available within the R statistical package (Mevik and Wehrens, 2007).

with λ values in the range 0–0.4.

System Comparison We compared the DRPs against the *existing way* of producing distributed trees (based on the recent paper described in (Zanzotto and Dell'Arciprete, 2012)): distributed trees are obtained using the output of a symbolic parser (SP) that is then transformed into a distributed tree using the DT with the appropriate λ. We refer to this chain as the Distributed Symbolic Parser (DSP). The DSP is then the chain $DSP(s) = DT(SP(s))$ (see Figure 1). As for the symbolic parser, we used Bikel's version (Bikel, 2004) of Collins' head-driven statistical parser (Collins, 2003). For a correct comparison, we used the Bikel's parser with oracle part-of-speech tags. We experimented with two versions: (1) a lexicalized method DSP_{lex}, i.e., the natural setting of the Collins/Bikel parser, and (2) a fully non-lexicalized version DSP_{no_lex} that exploits only part-of-speech tags. We obtained this last version by removing words in input sentences and leaving only part-of-speech tags. We trained these DSPs on PT_{train}.

Parameter estimation DRPs have two basic parameters: (1) parameter k of the pseudo-inverse, that is, the number of considered eigenvectors (see Section 3.3.2) and (2) the maximum length j of the n-grams considered by the encoder D_j (see Section 3.3.1). We performed the parameter estimation on the datasets derived from section PT_{24} by maximizing a pseudo f-measure. Section 4.2 reports both the definition of the measure and the results of the parameter estimation.

4.2 Parsing Performance

The first issue to explore is whether DRPs are actually good "distributed syntactic parsers". We compare DRPs against the distributed symbolic parsers by evaluating how well these "distributed syntactic parsers" reproduce oracle distributed trees.

Method A good DRP should produce distributed trees that are similar to oracle distributed trees. To capture this, we use the cosine similarity between the system and the oracle vectors:

$$cos(\vec{t}, \vec{o}) = \frac{\vec{t} \cdot \vec{o}}{||\vec{t}||||\vec{o}||}$$

where $\vec{t}$ is the system's distributed tree and $\vec{o}$ is the oracle distributed tree. We compute these the cosine similarity at the sentence-based (i.e., vector-based) granularity. Results report average values.

dim	*Model*	$\lambda = 0$	$\lambda = 0.2$	$\lambda = 0.4$
4096	DRP_1	0.6285	0.5697	0.542
	DRP_2	0.8011	0.7311	0.631
	DRP_3	0.8276‡	0.7552 ‡	0.6506‡
	DRP_4	0.8171	0.744	0.6419
	DRP_5	0.8045	0.7342	0.631
	DSP_{no_lex}	0.654	0.5884	0.4835
	DSP_{lex}	0.815	0.7813	0.7121
8192	DRP_3	0.8335‡	0.7605‡	0.6558‡
	DSP_{no_lex}	0.6584	0.5924	0.4873
	DSP_{lex}	0.8157	0.7815	0.7123

Table 1: Average *similarity* on PT_{23} of the DRPs (with different j) and the DSP on the *non-lexicalized data sets* with different λs and with the two dimensions of the distributed tree space (4096 and 8192). ‡ indicates significant difference wrt. DSP_{no_lex} ($p << .005$ computed with the Student's t test)

Model	$\lambda = 0$	$\lambda = 0.2$	$\lambda = 0.4$
DRP_3	0.7192	0.6406	0.0646
DSP_{lex}	0.9073	0.8564	0.6459

Table 2: Average *similarity* on PT_{23} of the DRP_3 and the DSP_{lex} on the *lexicalized data sets* with different λs on the distributed tree space with 4096 dimensions

Estimated parameters We estimated parameters k and j by training the different DRPs on the PT_{train} set and by maximizing the *similarity* of the DRPs on PT_{24}. The best pair of parameters is j=3 and k=3000. For completeness, we report also the best k values for the five different j we experimented with: $k = 47$ for j=1 (the linearly independent vectors representing pos-tags), $k = 1300$ for j=2, $k = 3000$ for j=3, $k = 4000$ for j=4, and $k = 4000$ for j=5. For comparison, some resulting tables report results for the different values of j.

Results Table 1 reports the results of the first set of experiments on the *non-lexicalized* data sets. The first block of rows (seven rows) reports the *average cosine similarity* of the different methods on the distributed tree spaces with 4096 dimensions. The second block (the last three rows) reports the performance on the space with 8192 dimensions. The *average cosine similarity* is computed on the PT_{23} set. Although we already selected j=3 as the best parameterization (i.e. DRP_3), the first

Output	Model	$\lambda = 0$	$\lambda = 0.2$	$\lambda = 0.4$
No lex	DRP_3	0.9490	0.9465	0.9408
	DSP_{no_lex}	0.9033	0.9001	0.8932
	DSP_{lex}	0.9627	0.9610	0.9566
Lex	DRP_3	0.9642	0.9599	0.0025
	DSP_{lex}	0.9845	0.9817	0.9451

Table 3: Average Spearman's Correlation: dim 4096 between the oracle's vector space and the systems' vector spaces (100 trials on lists of 1000 sentence pairs).

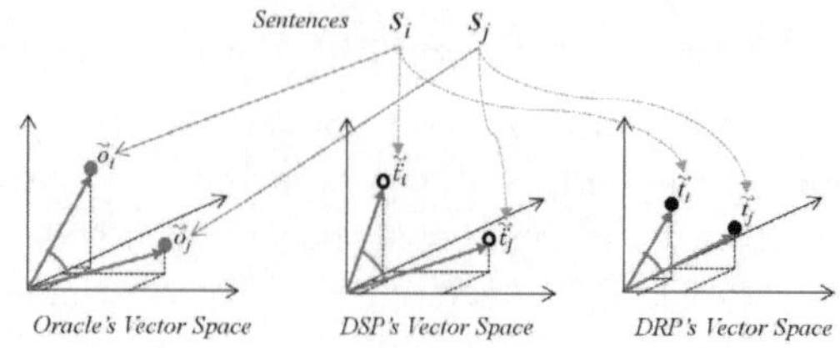

Figure 3: Topology of the resulting spaces derived with the three different methods: similarities between sentences

five rows of the first block report the results of the DRPs for five values of j. This gives an idea of how the different DRPs behave. The last two rows of this block report the results of the two DSPs.

We can observe some important facts. First, DRPs exploiting 2-grams, 3-grams, 4-grams, and 5-grams of part-of-speech tags behave significantly better than the 1-grams for all the values of λ. Distributed representation parsers need inputs that keep trace of sequences of pos-tags of sentences. But these sequences tend to confuse the model when too long. As expected, DRP_3 behaves better than all the other DRPs. Second, DRP_3 behaves significantly better than the comparable traditional parsing chain DSP_{no_lex} that uses only part-of-speech tags and no lexical information. This happens for all the values of λ. Third, DRP_3 behaves similarly to DSP_{lex} for λ=0. Both parsers use oracle pos tags to emit sentence interpretations but DSP_{lex} also exploits lexical information that DRP_3 does not access. For λ=0.2 and λ=0.4, the more informed DSP_{lex} behaves significantly better than DRP_3. But DRP_3 still behaves significantly better than the comparable DSP_{no_lex}. All these observations are valid also for the results obtained for 8192 dimensions.

Table 2 reports the results of the second set of experiments on the *lexicalized* data sets performed on a 4192-dimension space. The first row reports the *average cosine similarity* of DRP_3 trained on the lexicalized model and the second row reports the results of DSP_{lex}. In this case, DRP_3 is not behaving well with respect to DSP_{lex}. The additional problem DRP_3 has is that it has to reproduce input words in the output. This greatly complicates the work of the distributed representation parser. But, as we report in the next section, this preliminary result may be still satisfactory for λ=0 and λ=0.2.

4.3 Kernel-based Performance

This experiment investigates how DRPs preserve the topology of the oracle vector space. This correlation is an important quality factor of a distributed tree space. When using distributed tree vectors in learning classifiers, whether $\vec{o_i} \cdot \vec{o_j}$ in the oracle's vector space is similar to $\vec{t_i} \cdot \vec{t_j}$ in the DRP's vector space is more important than whether $\vec{o_i}$ is similar to $\vec{t_i}$ (see Figure 3). Sentences that are close using the oracle syntactic interpretations should also be close using DRP vectors. The topology of the vector space is more relevant than the actual quality of the vectors. The experiment on the parsing quality in the previous section does not properly investigate this property, as the performance of DRPs could be not sufficient to preserve distances among sentences.

Method We evaluate the coherence of the topology of two distributed tree spaces by measuring the Spearman's correlation between two lists of pairs of sentences (s_i, s_j), ranked according to the similarity between the two sentences. If the two lists of pairs are highly correlated, the topology of the two spaces is similar. The different methods and, thus, the different distributed tree spaces are compared against the oracle vector space (see Figure 3). Then, the first list always represents the oracle vector space and ranks pairs (s_i, s_j) according to $\vec{o}_i \cdot \vec{o}_j$. The second list instead represents the space obtained with a DSP or a DRP. Thus, it is respectively ranked with $\vec{\ddot{t}}_i \cdot \vec{\ddot{t}}_j$ or $\vec{t_i} \cdot \vec{t_j}$. In this way, we can comparatively evaluate the quality of the distributed tree vectors of our DRPs with respect to the other methods. We report average and standard deviation of the Spearman's correlation on 100 runs over lists of 1000 pairs. We used the testing set PT_{23} for extracting vectors.

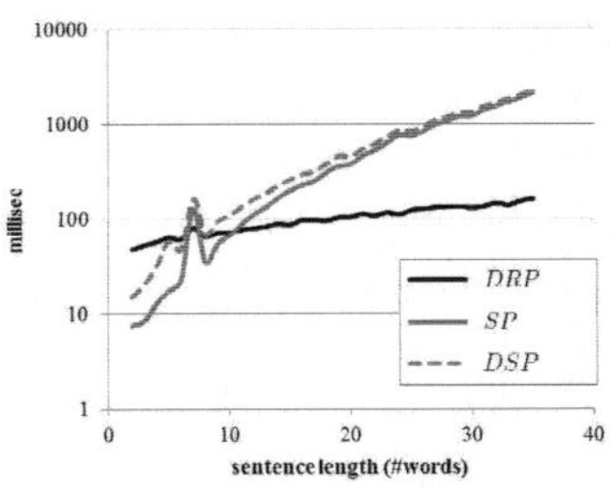

Figure 4: Running time with respect to the sentence length (dimension = 4092)

Results Table 3 reports results both on the non-lexicalized and on the lexicalized data set. For the non-lexicalized data set we report three methods (DRP_3, DSP_{no_lex}, and DSP_{lex}) and for the lexicalized dataset we report two methods (DRP_3 and DSP_{lex}). Columns represent different values of λ. Experiments are carried out on the 4096-dimension space. For the non-lexicalized data set, distributed representation parsers behave significantly better than DSP_{no_lex} for all the values of λ. The upper-bound of DSP_{lex} is not so far. For the harder lexicalized data set, the difference between DRP_3 and DSP_{lex} is smaller than the one based on the parsing performance. Thus, we have more evidence of the fact that we are in a good track. DRPs can substitute the *DSP* in generating vector spaces of distributed trees that adequately approximate the space defined by an oracle.

4.4 Running Time

In this last experiment, we compared the running time of the DRP with respect to the DSP. The analysis has been done on a dual-core processor and both systems are implemented in the same programming language, i.e. Java. Figure 4 plots the running time of the DRP, the SP, and the full $DSP = DT \circ SP$. The x-axis represents the sentence length in words and the y-axis represents the running time in milliseconds. The distance between SP and DSP shrinks as the plot is in a logarithmic scale. Figure 5 reports the average cosine similarity of DRP, DSP_{lex}, and DSP_{no_lex}, with respect to the sentence length, on the non-lexicalized data set with λ=0.4.

We observe that DRP becomes extremely convenient for sentences larger than 10 words (see Fig. 4) and the average cosine similarity difference between the different methods is nearly constant for the different sentence lengths (see Fig. 5). This test already makes DRPs very appealing methods for real time applications. But, if we consider that

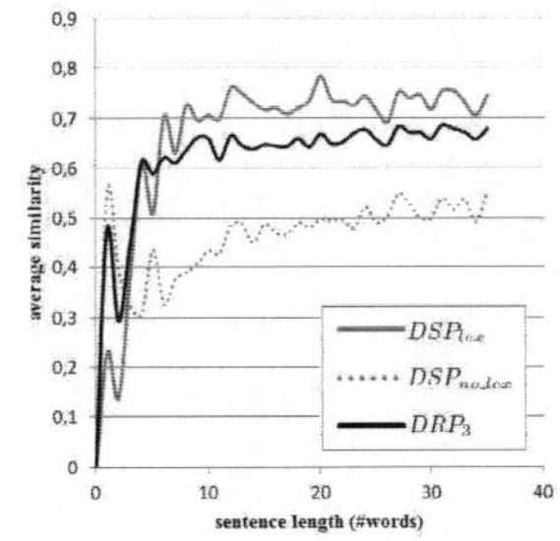

Figure 5: Average similarity with λ=0.4 with respect to the sentence length (dimension = 4092)

DRPs can run completely on Graphical Processing Units (GPUs), as dealing only with matrix products, fast-Fourier transforms, and random generators, we can better appreciate the potentials of the proposed methods.

5 Conclusions and Future Work

We presented Distributed Representation Parsers (DRP) as a novel path to use syntactic structures in feature spaces. We have shown that these "parsers" can be learnt using training data and that DRPs are competitive with respect to traditional methods of using syntax in feature spaces.

This novel path to use syntactic structures in feature spaces opens interesting and unexplored possibilities. First, DRPs tackle the issue of computational efficiency of structural kernel methods (Rieck et al., 2010; Shin et al., 2011) from another perspective. DRPs could reduce structural kernel computations to extremely efficient dot products. Second, the tight integration of parsing and feature vector generation lowers the computational cost of producing distributed representations from trees, as circular convolution is not applied on-line.

Finally, DRPs can contribute to treat syntax in deep learning models in a uniform way. Deep learning models (Bengio, 2009) are completely based on distributed representations. But when applied to natural language processing tasks (e.g., (Collobert et al., 2011; Socher et al., 2011)), syntactic structures are not represented in the neural networks in a distributed way. Syntactic information is generally used by exploiting symbolic parse trees, and this information positively impacts performances on final applications, e.g., in paraphrase detection (Socher et al., 2011) and in semantic role labeling (Collobert et al., 2011). Building on the results presented here, an interesting line of research is then the integration of distributed representation parsers and deep learning models.

References

James A. Anderson. 1973. A theory for the recognition of items from short memorized lists. *Psychological Review*, 80(6):417 – 438.

Yoshua Bengio. 2009. Learning deep architectures for ai. *Foundations and Trends in Machine Learning*, 2(1):1–127.

Daniel M. Bikel. 2004. Intricacies of collins' parsing model. *Comput. Linguist.*, 30:479–511, December.

Christian Bockermann, Martin Apel, and Michael Meier. 2009. Learning sql for database intrusion detection using context-sensitive modelling. In *Detection of Intrusions andMalware & Vulnerability Assessment (DIMVA)*, pages 196–205.

Eugene Charniak. 2000. A maximum-entropy-inspired parser. In *Proc. of the 1st NAACL*, pages 132–139, Seattle, Washington.

Naom Chomsky. 1957. *Aspect of Syntax Theory*. MIT Press, Cambridge, Massachussetts.

Michael Collins and Nigel Duffy. 2002. New ranking algorithms for parsing and tagging: Kernels over discrete structures, and the voted perceptron. In *Proceedings of ACL02*.

Michael Collins. 2003. Head-driven statistical models for natural language parsing. *Comput. Linguist.*, 29(4):589–637.

R. Collobert and J. Weston. 2008. A unified architecture for natural language processing: Deep neural networks with multitask learning. In *International Conference on Machine Learning, ICML*.

Ronan Collobert, Jason Weston, Léon Bottou, Michael Karlen, Koray Kavukcuoglu, and Pavel Kuksa. 2011. Natural language processing (almost) from scratch. *J. Mach. Learn. Res.*, 12:2493–2537, November.

Nello Cristianini and John Shawe-Taylor. 2000. *An Introduction to Support Vector Machines and Other Kernel-based Learning Methods*. Cambridge University Press, March.

Aron Culotta and Jeffrey Sorensen. 2004. Dependency tree kernels for relation extraction. In *Proceedings of the 42nd Annual Meeting on Association for Computational Linguistics*, ACL '04, Stroudsburg, PA, USA. Association for Computational Linguistics.

Patrick Düssel, Christian Gehl, Pavel Laskov, and Konrad Rieck. 2008. Incorporation of application layer protocol syntax into anomaly detection. In *Proceedings of the 4th International Conference on Information Systems Security*, ICISS '08, pages 188–202, Berlin, Heidelberg. Springer-Verlag.

Thomas Gärtner. 2003. A survey of kernels for structured data. *SIGKDD Explorations*.

Daniel Gildea and Daniel Jurafsky. 2002. Automatic Labeling of Semantic Roles. *Computational Linguistics*, 28(3):245–288.

Gene Golub and William Kahan. 1965. Calculating the singular values and pseudo-inverse of a matrix. *Journal of the Society for Industrial and Applied Mathematics, Series B: Numerical Analysis*, 2(2):205–224.

Kosuke Hashimoto, Ichigaku Takigawa, Motoki Shiga, Minoru Kanehisa, and Hiroshi Mamitsuka. 2008. Mining significant tree patterns in carbohydrate sugar chains. *Bioinformatics*, 24:i167–i173, August.

G. E. Hinton, J. L. McClelland, and D. E. Rumelhart. 1986. Distributed representations. In D. E. Rumelhart and J. L. McClelland, editors, *Parallel Distributed Processing: Explorations in the Microstructure of Cognition. Volume 1: Foundations*. MIT Press, Cambridge, MA.

Bill MacCartney, Trond Grenager, Marie-Catherine de Marneffe, Daniel Cer, and Christopher D. Manning. 2006. Learning to recognize features of valid textual entailments. In *Proceedings of the Human Language Technology Conference of the NAACL, Main Conference*, pages 41–48, New York City, USA, June. Association for Computational Linguistics.

M. P. Marcus, B. Santorini, and M. A. Marcinkiewicz. 1993. Building a large annotated corpus of english: The penn treebank. *Computational Linguistics*, 19:313–330.

Bjrn-Helge Mevik and Ron Wehrens. 2007. The pls package: Principal component and partial least squares regression in r. *Journal of Statistical Software*, 18(2):1–24, 1.

Alessandro Moschitti, Daniele Pighin, and Roberto Basili. 2008. Tree kernels for semantic role labeling. *Computational Linguistics*, 34(2):193–224.

Alessandro Moschitti. 2006. Efficient Convolution Kernels for Dependency and Constituent Syntactic Trees. In *Proceedings of The 17th European Conference on Machine Learning*, Berlin, Germany.

Bennet B. Murdock. 1983. A distributed memory model for serial-order information. *Psychological Review*, 90(4):316 – 338.

Joakim Nivre, Johan Hall, Jens Nilsson, Atanas Chanev, Glsen Eryigit, Sandra Kübler, Svetoslav Marinov, and Erwin Marsi. 2007. Maltparser: A language-independent system for data-driven dependency parsing. *Natural Language Engineering*, 13(2):95–135.

Roger Penrose. 1955. A generalized inverse for matrices. In *Proc. Cambridge Philosophical Society*.

T. A. Plate. 1994. *Distributed Representations and Nested Compositional Structure*. Ph.D. thesis.

Sameer Pradhan, Wayne Ward, Kadri Hacioglu, James H. Martin, and Daniel Jurafsky. 2005. Semantic role labeling using different syntactic views. In *ACL '05: Proceedings of the 43rd Annual Meeting on Association for Computational Linguistics*, pages 581–588. Association for Computational Linguistics, Morristown, NJ, USA.

J. Quinlan. 1993. *C4:5:programs for Machine Learning*. Morgan Kaufmann, San Mateo.

Konrad Rieck and Pavel Laskov. 2007. Language models for detection of unknown attacks in network traffic. *Journal in Computer Virology*, 2:243–256. 10.1007/s11416-006-0030-0.

Konrad Rieck, Tammo Krueger, Ulf Brefeld, and Klaus-Robert Müller. 2010. Approximate tree kernels. *J. Mach. Learn. Res.*, 11:555–580, March.

David E. Rumelhart and James L. Mcclelland. 1986. *Parallel Distributed Processing: Explorations in the Microstructure of Cognition : Foundations (Parallel Distributed Processing)*. MIT Press, August.

Magnus Sahlgren. 2005. An introduction to random indexing. In *Proceedings of the Methods and Applications of Semantic Indexing Workshop at the 7th International Conference on Terminology and Knowledge Engineering TKE*, Copenhagen, Denmark.

Kilho Shin, Marco Cuturi, and Tetsuji Kuboyama. 2011. Mapping kernels for trees. In Lise Getoor and Tobias Scheffer, editors, *Proceedings of the 28th International Conference on Machine Learning (ICML-11)*, ICML '11, pages 961–968, New York, NY, USA, June. ACM.

Richard Socher, Eric H. Huang, Jeffrey Pennington, Andrew Y. Ng, and Christopher D. Manning. 2011. Dynamic pooling and unfolding recursive autoencoders for paraphrase detection. In *Advances in Neural Information Processing Systems 24*.

Jean-Philippe Vert. 2002. A tree kernel to analyse phylogenetic profiles. *Bioinformatics*, 18(suppl 1):S276–S284, July.

S. V. N. Vishwanathan and Alexander J. Smola. 2002. Fast kernels for string and tree matching. In Suzanna Becker, Sebastian Thrun, and Klaus Obermayer, editors, *NIPS*, pages 569–576. MIT Press.

Rui Wang and Günter Neumann. 2007. Recognizing textual entailment using sentence similarity based on dependency tree skeletons. In *Proceedings of the ACL-PASCAL Workshop on Textual Entailment and Paraphrasing*, pages 36–41, Prague, June. Association for Computational Linguistics.

F.M. Zanzotto and L. Dell'Arciprete. 2012. Distributed tree kernels. In *Proceedings of International Conference on Machine Learning*, pages 193–200.

Fabio Massimo Zanzotto, Marco Pennacchiotti, and Alessandro Moschitti. 2009. A machine learning approach to textual entailment recognition. *NATURAL LANGUAGE ENGINEERING*, 15-04:551–582.

Dell Zhang and Wee Sun Lee. 2003. Question classification using support vector machines. In *Proceedings of the 26th annual international ACM SIGIR conference on Research and development in informaion retrieval*, SIGIR '03, pages 26–32, New York, NY, USA. ACM.

Min Zhang and Haizhou Li. 2009. Tree kernel-based SVM with structured syntactic knowledge for BTG-based phrase reordering. In *Proceedings of the 2009 Conference on Empirical Methods in Natural Language Processing*, pages 698–707, Singapore, August. Association for Computational Linguistics.

GuoDong Zhou, Min Zhang, DongHong Ji, and QiaoMing Zhu. 2007. Tree kernel-based relation extraction with context-sensitive structured parse tree information. In *Proceedings of the 2007 Joint Conference on Empirical Methods in Natural Language Processing and Computational Natural Language Learning (EMNLP-CoNLL)*, pages 728–736.

General estimation and evaluation of compositional distributional semantic models

Georgiana Dinu and **Nghia The Pham** and **Marco Baroni**
Center for Mind/Brain Sciences (University of Trento, Italy)
(georgiana.dinu|thenghia.pham|marco.baroni)@unitn.it

Abstract

In recent years, there has been widespread interest in *compositional* distributional semantic models (cDSMs), that derive meaning representations for phrases from their parts. We present an evaluation of alternative cDSMs under truly comparable conditions. In particular, we extend the idea of Baroni and Zamparelli (2010) and Guevara (2010) to use corpus-extracted examples of the target phrases for parameter estimation to the other models proposed in the literature, so that all models can be tested under the same training conditions. The linguistically motivated functional model of Baroni and Zamparelli (2010) and Coecke et al. (2010) emerges as the winner in all our tests.

1 Introduction

The need to assess similarity in meaning is central to many language technology applications, and distributional methods are the most robust approach to the task. These methods measure word similarity based on patterns of occurrence in large corpora, following the intuition that similar words occur in similar contexts. More precisely, vector space models, the most widely used distributional models, represent words as high-dimensional vectors, where the dimensions represent (functions of) context features, such as co-occurring context words. The relatedness of two words is assessed by comparing their vector representations.

The question of assessing meaning similarity *above the word level* within the distributional paradigm has received a lot of attention in recent years. A number of compositional frameworks have been proposed in the literature, each of these defining operations to combine word vectors into representations for phrases or even entire sentences. These range from simple but robust methods such as vector addition to more advanced methods, such as learning function words as tensors and composing constituents through inner product operations. Empirical evaluations in which alternative methods are tested in comparable settings are thus called for. This is complicated by the fact that the proposed compositional frameworks package together a number of choices that are conceptually distinct, but difficult to disentangle. Broadly, these concern (i) the input representations fed to composition; (ii) the composition operation proper; (iii) the method to estimate the parameters of the composition operation.

For example, Mitchell and Lapata in their classic 2010 study propose a set of composition operations (multiplicative, additive, etc.), but they also experiment with two different kinds of input representations (vectors recording co-occurrence with words vs. distributions over latent topics) and use supervised training via a grid search over parameter settings to estimate their models. Guevara (2010), to give just one further example, is not only proposing a different composition method with respect to Mitchell and Lapata, but he is also adopting different input vectors (word co-occurrences compressed via SVD) and an unsupervised estimation method based on minimizing the distance of composed vectors to their equivalents directly extracted from the source corpus.

Blacoe and Lapata (2012) have recently highlighted the importance of teasing apart the different aspects of a composition framework, presenting an evaluation in which different input vector representations are crossed with different composition methods. However, two out of three composition methods they evaluate are parameter-free, so that they can side-step the issue of fixing the parameter estimation method.

In this work, we evaluate *all* composition methods we know of, excluding a few that lag behind the state of the art or are special cases of those we consider, *while keeping the estimation method constant*. This evaluation is made possible by our extension to all target composition models of the corpus-extracted phrase approximation method originally proposed in *ad-hoc* settings by Baroni and Zamparelli (2010) and Guevara (2010). For the models for which it is feasible, we compare the phrase approximation approach to supervised estimation with crossvalidation, and show that phrase approximation is competitive, thus confirming that we are not comparing models under poor training conditions. Our tests are conducted over three tasks that involve different syntactic constructions and evaluation setups. Finally, we consider a range of parameter settings for the input vector representations, to insure that our results are not too brittle or parameter-dependent.[1]

2 Composition frameworks

Distributional semantic models (DSMs) approximate word meanings with vectors recording their patterns of co-occurrence with corpus contexts (e.g., other words). There is an extensive literature on how to develop such models and on their evaluation (see, e.g., Clark (2012), Erk (2012), Turney and Pantel (2010)). We focus here on *compositional* DSMs (**cDSMs**). After discussing some options pertaining to the input vectors, we review all the composition operations we are aware of (excluding only the tensor-product-based models shown by Mitchell and Lapata (2010) to be much worse than simpler models),[2] and then methods to estimate their parameters.

Input vectors Different studies have assumed different distributional inputs to composition. These include bag-of-words co-occurrence vectors, possibly mapped to lower dimensionality with SVD or other techniques (Mitchell and Lapata (2010) and many others), vectors whose dimensions record the syntactic link between targets and collocates (Erk and Padó, 2008; Thater et al., 2010), and most recently vectors based on neural language models (Socher et al., 2011; Socher et al., 2012). Blacoe and Lapata (2012) compared the three representations on phrase similarity and paraphrase detection, concluding that "simple is best", that is, the bag-of-words approach performs at least as good or better than either syntax-based or neural representations across the board. Here, we take their message home and we focus on bag-of-words representations, exploring the impact of various parameters within this approach.

Most frameworks assume that word vectors constitute rigid inputs fixed *before* composition, often using a separate word-similarity task independent of composition. The only exception is Socher et al. (2012), where the values in the input vectors are re-estimated during composition parameter optimization. Our re-implementation of their method assumes rigid input vectors instead.

Model	Composition function	Parameters
Add	$w_1\vec{u} + w_2\vec{v}$	w_1, w_2
Mult	$\vec{u}^{w_1} \odot \vec{v}^{w_2}$	w_1, w_2
Dil	$\|\|\vec{u}\|\|_2^2\vec{v} + (\lambda - 1)\langle\vec{u}, \vec{v}\rangle\vec{u}$	λ
Fulladd	$W_1\vec{u} + W_2\vec{v}$	$W_1, W_2 \in \mathbf{R}^{m\times m}$
Lexfunc	$A_u\vec{v}$	$A_u \in \mathbf{R}^{m\times m}$
Fulllex	$tanh([W_1, W_2] \begin{bmatrix} A_u\vec{v} \\ A_v\vec{u} \end{bmatrix})$	$W_1, W_2,$ $A_u, A_v \in \mathbf{R}^{m\times m}$

Table 1: Composition functions of inputs (u, v).

Composition operations Mitchell and Lapata (2008; 2010) present a set of simple but effective models in which each component of the output vector is a function of the corresponding components of the inputs. Given input vectors $\vec{u}$ and $\vec{v}$, the weighted additive model (**Add**) returns their weighted sum: $\vec{p} = w_1\vec{u} + w_2\vec{v}$. In the dilation model (**Dil**), the output vector is obtained by decomposing one of the input vectors, say $\vec{v}$, into a vector parallel to $\vec{u}$ and an orthogonal vector, and then dilating only the parallel vector by a factor λ before re-combining (formula in Table 1). Mitchell and Lapata also propose a simple multiplicative model in which the output components are obtained by component-wise multiplication of the corresponding input components. We introduce here its natural *weighted* extension (**Mult**), that takes w_1 and w_2 powers of the components before multiplying, such that each phrase component p_i is given by: $p_i = u_i^{w_1} v_i^{w_2}$.

[1]We made the software we used to construct semantic models and estimate and test composition methods available online at http://clic.cimec.unitn.it/composes/toolkit/

[2]Erk and Padó (2008) and Thater et al. (2010) use input vectors that have been adapted to their phrasal contexts, but then apply straightforward composition operations such as addition and multiplication to these contextualized vectors. Their approaches are thus not alternative cDSMs, but special ways to construct the input vectors. Grefenstette and Sadrzadeh (2011a; 2011b) and Kartsaklis et al. (2012) propose estimation techniques for the tensors in the functional model of Coecke et al. (2010). Turney (2012) does not compose representations but similarity scores.

Guevara (2010) and Zanzotto et al. (2010) explore a full form of the additive model (**Fulladd**), where the two vectors entering a composition process are pre-multiplied by weight matrices before being added, so that each output component is a weighted sum of *all* input components: $\vec{p} = W_1\vec{u} + W_2\vec{v}$.

Baroni and Zamparelli (2010) and Coecke et al. (2010), taking inspiration from formal semantics, characterize composition as *function application*. For example, Baroni and Zamparelli model adjective-noun phrases by treating the adjective as a function from nouns onto (modified) nouns. Given that linear functions can be expressed by matrices and their application by matrix-by-vector multiplication, a functor (such as the adjective) is represented by a matrix A_u to be composed with the argument vector $\vec{v}$ (e.g., the noun) by multiplication, returning the *lexical function* (**Lexfunc**) representation of the phrase: $\vec{p} = A_u\vec{v}$.

The method proposed by Socher et al. (2012) (see Socher et al. (2011) for an earlier proposal from the same team) can be seen as a combination and non-linear extension of Fulladd and Lexfunc (that we thus call **Fulllex**) in which *both* phrase elements act as functors (matrices) *and* arguments (vectors). Given input terms *u* and *v* represented by $(\vec{u}, A_u)$ and $(\vec{v}, A_v)$, respectively, their composition vector is obtained by applying first a linear transformation and then the hyperbolic tangent function to the concatenation of the products $A_u\vec{v}$ and $A_v\vec{u}$ (see Table 1 for the equation). Socher and colleagues also present a way to construct matrix representations for specific phrases, needed to scale this composition method to larger constituents. We ignore it here since we focus on the two-word case.

Estimating composition parameters If we have manually labeled example data for a target task, we can use supervised machine learning to optimize parameters. Mitchell and Lapata (2008; 2010), since their models have just a few parameters to optimize, use a direct grid search for the parameter setting that performs best on the training data. Socher et al. (2012) train their models using multinomial softmax classifiers.

If our goal is to develop a cDSM optimized for a specific task, supervised methods are undoubtedly the most promising approach. However, every time we face a new task, parameters must be re-estimated from scratch, which goes against the idea of distributional semantics as a general similarity resource (Baroni and Lenci, 2010). Moreover, supervised methods are highly composition-model-dependent, and for models such as Fulladd and Lexfunc we are not aware of proposals about how to estimate them in a supervised manner.

Socher et al. (2011) propose an *autoencoding* strategy. Given a decomposition function that reconstructs the constituent vectors from a phrase vector (e.g., it re-generates *green* and *jacket* vectors from the composed *green jacket* vector), the composition parameters minimize the distance between the original and reconstructed input vectors. This method does not require hand-labeled training data, but it is restricted to cDSMs for which an appropriate decomposition function can be defined, and even in this case the learning problem might lack a closed-form solution.

Guevara (2010) and Baroni and Zamparelli (2010) optimize parameters using examples of how the output vectors should look like that are directly extracted from the corpus. To learn, say, a Lexfunc matrix representing the adjective *green*, we extract from the corpus example vectors of ⟨*N, green N*⟩ pairs that occur with sufficient frequency (⟨*car, green car*⟩, ⟨*jacket, green jacket*⟩, ⟨*politician, green politician*⟩, ...). We then use least-squares methods to find weights for the *green* matrix that minimize the distance between the *green N* vectors generated by the model given the input *N* and the corresponding corpus-observed phrase vectors. This is a very general approach, it does not require hand-labeled data, and it has the nice property that corpus-harvested phrase vectors provide direct evidence of the polysemous behaviour of functors (the *green jacket* vs. *politician* contexts, for example, will be very different). In the next section, we extend the **corpus-extracted phrase approximation** method to all cDSMs described above, with closed-form solutions for all but the Fulllex model, for which we propose a rapidly converging iterative estimation method.

3 Least-squares model estimation using corpus-extracted phrase vectors[3]

Notation Given two matrices $X, Y \in \mathbf{R}^{m\times n}$ we denote their inner product by $\langle X, Y\rangle$, ($\langle X, Y\rangle = \sum_{i=1}^{m}\sum_{j=1}^{n} x_{ij}y_{ij}$). Similarly we denote by $\langle u, v\rangle$ the dot product of two vectors $u, v \in \mathbf{R}^{m\times 1}$ and by $||u||$ the Euclidean norm of a vector:

[3]Proofs omitted due to space constraints.

$||u|| = \langle u, u\rangle^{1/2}$. We use the following Frobenius norm notation: $||X||_F = \langle X, X\rangle^{1/2}$. Vectors are assumed to be column vectors and we use x_i to stand for the i-th $(m \times 1)$-dimensional column of matrix X. We use $[X, Y] \in \mathbf{R}^{m\times 2n}$ to denote the horizontal concatenation of two matrices while $\begin{bmatrix} X \\ Y \end{bmatrix} \in \mathbf{R}^{2m\times n}$ is their vertical concatenation.

General problem statement We assume vocabularies of constituents $\mathcal{U}$, $\mathcal{V}$ and that of resulting phrases $\mathcal{P}$. The training data consist of a set of tuples (u, v, p) where p stands for the phrase associated to the constituents u and v:

$$T = \{(u_i, v_i, p_i) | (u_i, v_i, p_i) \in \mathcal{U}\times\mathcal{V}\times\mathcal{P}, 1 \leq i \leq k\}$$

We build the matrices $U, V, P \in \mathbf{R}^{m\times k}$ by concatenating the vectors associated to the training data elements as columns.[4]

Given the training data matrices, the general problem can be stated as:

$$\boldsymbol{\theta}^* = \arg\min_{\boldsymbol{\theta}} ||P - fcomp_{\boldsymbol{\theta}}(U, V)||_F$$

where $fcomp_{\boldsymbol{\theta}}$ is a composition function and $\boldsymbol{\theta}$ stands for a list of parameters that this composition function is associated to. The composition functions are defined: $fcomp_{\boldsymbol{\theta}} : \mathbf{R}^{m\times 1} \times \mathbf{R}^{m\times 1} \rightarrow \mathbf{R}^{m\times 1}$ and $fcomp_{\boldsymbol{\theta}}(U, V)$ stands for their natural extension when applied on the individual columns of the U and V matrices.

Add The weighted additive model returns the sum of the composing vectors which have been re-weighted by some scalars w_1 and w_2: $\vec{p} = w_1\vec{u} + w_2\vec{v}$. The problem becomes:

$$w_1^*, w_2^* = \arg\min_{w_1, w_2 \in \mathbf{R}} ||P - w_1 U - w_2 V||_F$$

The optimal w_1 and w_2 are given by:

$$w_1^* = \frac{||V||_F^2\langle U, P\rangle - \langle U, V\rangle\langle V, P\rangle}{||U||_F^2||V||_F^2 - \langle U, V\rangle^2} \quad (1)$$

$$w_2^* = \frac{||U||_F^2\langle V, P\rangle - \langle U, V\rangle\langle U, P\rangle}{||U||_F^2||V||_F^2 - \langle U, V\rangle^2} \quad (2)$$

[4]In reality, not all composition models require u, v and p to have the same dimensionality.

Dil Given two vectors $\vec{u}$ and $\vec{v}$, the dilation model computes the phrase vector $\vec{p} = ||\vec{u}||^2\vec{v} + (\lambda - 1)\langle\vec{u}, \vec{v}\rangle\vec{u}$ where the parameter λ is a scalar. The problem becomes:

$$\lambda^* = \arg\min_{\lambda\in\mathbf{R}} ||P - VD_{||u_i||^2} - UD_{(\lambda-1)\langle u_i, v_i\rangle}||_F$$

where by $D_{||u_i||^2}$ and $D_{(\lambda-1)\langle u_i, v_i\rangle}$ we denote diagonal matrices with diagonal elements (i, i) given by $||u_i||^2$ and $(\lambda - 1)\langle u_i, v_i\rangle$ respectively. The solution is:

$$\lambda^* = 1 - \frac{\sum_{i=1}^k \langle u_i, (||u_i||^2 v_i - p_i)\rangle\langle u_i, v_i\rangle}{\sum_{i=1}^k \langle u_i, v_i\rangle^2 ||u_i||^2}$$

Mult Given two vectors $\vec{u}$ and $\vec{v}$, the weighted multiplicative model computes the phrase vector $\vec{p} = \vec{u}^{w_1} \odot \vec{v}^{w_2}$ where $\odot$ stands for component-wise multiplication. We assume for this model that $U, V, P \in \mathbf{R}_{++}^{m\times n}$, i.e. that the entries are strictly larger than 0: in practice we add a small smoothing constant to all elements to achieve this (Mult performs badly on negative entries, such as those produced by SVD). We use the w_1 and w_2 weights obtained when solving the much simpler related problem:[5]

$$w_1^*, w_2^* = \arg\min_{w_1, w_2\in\mathbf{R}} ||log(P) - log(U.^\wedge w_1 \odot V.^\wedge w_2)||_F$$

where $.^\wedge$ stands for the component-wise power operation. The solution is the same as that for Add, given in equations (1) and (2), with $U \rightarrow log(U)$, $V \rightarrow log(V)$ and $P \rightarrow log(P)$.

Fulladd The full additive model assumes the composition of two vectors to be $\vec{p} = W_1\vec{u} + W_2\vec{v}$ where $W_1, W_2 \in \mathbf{R}^{m\times m}$. The problem is:

$$[W_1, W_2]^* = \arg\min_{[W_1, W_2]\in\mathbf{R}^{m\times 2m}} ||P - [W_1 W_2]\begin{bmatrix} U \\ V \end{bmatrix}||$$

This is a multivariate linear regression problem (Hastie et al., 2009) for which the least squares estimate is given by: $[W_1, W_2] = ((X^T X)^{-1} X^T Y)^T$ where we use $X = [U^T, V^T]$ and $Y = P^T$.

Lexfunc The lexical function composition method learns a matrix representation for each functor (given by $\mathcal{U}$ here) and defines composition as matrix-vector multiplication. More precisely:

[5]In practice training Mult this way achieves similar or lower errors in comparison to Add.

$\vec{p} = A_u\vec{v}$ where A_u is a matrix associated to each functor $u \in \mathcal{U}$. We denote by T_u the training data subset associated to an element u, which contains only tuples which have u as first element. Learning the matrix representations amounts to solving the set of problems:

$$A_u = \underset{A_u \in \mathbf{R}^{m \times m}}{\arg\min} ||P_u - A_u V_u||$$

for each $u \in \mathcal{U}$ where $P_u, V_u \in \mathbf{R}^{m \times |T_u|}$ are the matrices corresponding to the T_u training subset. The solutions are given by: $A_u = ((V_u V_u^T)^{-1} V_u P_u^T)^T$. This composition function does not use the functor vectors.

Fulllex This model can be seen as a generalization of Lexfunc which makes no assumption on which of the constituents is a functor, so that both words get a matrix and a vector representation. The composition function is:

$$\vec{p} = tanh([W_1, W_2] \begin{bmatrix} A_u\vec{v} \\ A_v\vec{u} \end{bmatrix})$$

where A_u and A_v are the matrices associated to constituents u and v and $[W_1, W_2] \in \mathbf{R}^{m \times 2m}$. The estimation problem is given in Figure 1.

This is the only composition model which does not have a closed-form solution. We use a block coordinate descent method, in which we fix each of the matrix variables but one and solve the corresponding least-squares linear regression problem, for which we can use the closed-form solution. Fixing everything but $[W_1, W_2]$:

$$[W_1^*, W_2^*] = ((X^T X)^{-1} X^T Y)^T$$
$$X = \begin{bmatrix} [A_{u_1}\vec{v_1}, ..., A_{u_k}\vec{v_k}] \\ [A_{v_1}\vec{u_1}, ..., A_{v_k}\vec{u_k}] \end{bmatrix}^T$$
$$Y = atanh(P^T)$$

Fixing everything but A_u for some element u, the objective function becomes:

$$||atanh(P_u) - W_1 A_u V_u - W_2[A_{v_1}\vec{u}, ..., A_{v_{k'}}\vec{u}]||_F$$

where $v_1 ... v_{k'} \in \mathcal{V}$ are the elements occurring with u in the training data and V_u the matrix resulting from their concatenation. The update formula for the A_u matrices becomes:

$$A_u^* = W_1^{-1}((X^T X)^{-1} X^T Y)^T$$
$$X = V_u^T$$
$$Y = (atanh(P_u) - W_2[A_{v_1}\vec{u}, ..., A_{v_{k'}}\vec{u}])^T$$

In all our experiments, Fulllex estimation converges after very few passes though the matrices. Despite the very large number of parameters of this model, when evaluating on the test data we observe that using a higher dimensional space (such as 200 dimensions) still performs better than a lower dimensional one (e.g., 50 dimensions).

4 Evaluation setup and implementation

4.1 Datasets

We evaluate the composition methods on three phrase-based benchmarks that test the models on a variety of composition processes and similarity-based tasks.

Intransitive sentences The first dataset, introduced by Mitchell and Lapata (2008), focuses on simple sentences consisting of intransitive verbs and their noun subjects. It contains a total of 120 sentence pairs together with human similarity judgments on a 7-point scale. For example, *conflict erupts/conflict bursts* is scored 7, *skin glows/skin burns* is scored 1. On average, each pair is rated by 30 participants. Rather than evaluating against mean scores, we use each rating as a separate data point, as done by Mitchell and Lapata. We report Spearman correlations between human-assigned scores and model cosine scores.

Adjective-noun phrases Turney (2012) introduced a dataset including both noun-noun compounds and adjective-noun phrases (ANs). We focus on the latter, and we frame the task differently from Turney's original definition due to data sparsity issues.[6] In our version, the dataset contains 620 ANs, each paired with a single-noun paraphrase. Examples include: *archaeological site/dig*, *spousal relationship/marriage* and *dangerous undertaking/adventure*. We evaluate a model by computing the cosine of all 20K nouns in our semantic space with the target AN, and looking at the rank of the correct paraphrase in this list. The lower the rank, the better the model. We report median rank across the test items.

Determiner phrases The last dataset, introduced in Bernardi et al. (2013), focuses on a class of *grammatical* terms (rather than content

[6]Turney used a corpus of about 50 billion words, almost 20 times larger than ours, and we have very poor or no coverage of many original items, making the "multiple-choice" evaluation proposed by Turney meaningless in our case.

$$W_1^*, W_2^*, A_{u_1}^*, ..., A_{v_1}^*, ... = \underset{\mathbf{R}^{m \times m}}{\arg\min} ||atanh(P^T) - [W_1, W_2] \begin{bmatrix} [A_{u_1}\vec{v_1}, ..., A_{u_k}\vec{v_k}] \\ [A_{v_1}\vec{u_1}, ..., A_{v_k}\vec{u_k}] \end{bmatrix} ||_F$$
$$= \underset{\mathbf{R}^{m \times m}}{\arg\min} ||atanh(P^T) - W_1[A_{u_1}\vec{v_1}, ..., A_{u_k}\vec{v_k}] - W_2[A_{v_1}\vec{u_1}, ..., A_{v_k}\vec{u_k}]||_F$$

Figure 1: Fulllex estimation problem.

words), namely determiners. It is a multiple-choice test where target nouns (e.g., *amnesia)* must be matched with the most closely related determiner(-noun) phrases (DPs) (e.g., *no memory*). The task differs from the previous one also because here the targets are single words, and the related items are composite. There are 173 target nouns in total, each paired with one correct DP response, as well as 5 foils, namely the determiner (*no*) and noun (*memory*) from the correct response and three more DPs, two of which contain the same noun as the correct phrase (*less memory, all memory*), the third the same determiner (*no repertoire*). Other examples of targets/related-phrases are *polysemy/several senses* and *trilogy/three books*. The models compute cosines between target noun and responses and are scored based on their accuracy at ranking the correct phrase first.

4.2 Input vectors

We extracted distributional semantic vectors using as source corpus the concatenation of ukWaC, Wikipedia (2009 dump) and BNC, 2.8 billion tokens in total.[7] We use a bag-of-words approach and we count co-occurrences within sentences and with a limit of maximally 50 words surrounding the target word. By tuning on the MEN lexical relatedness dataset,[8] we decided to use the top 10K most frequent content lemmas as context features (vs. top 10K inflected forms), and we experimented with positive Pointwise and Local Mutual Information (Evert, 2005) as association measures (vs. raw counts, log transform and a probability ratio measure) and dimensionality reduction by Non-negative Matrix Factorization (NMF, Lee and Seung (2000)) and Singular Value Decomposition (SVD, Golub and Van Loan (1996)) (both outperforming full dimensionality vectors on MEN). For both reduction techniques, we varied the number of dimensions to be preserved from 50 to 300 in 50-unit intervals. As Local Mutual Information performed very poorly across composition experiments and other parameter choices, we dropped it. We will thus report, for each experiment and composition method, the distribution of the relevant performance measure across 12 input settings (NMF vs. SVD times 6 dimensionalities). However, since the Mult model, as expected, worked very poorly when the input vectors contained negative values, as is the case with SVD, for this model we report result distributions across the 6 NMF variations only.

4.3 Composition model estimation

Training by approximating the corpus-extracted phrase vectors requires corpus-based examples of input (constituent word) and output (phrase) vectors for the composition processes to be learned. In all cases, training examples are simply selected based on corpus frequency. For the first experiment, we have 42 distinct target verbs and a total of ≈20K training instances, that is, ⟨⟨*noun*, *verb*⟩, *noun-verb*⟩ tuples (505 per verb on average). For the second experiment, we have 479 adjectives and ≈1 million ⟨⟨*adjective*, *noun*⟩, *adjective-noun*⟩ training tuples (2K per adjective on average). In the third, 50 determiners and 50K ⟨⟨*determiner*, *noun*⟩, *determiner-noun*⟩ tuples (1K per determiner). For all models except Lexfunc and Fulllex, training examples are pooled across target elements to learn a single set of parameters. The Lexfunc model takes only argument word vectors as inputs (the functors in the three datasets are verbs, adjectives and determiners, respectively). A separate weight matrix is learned for each functor, using the corresponding training data.[9] The Fulllex method jointly learns distinct matrix representations for both left- and right-hand side con-

[7] http://wacky.sslmit.unibo.it; http://www.natcorp.ox.ac.uk

[8] http://clic.cimec.unitn.it/~elia.bruni/MEN

[9] For the Lexfunc model we have experimented with least squeares regression with and without regularization, obtaining similar results.

stituents. For this reason, we must train this model on balanced datasets. More precisely, for the intransitive verb experiments, we use training data containing noun-verb phrases in which the verbs and the nouns are present in the lists of 1,500 most frequent verbs/nouns respectively, adding to these the verbs and nouns present in our dataset. We obtain 400K training tuples. We create the training data similarity for the other datasets obtaining 440K adjective-noun and 50K determiner phrase training tuples, respectively (we also experimented with Fulllex trained on the same tuples used for the other models, obtaining considerably worse results than those reported). Finally, for Dil we treat direction of stretching as a further parameter to be optimized, and find that for intransitives it is better to stretch verbs, in the other datasets nouns.

For the simple composition models for which parameters consist of one or two scalars, namely Add, Mult and Dil, we also tune the parameters through 5-fold crossvalidation on the datasets, directly optimizing the parameters on the target tasks. For Add and Mult, we search w_1, w_2 through the crossproduct of the interval $[0:5]$ in 0.2-sized steps. For Dil we use $\lambda \in [0:20]$, again in 0.2-sized steps.

5 Evaluation results

We begin with some remarks pertaining to the overall quality of and motivation for corpus-phrase-based estimation. In seven out of nine comparisons of this unsupervised technique with fully supervised crossvalidation (3 "simple" models –Add, Dil and Mult– times 3 test sets), there was no significant difference between the two estimation methods.[10] Supervised estimation outperformed the corpus-phrase-based method only for Dil on the intransitive sentence and AN benchmarks, but crossvalidated Dil was outperformed by at least one phrase-estimated simple model on both benchmarks.

The rightmost boxes in the panels of Figure 2 depict the performance distribution for using phrase vectors directly extracted from the corpus to tackle the various tasks. This non-compositional approach outperforms all compositional methods in two tasks over three, and it is one of the best approaches in the third, although in all cases even its top scores are far from the theoretical ceiling. Still, performance is impressive, especially in light of the fact that the non-compositional approach suffers of serious data-sparseness problems. Performance on the intransitive task is above state-of-the-art despite the fact that for almost half of the cases one test phrase is not in the corpus, resulting in 0 vectors and consequently 0 similarity pairs. The other benchmarks have better corpus-phrase coverage (nearly perfect AN coverage; for DPs, about 90% correct phrase responses are in the corpus), but many target phrases occur only rarely, leading to unreliable distributional vectors. We interpret these results as a good motivation for corpus-phrase-based estimation. On the one hand they show how good these vectors are, and thus that they are sensible targets of learning. On the other hand, they do not suffice, since natural language is infinitely productive and thus no corpus can provide full phrase coverage, justifying the whole compositional enterprise.

The other boxes in Figure 2 report the performance of the composition methods trained by corpus phrase approximation. Nearly all models are significantly above chance in all tasks, except for Fulladd on intransitive sentences. To put AN median ranks into perspective, consider that a median rank as high as 8,300 has near-0 probability to occur by chance. For DP accuracy, random guessing gets 0.17% accuracy.

Lexfunc emerges consistently as the best model. On intransitive constructions, it significantly outperforms all other models except Mult, but the difference approaches significance even with respect to the latter ($p = 0.071$). On this task, Lexfunc's *median* correlation (0.26) is nearly equivalent to the *best* correlation across a wide range of parameters reported by Erk and Padó (2008) (0.27). In the AN task, Lexfunc significantly outperforms Fulllex and Dil and, visually, its distribution is slightly more skewed towards lower (better) ranks than any other model. In the DP task, Lexfunc significantly outperforms Add and Mult and, visually, most of its distribution lies above that of the other models. Most importantly, Lexfunc is the only model that is consistent across the three tasks, with all other models displaying instead a brittle performance pattern.[11]

Still, the top-performance range of all models

[10]Significance assessed through Tukey Honestly Significant Difference tests (Abdi and Williams, 2010), $\alpha = 0.05$.

[11]No systematic trend emerged pertaining to the input vector parameters (SVD vs. NMF and retained dimension number).

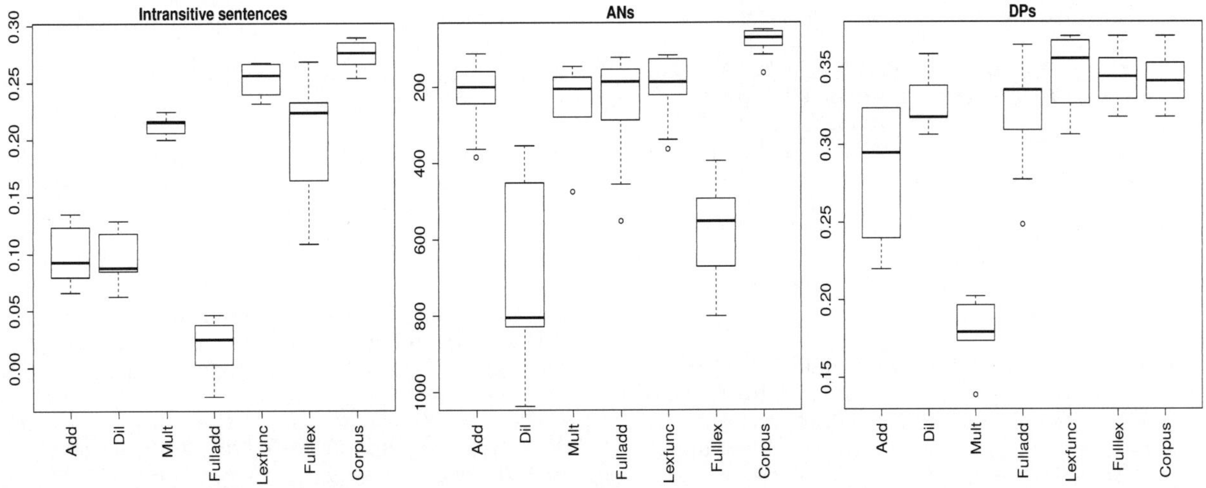

Figure 2: Boxplots displaying composition model performance distribution on three benchmarks, across input vector settings (6 datapoints for Mult, 12 for all other models). For intransitive sentences, figure of merit is Spearman correlation, for ANs median rank of correct paraphrase, and for DPs correct response accuracy. The boxplots display the distribution median as a thick horizontal line within a box extending from first to third quartile. Whiskers cover 1.5 of interquartile range in each direction from the box, and extreme outliers outside this extended range are plotted as circles.

on the three tasks is underwhelming, and none of them succeeds in exploiting compositionality to do significantly better than using whatever phrase vectors can be extracted from the corpus directly. Clearly, much work is still needed to develop truly successful cDSMs.

The AN results might look particularly worrying, considering that even the top (lowest) median ranks are above 100. A qualitative analysis, however, suggests that the actual performance is not as bad as the numerical scores suggest, since often the nearest neighbours of the ANs to be paraphrased are nouns that are as strongly related to the ANs as the gold standard response (although not necessarily proper paraphrases). For example, the gold response to *colorimetric analysis* is *colorimetry*, whereas the Lexfunc (NMF, 300 dimensions) nearest neighbour is *chromatography*; the gold response to *heavy particle* is *baryon*, whereas Lexfunc proposes *muon*; for *melodic phrase* the gold is *tune* and Lexfunc has *appoggiatura*; for *indoor garden*, the gold is *hothouse* but Lexfunc proposes *glasshouse* (followed by the more sophisticated *orangery*!), and so on and so forth.

6 Conclusion

We extended the unsupervised corpus-extracted phrase approximation method of Guevara (2010) and Baroni and Zamparelli (2010) to estimate all known state-of-the-art cDSMs, using closed-form solutions or simple iterative procedures in all cases. Equipped with a general estimation approach, we thoroughly evaluated the cDSMs in a comparable setting. The linguistically motivated Lexfunc model of Baroni and Zamparelli (2010) and Coecke et al. (2010) was the winner across three composition tasks, also outperforming the more complex Fulllex model, our re-implementation of Socher et al.'s (2012) composition method (of course, the composition method is only one aspect of Socher et al.'s architecture). All other composition methods behaved inconsistently.

In the near future, we want to focus on improving estimation itself. In particular, we want to explore ways to automatically select good phrase examples for training, beyond simple frequency thresholds. We tested composition methods on two-word phrase benchmarks. Another natural next step is to apply the composition rules recursively, to obtain representations of larger chunks, up to full sentences, coming, in this way, nearer to the ultimate goal of compositional distributional semantics.

Acknowledgments

We acknowledge ERC 2011 Starting Independent Research Grant n. 283554 (COMPOSES).

References

Hervé Abdi and Lynne Williams. 2010. Newman-Keuls and Tukey test. In Neil Salkind, Bruce Frey, and Dondald Dougherty, editors, *Encyclopedia of Research Design*, pages 897–904. Sage, Thousand Oaks, CA.

Marco Baroni and Alessandro Lenci. 2010. Distributional Memory: A general framework for corpus-based semantics. *Computational Linguistics*, 36(4):673–721.

Marco Baroni and Roberto Zamparelli. 2010. Nouns are vectors, adjectives are matrices: Representing adjective-noun constructions in semantic space. In *Proceedings of EMNLP*, pages 1183–1193, Boston, MA.

Raffaella Bernardi, Georgiana Dinu, Marco Marelli, and Marco Baroni. 2013. A relatedness benchmark to test the role of determiners in compositional distributional semantics. In *Proceedings of ACL (Short Papers)*, Sofia, Bulgaria. In press.

William Blacoe and Mirella Lapata. 2012. A comparison of vector-based representations for semantic composition. In *Proceedings of EMNLP*, pages 546–556, Jeju Island, Korea.

Stephen Clark. 2012. Vector space models of lexical meaning. In Shalom Lappin and Chris Fox, editors, *Handbook of Contemporary Semantics, 2nd edition*. Blackwell, Malden, MA. In press.

Bob Coecke, Mehrnoosh Sadrzadeh, and Stephen Clark. 2010. Mathematical foundations for a compositional distributional model of meaning. *Linguistic Analysis*, 36:345–384.

Katrin Erk and Sebastian Padó. 2008. A structured vector space model for word meaning in context. In *Proceedings of EMNLP*, pages 897–906, Honolulu, HI.

Katrin Erk. 2012. Vector space models of word meaning and phrase meaning: A survey. *Language and Linguistics Compass*, 6(10):635–653.

Stefan Evert. 2005. *The Statistics of Word Cooccurrences*. Dissertation, Stuttgart University.

Gene Golub and Charles Van Loan. 1996. *Matrix Computations (3rd ed.)*. JHU Press, Baltimore, MD.

Edward Grefenstette and Mehrnoosh Sadrzadeh. 2011a. Experimental support for a categorical compositional distributional model of meaning. In *Proceedings of EMNLP*, pages 1394–1404, Edinburgh, UK.

Edward Grefenstette and Mehrnoosh Sadrzadeh. 2011b. Experimenting with transitive verbs in a DisCoCat. In *Proceedings of GEMS*, pages 62–66, Edinburgh, UK.

Emiliano Guevara. 2010. A regression model of adjective-noun compositionality in distributional semantics. In *Proceedings of GEMS*, pages 33–37, Uppsala, Sweden.

Trevor Hastie, Robert Tibshirani, and Jerome Friedman. 2009. *The Elements of Statistical Learning, 2nd ed.* Springer, New York.

Dimitri Kartsaklis, Mehrnoosh Sadrzadeh, and Stephen Pulman. 2012. A unified sentence space for categorical distributional-compositional semantics: Theory and experiments. In *Proceedings of COLING: Posters*, pages 549–558, Mumbai, India.

Daniel Lee and Sebastian Seung. 2000. Algorithms for Non-negative Matrix Factorization. In *Proceedings of NIPS*, pages 556–562.

Jeff Mitchell and Mirella Lapata. 2008. Vector-based models of semantic composition. In *Proceedings of ACL*, pages 236–244, Columbus, OH.

Jeff Mitchell and Mirella Lapata. 2010. Composition in distributional models of semantics. *Cognitive Science*, 34(8):1388–1429.

Richard Socher, Eric Huang, Jeffrey Pennin, Andrew Ng, and Christopher Manning. 2011. Dynamic pooling and unfolding recursive autoencoders for paraphrase detection. In *Proceedings of NIPS*, pages 801–809, Granada, Spain.

Richard Socher, Brody Huval, Christopher Manning, and Andrew Ng. 2012. Semantic compositionality through recursive matrix-vector spaces. In *Proceedings of EMNLP*, pages 1201–1211, Jeju Island, Korea.

Stefan Thater, Hagen Fürstenau, and Manfred Pinkal. 2010. Contextualizing semantic representations using syntactically enriched vector models. In *Proceedings of ACL*, pages 948–957, Uppsala, Sweden.

Peter Turney and Patrick Pantel. 2010. From frequency to meaning: Vector space models of semantics. *Journal of Artificial Intelligence Research*, 37:141–188.

Peter Turney. 2012. Domain and function: A dual-space model of semantic relations and compositions. *Journal of Artificial Intelligence Research*, 44:533–585.

Fabio Zanzotto, Ioannis Korkontzelos, Francesca Falucchi, and Suresh Manandhar. 2010. Estimating linear models for compositional distributional semantics. In *Proceedings of COLING*, pages 1263–1271, Beijing, China.

Applicative structure in vector space models

Márton Makrai **Dávid Nemeskey** **András Kornai**
HAS Computer and Automation Research Institute
H-1111 Kende u 13-17, Budapest
{makrai,ndavid,kornai}@sztaki.hu

Abstract

We introduce a new 50-dimensional embedding obtained by spectral clustering of a graph describing the conceptual structure of the lexicon. We use the embedding directly to investigate sets of antonymic pairs, and indirectly to argue that function application in CVSMs requires not just vectors but two transformations (corresponding to subject and object) as well.

1 Introduction

Commutativity is a fundamental property of vector space models. As soon as we encode *king* by $\vec{k}$, *queen* by $\vec{q}$, *male* by $\vec{m}$, and *female* by $\vec{f}$, if we expect $\vec{k} - \vec{q} = \vec{m} - \vec{f}$, as suggested in Mikolov et al. (2013), we will, by commutativity, also expect $\vec{k} - \vec{m} = \vec{q} - \vec{f}$ 'ruler, gender unspecified'. When the meaning decomposition involves function application, commutativity no longer makes sense: consider *Victoria* as $\vec{q}\oslash$*England* and *Victor* as $\vec{k}\oslash$*Italy*. If the function application operator $\oslash$ is simply another vector to be added to the representation, the same logic would yield that Italy is the male counterpart of female England. To make matters worse, performing the same operations on *Albert*, $\vec{k}\oslash$*England* and *Elena*, $\vec{q}\oslash$*Italy* would yield that Italy is the female counterpart of male England.

Section 2 offers a method to treat antonymy in continuous vector space models (CVSMs). Section 3 describes a new embedding, 4lang, obtained by spectral clustering from the definitional framework of the Longman Dictionary of Contemporary English (LDOCE, see Chapter 13 of McArtur 1998), and Section 4 shows how to solve the problem outlined above by treating $\oslash$ and $\otimes$ not as a vectors but as transformations.

2 Diagnostic properties of additive decomposition

The standard model of lexical decomposition (Katz and Fodor, 1963) divides lexical meaning in a systematic component, given by a tree of (generally binary) features, and an accidental component they call the *distinguisher*. Figure 1 gives an example.

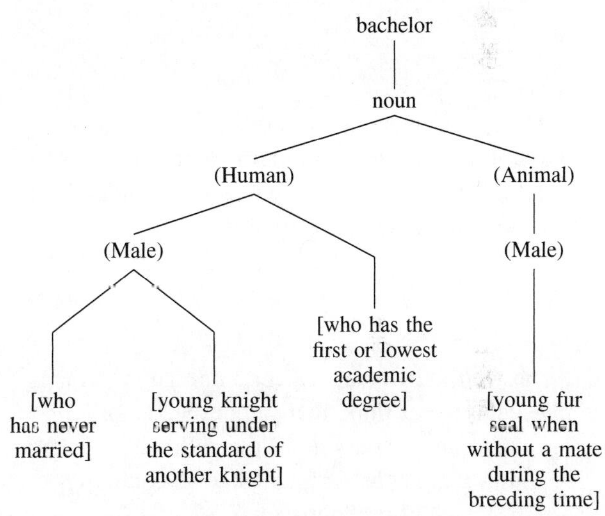

Figure 1: Decomposition of lexical items to features (Katz and Fodor, 1963)

This representation has several advantages: for example *bachelor*$_3$ 'holder of a BA or BSc degree' neatly escapes being *male* by definition. We tested which putative semantic features like GENDER are captured by CVSMs. We assume that the difference between two vectors, for antonyms, distills the actual property which is the opposite in each member of a pair of antonyms. So, for example, for a set of male and female words, such as ⟨king, queen⟩, ⟨actor, actress⟩, etc., the difference between words in each pair should represent the idea of gender. To test the hypothesis, we as-

GOOD		VERTICAL	
safe	out	raise	level
peace	war	tall	short
pleasure	pain	rise	fall
ripe	green	north	south
defend	attack	shallow	deep
conserve	waste	ascending	descending
affirmative	negative	superficial	profound
⋮	⋮	⋮	⋮

Table 1: Word pairs associated to features GOOD and VERTICAL

sociated antonymic word pairs from the WordNet (Miller, 1995) to 26 classes e.g. END/BEGINNING, GOOD/BAD, ..., see Table 1 and Table 3 for examples. The intuition to be tested is that the first member of a pair relates to the second one in the same way among all pairs associated to the same feature. For k pairs $\vec{x}_i, \vec{y}_i$ we are looking for a common vector $\vec{a}$ such that

$$\vec{x_i} - \vec{y_i} = \vec{a} \quad (1)$$

Given the noise in the embedding, it would be naive in the extreme to assume that (1) can be a strict identity. Rather, our interest is with the best $\vec{a}$ which minimizes the error

$$Err = \sum_i ||\vec{x_i} - \vec{y_i} - \vec{a}||^2 \quad (2)$$

As is well known, E will be minimal when $\vec{a}$ is chosen as the arithmetic mean of the vectors $\vec{x_i} - \vec{y_i}$. The question is simply the following: is the minimal E_m any better than what we could expect from a bunch of random $\vec{x_i}$ and $\vec{y_i}$?

Since the sets are of different sizes, we took 100 random pairings of the words appearing on either sides of the pairs to estimate the error distribution, computing the minima of

$$Err_{rand} = \sum_i ||\vec{x_i}' - \vec{y_i} - \vec{a}||^2 \quad (3)$$

For each distribution, we computed the mean and the variance of Err_{rand}, and checked whether the error of the correct pairing, Err is at least 2 or 3 σs away from the mean.

Table 2 summarizes our results for three embeddings: the original and the scaled HLBL (Mnih and Hinton, 2009) and SENNA (Collobert et al., 2011). The first two columns give the number of pairs considered for a feature and the name of the feature. For each of the three embeddings, we report the error Err of the unpermuted arrangement, the mean m and variance σ of the errors obtained under random permutations, and the ratio

$$r = \frac{|m - Err|}{\sigma}.$$

PRIMARY		ANGULAR	
leading	following	square	round
preparation	resolution	sharp	flat
precede	follow	curved	straight
intermediate	terminal	curly	straight
antecedent	subsequent	angular	rounded
precede	succeed	sharpen	soften
question	answer	angularity	roundness
⋮	⋮	⋮	⋮

Table 3: Features that fail the test

Horizontal lines divide the features to three groups: for the upper group, $r \geqslant 3$ for at least two of the three embeddings, and for the middle group $r \geqslant 2$ for at least two.

For the features above the first line we conclude that the antonymic relations are well captured by the embeddings, and for the features below the second line we assume, conservatively, that they are not. (In fact, looking at the first column of Table 2 suggests that the lack of significance at the bottom rows may be due primarily to the fact that WordNet has more antonym pairs for the features that performed well on this test than for those features that performed badly, but we didn't want to start creating antonym pairs manually.) For example, the putative sets in Table 3 does not meet the criterion and gets rejected.

3 Embedding based on conceptual representation

The 4lang embedding is created in a manner that is notably different from the others. Our input is a graph whose nodes are concepts, with edges running from A to B iff B is used in the definition of A. The base vectors are obtained by the spectral clustering method pioneered by (Ng et al., 2001): the incidence matrix of the conceptual network is replaced by an affinity matrix whose ij-th element is formed by computing the cosine distance of the ith and jth row of the original matrix, and the first few (in our case, 100) eigenvectors are used as a basis.

Since the concept graph includes the entire Longman Defining Vocabulary (LDV), each LDV

# pairs	feature name	HLBL original				HLBL scaled				SENNA			
		Err	m	σ	r	Err	m	σ	r	Err	m	σ	r
156	good	1.92	2.29	0.032	11.6	4.15	4.94	0.0635	12.5	50.2	81.1	1.35	22.9
42	vertical	1.77	2.62	0.0617	13.8	3.82	5.63	0.168	10.8	37.3	81.2	2.78	15.8
49	in	1.94	2.62	0.0805	8.56	4.17	5.64	0.191	7.68	40.6	82.9	2.46	17.2
32	many	1.56	2.46	0.0809	11.2	3.36	5.3	0.176	11	43.8	76.9	3.01	11
65	active	1.87	2.27	0.0613	6.55	4.02	4.9	0.125	6.99	50.2	84.4	2.43	14.1
48	same	2.23	2.62	0.0684	5.63	4.82	5.64	0.14	5.84	49.1	80.8	2.85	11.1
28	end	1.68	2.49	0.124	6.52	3.62	5.34	0.321	5.36	34.7	76.7	4.53	9.25
32	sophis	2.34	2.76	0.105	4.01	5.05	5.93	0.187	4.72	43.4	78.3	2.9	12
36	time	1.97	2.41	0.0929	4.66	4.26	5.2	0.179	5.26	51.4	82.9	3.06	10.3
20	progress	1.34	1.71	0.0852	4.28	2.9	3.72	0.152	5.39	47.1	78.4	4.67	6.7
34	yes	2.3	2.7	0.0998	4.03	4.96	5.82	0.24	3.6	59.4	86.8	3.36	8.17
23	whole	1.96	2.19	0.0718	3.2	4.23	4.71	0.179	2.66	52.8	80.3	3.18	8.65
18	mental	1.86	2.14	0.0783	3.54	4.02	4.6	0.155	3.76	51.9	73.9	3.52	6.26
14	gender	1.27	1.68	0.126	3.2	2.74	3.66	0.261	3.5	19.8	57.4	5.88	6.38
12	color	1.2	1.59	0.104	3.7	2.59	3.47	0.236	3.69	46.1	70	5.91	4.04
17	strong	1.41	1.69	0.0948	2.92	3.05	3.63	0.235	2.48	49.5	74.9	3.34	7.59
16	know	1.79	2.07	0.0983	2.88	3.86	4.52	0.224	2.94	47.6	74.2	4.29	6.21
12	front	1.48	1.95	0.17	2.74	3.19	4.21	0.401	2.54	37.1	63.7	5.09	5.23
22	size	2.13	2.69	0.266	2.11	4.6	5.86	0.62	2.04	45.9	73.2	4.39	6.21
10	distance	1.6	1.76	0.0748	2.06	3.45	3.77	0.172	1.85	47.2	73.3	4.67	5.58
10	real	1.45	1.61	0.092	1.78	3.11	3.51	0.182	2.19	44.2	64.2	5.52	3.63
14	primary	2.22	2.43	0.154	1.36	4.78	5.26	0.357	1.35	59.4	80.9	4.3	5
8	single	1.57	1.82	0.19	1.32	3.38	3.83	0.32	1.4	40.3	70.7	6.48	4.69
8	sound	1.65	1.8	0.109	1.36	3.57	3.88	0.228	1.37	46.2	62.7	6.17	2.67
7	hard	1.46	1.58	0.129	0.931	3.15	3.41	0.306	0.861	42.5	60.4	8.21	2.18
10	angular	2.34	2.45	0.203	0.501	5.05	5.22	0.395	0.432	46.3	60	6.18	2.2

Table 2: Error of approximating real antonymic pairs (Err), mean and standard deviation (m, σ) of error with 100 random pairings, and the ratio $r = \frac{|Err-m|}{\sigma}$ for different features and embeddings

element w_i corresponds to a base vector b_i. For the vocabulary of the whole dictionary, we simply take the Longman definition of any word w, strip out the stopwords (we use a small list of 19 elements taken from the top of the frequency distribution), and form $V(w)$ as the sum of the b_i for the w_is that appeared in the definition of w (with multiplicity).

We performed the same computations based on this embedding as in Section 2: the results are presented in Table 4. Judgment columns under the four three embeddings in the previous section and 4lang are highly correlated, see table 5.

Unsurprisingly, the strongest correlation is between the original and the scaled HLBL results. Both the original and the scaled HLBL correlate notably better with 4lang than with SENNA, making the latter the odd one out.

4 Applicativity

So far we have seen that a dictionary-based embedding, when used for a purely semantic task, the analysis of antonyms, does about as well as the more standard embeddings based on cooccurrence data. Clearly, a CVSM could be obtained by the same procedure from any machine-readable dic-

# pairs	feature name	4lang			
		Err	m	σ	r
49	in	0.0553	0.0957	0.00551	7.33
156	good	0.0589	0.0730	0.00218	6.45
42	vertical	0.0672	0.1350	0.01360	4.98
34	yes	0.0344	0.0726	0.00786	4.86
23	whole	0.0996	0.2000	0.02120	4.74
28	end	0.0975	0.2430	0.03410	4.27
32	many	0.0516	0.0807	0.00681	4.26
14	gender	0.0820	0.2830	0.05330	3.76
36	time	0.0842	0.1210	0.00992	3.74
65	active	0.0790	0.0993	0.00553	3.68
20	progress	0.0676	0.0977	0.00847	3.56
18	mental	0.0486	0.0601	0.00329	3.51
48	same	0.0768	0.0976	0.00682	3.05
22	size	0.0299	0.0452	0.00514	2.98
16	know	0.0598	0.0794	0.00706	2.77
32	sophis	0.0665	0.0879	0.00858	2.50
12	front	0.0551	0.0756	0.01020	2.01
10	real	0.0638	0.0920	0.01420	1.98
8	single	0.0450	0.0833	0.01970	1.95
7	hard	0.0312	0.0521	0.01960	1.06
10	angular	0.0323	0.0363	0.00402	0.999
12	color	0.0564	0.0681	0.01940	0.600
8	sound	0.0565	0.0656	0.01830	0.495
17	strong	0.0693	0.0686	0.01111	0.0625
14	primary	0.0890	0.0895	0.00928	0.0529
10	distance	0.0353	0.0351	0.00456	0.0438

Table 4: The results on 4lang

	HLBL original	HLBL scaled	SENNA	4lang
HLBL original	1	0.925	0.422	0.856
HLBL scaled	0.925	1	0.390	0.772
SENNA	0.422	0.390	1	0.361
4lang	0.856	0.772	0.361	1

Table 5: Correlations between judgments based on different embeddings

tionary. Using LDOCE is computationally advantageous in that the core vocabulary is guaranteed to be very small, but finding the eigenvectors for an 80k by 80k sparse matrix would also be within CPU reach. The main advantage of starting with a conceptual graph lies elsewhere, in the possibility of investigating the function application issue we started out with.

The 4lang conceptual representation relies on a small number of basic elements, most of which correspond to what are called unary predicates in logic. We have argued elsewhere (Kornai, 2012) that meaning of linguistic expressions can be formalized using predicates with at most two arguments (there are no ditransitive or higher arity predicates on the semantic side). The x and y slots of binary elements such as *x has y* or *x kill y*, (Kornai and Makrai 2013) receive distinct labels called NOM and ACC in case grammar (Fillmore, 1977); 1 and 2 in relational grammar (Perlmutter, 1983); or AGENT and PATIENT in linking theory (Ostler, 1979). The label names themselves are irrelevant, what matters is that these elements are not part of the lexicon the same way as the words are, but rather constitute transformations of the vector space.

Here we will use the binary predicate *x has y* to reformulate the puzzle we started out with, analyzing *queen of England, king of Italy* etc. in a compositional (additive) manner, but escaping the commutativity problem. For the sake of concreteness we use the traditional assumption that it is the king who possesses the realm and not the other way around, but what follows would apply just as well if the roles were reversed. What we are interested in is the asymmetry of expressions like *Albert has England* or *Elena has Italy*, in contrast to largely symmetric predicates. *Albert marries Victoria* will be true if and only if *Victoria marries Albert* is true, but from *James has a martini* it does not follow that *?A martini has James*.

While the fundamental approach of CVSM is quite correct in assuming that nouns (unaries) and verbs (binaries) can be mapped on the same space, we need two transformations T_1 and T_2 to regulate the linking of arguments. A form like *James kills* has *James* as agent, so we compute $V(\text{James})+T_1V(\text{kill})$, while *kills James* is obtained as $V(\text{James})+T_2V(\text{kill})$. The same two transforms can distinguish agent and patient relatives as in *the man that killed James* versus *the man that James killed*.

Such forms are compositional, and in languages that have overt case markers, even 'surface compositional' (Hausser, 1984). All input and outputs are treated as vectors in the same space where the atomic lexical entries get mapped, but the applicative paradox we started out with goes away. As long as the transforms T_1 ($\oslash$) and T_2 ($\oslash$) take different values on *kill, has,* or any other binary, the meanings are kept separate.

Acknowledgments

Makrai did the work on antonym set testing, Nemeskey built the embedding, Kornai advised. We would like to thank Zsófia Tardos (BUTE) and the anonymous reviewers for useful comments. Work supported by OTKA grant #82333.

References

R. Collobert, J. Weston, L. Bottou, M. Karlen, K. Kavukcuoglu, and P. Kuksa. 2011. Natural language processing (almost) from scratch. *Journal of Machine Learning Research (JMLR)*.

Charles Fillmore. 1977. The case for case reopened. In P. Cole and J.M. Sadock, editors, *Grammatical Relations*, pages 59–82. Academic Press.

Roland Hausser. 1984. *Surface compositional grammar*. Wilhelm Fink Verlag, München.

J. Katz and Jerry A. Fodor. 1963. The structure of a semantic theory. *Language*, 39:170–210.

András Kornai and Márton Makrai. 2013. A 4lang fogalmi szótár [the 4lang concept dictionary]. In A. Tanács and V. Vincze, editors, *IX. Magyar Számítógépes Nyelvészeti Konferencia [Ninth Conference on Hungarian Computational Linguistics]*, pages 62–70.

András Kornai. 2012. Eliminating ditransitives. In Ph. de Groote and M-J Nederhof, editors, *Revised and Selected Papers from the 15th and 16th Formal Grammar Conferences*, LNCS 7395, pages 243–261. Springer.

Tom McArthur. 1998. *Living Words: Language, Lexicography, and the Knowledge Revolution*. Exeter Language and Lexicography Series. University of Exeter Press.

Tomas Mikolov, Kai Chen, Greg Corrado, and Jeffrey Dean. to appear. Efficient estimation of word representations in vector space. In Y. Bengio, , and Y. LeCun, editors, *Proc. ICLR 2013*.

George A. Miller. 1995. Wordnet: a lexical database for english. *Communications of the ACM*, 38(11):39–41.

Andriy Mnih and Geoffrey E Hinton. 2009. A scalable hierarchical distributed language model. *Advances in neural information processing systems*, 21:1081–1088.

Andrew Y. Ng, Michael I. Jordan, and Yair Weiss. 2001. On spectral clustering: Analysis and an algorithm. In *Advances in neural information processing systems*, pages 849–856. MIT Press.

Nicholas Ostler. 1979. *Case-Linking: a Theory of Case and Verb Diathesis Applied to Classical Sanskrit*. PhD thesis, MIT.

David M. Perlmutter. 1983. *Studies in Relational Grammar*. University of Chicago Press.

Determining Compositionality of Word Expressions Using Various Word Space Models and Measures

Lubomír Krčmář[1,2]
[1]University of West Bohemia, Faculty of Applied Sciences, NTIS – New Technologies for the Information Society, Pilsen, Czech Republic
lkrcmar@kiv.zcu.cz

Karel Ježek[2]
[2]University of West Bohemia, Faculty of Applied Sciences, Department of Computer Science and Engineering, Pilsen, Czech Republic
jezek_ka@kiv.zcu.cz

Pavel Pecina[3]
[3]Charles University in Prague, Faculty of Mathematics and Physics, Institute of Formal and Applied Linguistics, Prague, Czech Republic
pecina@ufal.mff.cuni.cz

Abstract

This paper presents a comparative study of 5 different types of Word Space Models (WSMs) combined with 4 different compositionality measures applied to the task of automatically determining semantic compositionality of word expressions. Many combinations of WSMs and measures have never been applied to the task before.

The study follows Biemann and Giesbrecht (2011) who attempted to find a list of expressions for which the compositionality assumption – the meaning of an expression is determined by the meaning of its constituents and their combination – does not hold. Our results are very promising and can be appreciated by those interested in WSMs, compositionality, and/or relevant evaluation methods.

1 Introduction

Our understanding of WSM is in agreement with Sahlgren (2006): "The word space model is a computational model of word meaning that utilizes the distributional patterns of words collected over large text data to represent semantic similarity between words in terms of spatial proximity". There are many types of WSMs built by different algorithms. WSMs are based on the Harris distributional hypothesis (Harris, 1954), which assumes that words are similar to the extent to which they share similar linguistic contexts. WSM can be viewed as a set of words associated with vectors representing contexts in which the words occur. Then, similar vectors imply (semantic) similarity of the words and vice versa. Consequently, WSMs provide a means to find words semantically similar to a given word. This capability of WSMs is exploited by many Natural Language Processing (NLP) applications as listed e.g. by Turney and Pantel (2010).

This study follows Biemann and Giesbrecht (2011), who attempted to find a list of non-compositional expressions whose meaning is not fully determined by the meaning of its constituents and their combination. The task turned out to be frustratingly hard (Johannsen et al., 2011). Biemann's idea and motivation is that noncompositional expressions could be treated as single units in many NLP applications such as Information Retrieval (Acosta et al., 2011) or Machine Translation (Carpuat and Diab, 2010). We extend this motivation by stating that WSMs could also benefit from a set of non-compositional expressions. Specifically, WSMs could treat semantically non-compositional expressions as single units. As an example, consider "kick the bucket", "hot dog", or "zebra crossing". Treating such expressions as single units might improve the quality of WSMs since the neighboring words of these expressions should not be related to their constituents ("kick", "bucket", "dog" or "zebra"), but instead to the whole expressions.

Recent works, including that of Lin (1999), Baldwin et al. (2003), Biemann and Giesbrecht (2011), Johannsen et al. (2011), Reddy et al. (2011a), Krčmář et al. (2012), and Krčmář et al. (2013), show the applicability of WSMs in determining the compositionality of word expressions. The proposed methods exploit various types of WSMs combined with various measures for determining the compositionality applied to various datasets. First, this leads to non-directly comparable results and second, many combinations of

WSMs and measures have never before been applied to the task. The main contribution and novelty of our study lies in systematic research of several basic and also advanced WSMs combined with all the so far, to the best of our knowledge, proposed WSM-based measures for determining the semantic compositionality.

The explored WSMs, described in more detail in Section 2, include the Vector Space Model, Latent Semantic Analysis, Hyperspace Analogue to Language, Correlated Occurrence Analogue to Lexical Semantics, and Random Indexing. The measures, including substitutability, endocentricity, compositionality, and neighbors-in-common-based, are described in detail in Section 3. Section 4 describes our experiments performed on the manually annotated datasets – Distributional Semantics and Compositionality dataset (DISCO) and the dataset built by Reddy et al. (2011a). Section 5 summarizes the results and Section 6 concludes the paper.

2 Word Space Models

The simplest and oldest types of WSMs[1] are the Vector Space Model (VSM) and Hyperspace Analogue to Language (HAL). More recent and advanced models include Latent Semantic Analysis (LSA), which is based on VSM, and Correlated Occurrence Analogue to Lexical Semantics (COALS), which originates from HAL. Random Indexing (RI) is WSM joining the principles of LSA and HAL. Many other WSMs have been proposed too. Their description is outside the scope of this paper and can be found e.g. in Turney and Pantel (2010) or Jurgens and Stevens (2010).

VSM is based on the assumption that similar (related) words tend to occur in the same documents.[2] VSM stores occurrence counts of all word types in documents a given corpus in a co-occurrence matrix **C**. The row vectors of the matrix correspond to the word types and the columns to the documents in the corpus. The numbers of occurrences c_{ij} in **C** are usually weighted by the product of the local and global weighting functions (Nakov et al., 2001). The local function weights c_{ij} by the same mathematical function; typically none (further denoted as no), $\log(c_{ij}+1)$ (denoted as log) or $\sqrt{c_{ij}}$ (denoted as $sqrt$). The purpose of local weighting is to lower the importance of highly occurring words in the document. The global function weights every value in row i of **C** by the same value calculated for row i. Typically: none (denoted as No), Inverse Document Frequency (denoted as Idf) or a function referred to as Entropy (Ent). Idf is calculated as $1 + \log(ndocs/df(i))$ and Ent as $1 + \{\sum_j p(i,j) \log p(i,j)\}/\log ndocs$, where $ndocs$ is the number of documents in the corpora, $df(i)$ is the number of documents containing word type i, and $p(i,j)$ is the probability of occurrence of word type i in document j.

LSA builds on VSM and was introduced by Landauer and Dumais (1997). The LSA algorithm works with the same co-occurrence matrix **C** which can be weighted in the same manner as in VSM. The matrix is than transformed by Singular Value Decomposition (SVD) (Deerwester et al., 1990) into **C**. The purpose of SVD is to project the row vectors and column vectors of **C** into a lower-dimensional space and thus bring the vectors of word types and vectors of documents, respectively, with similar meanings near to each other.[3] The output number of dimensions is a parameter of SVD and typically ranges from 200 to 1000 (Landauer and Dumais, 1997; Rohde et al., 2005).

HAL was first explored by Lund and Burgess (1996). It differs from VSM and LSA in that it only exploits neighboring words as contexts for word types. HAL processes the corpus by moving a sliding double-sided window with a size ranging from 1 to 5 around the word type in focus and accumulating the weighted co-occurrences of the preceding and following words into a matrix. Typically, the linear weighting function is used to ensure that the occurrences of words which are closer to the word type in focus are more significant. The dimensions of the resulting co-occurrence matrix are of size $|V|$ and $2|V|$, where V denotes the vocabulary consisting of all the word types occurring in the processed corpora. Finally, the HAL co-occurrence matrix can be reduced by retaining the most informative columns only. The columns with the highest values of entropy ($-\sum_j p_j \log p_j$, where p_j denotes the prob-

[1] WSMs are also referred to as distributional models of semantics, vector space models, or semantic spaces.

[2] VSM was originally developed for the SMART information retrieval system (Salton, 1971).

[3] In this way, LSA is able to capture higher-order co-occurrences.

ability of a word in the investigated column j) can be considered as the most informative. The alternatives and their description can be found e.g. in Song et al. (2004).

COALS was introduced by Rohde et al. (2005). Compared to HAL, COALS also processes a corpus by using a sliding window and linear weighting, but differs in several aspects: the window size of COALS is 4 and this value is fixed; COALS does not distinguish between the preceding and following words and treats them equally; applying COALS supposes that all but the most frequent m columns reflecting the most common open-class words are discarded; COALS transforms weighted counts in the co-occurrence matrix in a special way (all the word pair correlations are calculated, negative values are set to 0, and non-negative ones are square rooted – $corr$); and optionally, Singular Value Decomposition (Deerwester et al., 1990) can be applied to the COALS co-occurrence matrix.

RI is described in Sahlgren (2005) and can be viewed as a mixture of HAL and LSA. First, RI assigns random vectors to each word type in the corpus. The random vectors, referred to as index vectors, are very sparse, typically with a length of thousands, and contain only several (e.g. 7) non-zero values from the {-1,1} set. Second, RI processes the corpus by exploiting a sliding window like HAL and COALS. However, RI does not accumulate the weighted co-occurrence counts of neighboring words to the vector of the word type in focus. Instead, RI accumulates the index vectors of the co-occurring words. For accounting the word order, the permutation variant of RI was also developed (Sahlgren et al., 2008). This variant permutes the index vectors of neighboring words of the word type in focus according to the word order.

3 Compositionality Measures

We experimented with four basically different compositionality measures (further referred to as Measures) (Krčmář et al., 2013). Each Measure employs a function to measure similarity of WSM vectors. We experimented with the following ones: cosine (*cos*), Euclidian (inverse to Euclidian distance) (*euc*), and Pearson correlation (*cor*). The mathematical formulas are presented below.

$$cos(\mathbf{a},\mathbf{b}) = \frac{\sum_{i=1}^{n} a_i b_i}{\sqrt{\sum_{i=1}^{n}(a_i)^2 \sum_{i=1}^{n}(b_i)^2}}$$

$$euc(\mathbf{a},\mathbf{b}) = \frac{1}{1+\sqrt{\sum_{i=1}^{n}(a_i-b_i)^2}}$$

$$cor(\mathbf{a},\mathbf{b}) = \frac{\sum_{i=1}^{n}(a_i-\bar{a})(b_i-\bar{b})}{\sqrt{\sum_{i=1}^{n}(a_i-\bar{a})^2 \sum_{i=1}^{n}(b_i-\bar{b})^2}}$$

$$\text{where } \bar{a} = \frac{\sum_{i=1}^{n} a_i}{n}, \quad \bar{b} = \frac{\sum_{i=1}^{n} b_i}{n}$$

SU The substitutability-based Measure is based on the fact that the replacement of non-compositional expressions' constituents by the words similar to them leads to anti-collocations (Pearce, 2002). The compositionality of expressions is calculated as the ratio between the number of occurrences of the expression in a corpora and the sum of occurrences of its alternatives – possibly anti-collocations. In a similar way, we can compare pointwise mutual information scores (Lin, 1999). As an example, consider the possible occurrences of "hot dog" and "warm dog" in the corpora.

Formally, adopted from Krčmář et al. (2012), we calculate the compositionality score c_{su} for an examined expression as follows:

$$c_{su} = \frac{\sum_{i=1}^{H} W\langle a_i^h, m\rangle * \sum_{j=1}^{M} W\langle h, a_j^m\rangle}{W\langle h,m\rangle},$$

where $\langle h,m\rangle$ denotes the number of corpora occurrences of the examined expression consisting of a head and a modifying word, a_i^h and a_j^m denote i-th and j-th most similar word[4] in a certain WSM to the head and modifying word of the expression, respectively. W stands for a weighting function; following Krčmář et al. (2012), we experimented with no (no) and logarithm (log) weighting. The $*$ symbol stands for one of the two operators: addition (*plus*) and multiplication (*mult*).

EN The endocentricity-based Measure, also referred to as component or constituent-based, compares the WSM vectors of the examined expressions and their constituents. The vectors expected to be different from each other are e.g. the vector representing the expression "hot dog" and the vector representing the word "dog". Formally, the

[4]When exploiting POS tags, we constrained the similar words to be of the same POS category in our experiments.

compositionality score c_{en} can be calculated as follows:

$$c_{en} = f(x_h, x_m) \ ,$$

where x_h and x_m denote the similarity (*sim*) or inverse rank distance (*–dist*) between the examined expression and its head and modifying constituent, respectively, with regards to a certain WSM. Function f stands for a combination of its parameters: $0.5x_h + 0.5x_m$ (*avg*), $0x_h + 1x_m$ (*mOnly*), $1x_h + 0x_m$ (*hOnly*), $\min(x_h, x_m)$ (*min*), and $\max(x_h, x_m)$ (*max*).

CO The compositionality-based Measure compares the true co-occurrence vector of the examined expression and the vector obtained from the vectors corresponding to the constituents of the expression using some compositionality function (Reddy et al., 2011a). Commonly used compositionality functions are vector addition ($\oplus$) and pointwise vector multiplication ($\otimes$) (Mitchell and Lapata, 2008). The vectors expected to be different from each other are e.g. "hot dog" and "hot"$\oplus$"dog". Formally,

$$c_{co} = s(v_e, v_h * v_m) \ ,$$

where v_e, v_h, and v_m stand for vectors of an examined expression, its head and modifying constituents, respectively. $*$ stands for a vector operation.

NE The neighbors-in-common-based Measure is based on overlap of the most similar words to the examined expression and to its constituents (McCarthy et al., 2003). As an example, consider that "hot dog" is similar to "food" or "chips" and "dog" is similar to "cat" or "bark". On the other hand, the list of neighbors of a semantically compositional expression such as "black dog" is supposed to overlap with at least one of the lists of neighbors of both the expression constituents. Formally,

$$c_{ne} = o_N^h + o_N^m \ ,$$

where o_N^h and o_N^m stand for the number of same words occurring in the list of the most similar words to the examined expression and to its head and modifying constituent, respectively.

4 Experiments

We evaluated the ability of various combinations of WSMs and Measures to rank expressions as the human annotators had done ahead of time.

Datasets We experimented with the DISCO (Biemann and Giesbrecht, 2011) and Reddy (Reddy et al., 2011a) human annotated datasets, built for the task of automatic determining of semantic compositionality. The DISCO and Reddy datasets consist of manually scored expressions of adjective-noun (AN), verb-object (VO), and subject-verb (SV) types and the noun-noun (NN) type, respectively. The DISCO dataset consists of 349 expressions divided into training, validation, and test data (TestD); the Reddy dataset consists of one set containing 90 expressions. Since the DISCO validation data are of low size (35), we concatenated them with the training data (TrValD). To TrValD and TestD we added the Reddy dataset, which we had divided stratifically ahead of time. Numbers of expressions of all the different types are summarized in Table 1.

dataset	AN-VO-SV	AN	VO	SV	NN
TrValD	175	68	68	39	45
TestD	174	77	62	35	45

Table 1: Numbers of expressions of all the different types from the DISCO and Reddy datasets.

WSM construction Since the DISCO and Reddy data were extracted from the ukWaC corpus (Baroni et al., 2009), we also build our WSMs from the same corpus. We use our own modification of the S-Space package (Jurgens and Stevens, 2010). The modification lies in treating multiword expressions and handling stopwords. Specifically, we extended the package with the capability of building WSM vectors for the examined expressions in such a way that the WSM vectors previously built for words are preserved. This differentiates our approach e.g. from Baldwin et al. (2003), who label the expressions in the corpus ahead of time and treat them as single words.[5] As for treating stopwords, we map trigrams containing determiners as the middle word into bigrams without the determiners. The intuition is to extract better co-occurrence statistics for VO expressions often containing an intervening determiner. As an example, compare the occurrences of "reinvent (de-

[5]Since many single word occurrences disappear, the WSM vectors for words change. The more expressions are treated as single words, the more WSM changes. Consequently, we believe that this approach cannot be used for building a list of all expressions occurring in an examined corpus ordered by their compositionality score.

terminer) wheel" and "reinvent wheel" in ukWaC being 623 and 27, respectively.

We experimented with lemmas (*noT*) or with lemmas concatenated with their part of speech (POS) tags (*yesT*). We labeled the following strings in ukWaC as stopwords: low-frequency words (lemmas with frequency < 50), strings containing two adjacent non-letter characters (thus omitting sequences of various symbols), and closed-class words.

For our experiments, we built WSMs using various parameters examined in previous works (see Section 2) and parameters which are implied from our own experience with WSMs. Figure 1 summarizes all the parameters we used for building WSMs.

Measure settings We examined various Measure settings (see Section 3), summarized in Table 2. For all the vector comparisons, we used the *cos* similarity. Only for HAL we also examined *euc* and for COALS *cor*, since these are the recommended similarity functions for these particular WSMs (Lund and Burgess, 1996; Rohde et al., 2005).

Met.	par.	possible values
all	sim.	*cos*, *euc* if HAL, *cor* if COALS
SU	H	0,1,...,20,30,...,100
SU	M	0,1,...,20,30,...,100
SU	W	*no*, *log*
SU	$*$	*plus*, *mult*
EN	x	*sim*, *–dist*
EN	f	*avg*, *mOnly*, *hOnly*, *min*, *max*
CO	$*$	$\oplus$, $\otimes$
NE	N	10,20,...,50,100,200,...,500,1000

Table 2: All the parameters of Measures for determining semantic compositionality described in Section 3 used in our experiments.

Experimental setup Following Biemann and Giesbrecht (2011), Reddy et al. (2011a), Krčmář et al. (2012), and Krčmář et al. (2013), we use the Spearman correlation (ρ) for the evaluation of all the combinations of WSMs and Measures (Setups). Since the distribution of scores assigned to Reddy's NN dataset might not have corresponded to the distribution of DISCO scores, we decided not to map them to the same scale. Thus, we do not create a single list consisting of all the examined expressions. Instead, we order our Setups according to the weighted average of Spearman correlations calculated across all the expression types. The weights are directly proportional to the frequencies of the particular expression types. Thus, the Setup score (*wAvg*) is calculated as follows:

$$wAvg = \frac{|AN|\rho_{AN} + |VO|\rho_{VO} + |SV|\rho_{SV} + |NN|\rho_{NN}}{|AN| + |VO| + |SV| + |NN|}.$$

Having the evaluation testbed, we tried to find the optimal parameter settings for all WSMs combined with all Measures with the help of TrValD. Then, we applied the found Setups to TestD.

Notes Because several expressions or their constituents concatenated with their POS tags did not occur sufficiently often (for expressions: ≥ 0, for constituents: ≥ 50) in ukWaC, we removed them from the experiments; we removed "number crunching", "pecking order", and "sacred cow" from TrValD and "leading edge", "broken link", "spinning jenny", and "sitting duck" from TestD.

5 Results

The Setups achieving the highest *wAvg* when applied to TrValD are depicted in Table 3. The same Setups and their results when applied to TestD are depicted in Table 4. The values of Spearman correlations in TestD confirm many of the observations from TrValD[6]:

Almost all the combinations of WSMs and Measures achieve correlation values which are statistically significant. This is best illustrated by the $\rho(AN - VO - SV)$ column in Table 4, where a lot of correlation values are statistically ($p < 0.05$) or highly statistically ($p < 0.001$) significant, with regards to the number of expressions (172).

The results suggest that for every expression type, the task of determining compositionality is of varying difficulty. While determining the compositionality of the NN expression type seems to be the simplest (the highest correlations observed), determining the compositionality of the SV expression type seems to be hard since the majority of values in the ρSV column are not statistically significant; taking into account the number of SV expressions in TestD – 35, the statistically significant value of ρ at the $p < 0.05$ level is 0.34.

The correlation values differ with regards to the expression type. Certain WSMs combined with

[6]A test of statistical difference between two values of the Spearman correlation is adopted from Papoulis (1990).

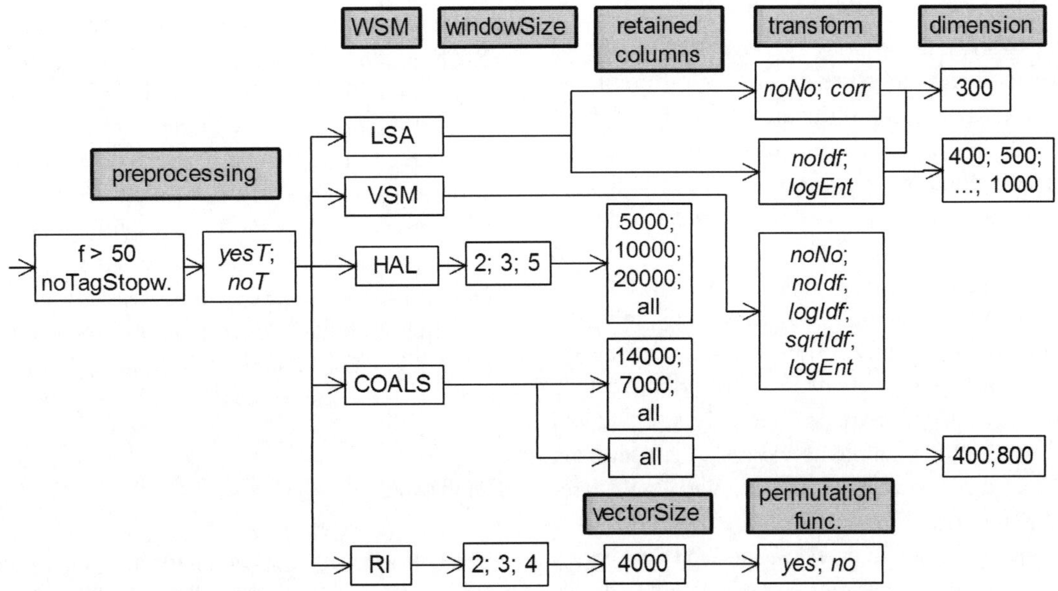

Figure 1: All the parameters of WSMs described in Section 2 used in all our experiments. Semicolon denotes OR. All the examined combinations of parameters are implied from reading the diagram from left to right.

certain Measures, although achieving high correlations upon certain expression types, fail to correlate with the rest of the expression types. Compare e.g. the correlation values of VSM and LSA combined with the SU Measure upon the AN and SV types with the correlation values upon the VO and NN types.

The results, as expected, illustrate that employing more advanced alternatives of basic WSMs is more appropriate. Specifically, LSA outperforms VSM and COALS outperforms HAL in 21 and 23 correlation values out of 24, respectively. Concerning RI, the values of correlations seem to be close to the values of VSM and HAL.

An interesting observation showing the appropriateness of using $wAvg(of\rho)$ as a good evaluation score is supported by a comparison of the $wAvg(of\rho)$ and $\rho(AN{-}VO{-}SV)$ columns. The columns suggest that some Setups might only be able to order the expressions of the same type and might not be able to order the expressions of different types among each other. As an example, compare the value of $\rho = 0.42$ in $wAvg(of\rho)$ with $\rho = 0.28$ in $\rho(AN{-}VO{-}SV)$ in the row corresponding to COALS combined with SU. Consider also that all the values of correlations are higher or equal to the value in $\rho(AN{-}VO{-}SV)$.

As for the parameters learned from applying all the combinations of differently set WSM algorithms and Measures to TrValD, their diversity is well illustrated in Tables 5 and 6. Due to this diversity, we cannot recommend any particular settings except for one. All our SU Measures benefit from weighting numbers of expression occurrences by logarithm.

The correlation values in TestD are slightly lower – probably due to overfitting – than the ones observed in TrValD. HAL combined with the Measures using euc similarity was not as successful as when combined with cos.[7]

For comparison, the results of Reddy et al. (2011b) and Chakraborty et al. (2011) as the results of the best performing Setups based on WSMs and association measures, respectively, applied to the DISCO data, are presented (Biemann and Giesbrecht, 2011). The correlation values of our Setups based on LSA and COALS, respectively, are mostly higher. However, the improvements are not statistically significant. Also, the recent results achieved by Krčmář et al. (2012) employing COALS and Krčmář et al. (2013) employ-

[7]However, using HAL combined with euc, we observed significant negative correlations which deserve further exploration.

ing LSA are depicted.

Discussion As described above, we observed different values of correlations for different expression types. This motivates us to think about other classes of expressions different from types; Measures could be e.g. varyingly successful with regards to different occurrence frequency classes of expressions (Evert, 2005). However, with such small datasets, as shown e.g. by the fact that the majority of our results are statistically indistinguishable, we cannot carry out any deeper investigations. A large dataset would provide a more reliable comparison. Ideally, this would consist of all the candidate expressions occurring in some smaller corpus. Also, we would prefer the annotated dataset not to be biased towards non-compositional expressions and to be provided with an inner-annotator agreement (Pecina, 2008); which is unfortunately not the case of the DISCO dataset.

6 Conclusion

Our study suggests that different WSMs combined with different Measures perform reasonably well in the task of determining the semantic compositionality of word expressions of different types. Especially, LSA and COALS perform well in our experiments since their results are better than those of their basic variants (VSM and HAL, respectively) and, although not statistically significantly, they outperform the best results of the previously proposed approaches (Table 4).

Importantly, our results demonstrate (Section 5) that the datasets used for the experiments are small for: first, a statistical learning of optimal parameters of both WSM algorithms and Measures; second, a thorough (different types) and reliable (statistically significant) comparison of our and the previously proposed approaches.

Therefore, we plan to build a larger manually-annotated dataset. Finally, we plan to extract a list of semantically non-compositional expressions from a given corpus and experiment with using it in NLP applications.

Acknowledgments

We thank to Vít Suchomel for providing the ukWaC corpus and the anonymous reviewers for their helpful comments and suggestions. This work was supported by the European Regional Development Fund (ERDF), project NTIS – New Technologies for the Information Society, European Centre of Excellence, CZ.1.05/1.1.00/02.0090; by Advanced Computing and Information Systems (grant no. SGS-2013-029); and by the Czech Science Foundation (grant no. P103/12/G084). Also, the access to the CERIT-SC computing facilities provided under the programme Center CERIT Scientific Cloud, part of the Operational Program Research and Development for Innovations, reg. no. CZ.1.05/3.2.00/08.0144 is highly appreciated.

References

Otavio Costa Acosta, Aline Villavicencio, and Viviane P. Moreira. 2011. Identification and treatment of multiword expressions applied to information retrieval. In *Proceedings of the Workshop on Multiword Expressions: from Parsing and Generation to the Real World*, MWE '11, pages 101–109, Stroudsburg, PA, USA.

Timothy Baldwin, Colin Bannard, Takaaki Tanaka, and Dominic Widdows. 2003. An empirical model of multiword expression decomposability. *Proceedings of the ACL 2003 workshop on Multiword expressions analysis acquisition and treatment*, pages 89–96.

Marco Baroni, Silvia Bernardini, Adriano Ferraresi, and Eros Zanchetta. 2009. The WaCky wide web: a collection of very large linguistically processed web-crawled corpora. *Journal of Language Resources And Evaluation*, 43(3):209–226.

Chris Biemann and Eugenie Giesbrecht. 2011. Distributional semantics and compositionality 2011: shared task description and results. In *Proceedings of the Workshop on Distributional Semantics and Compositionality*, DiSCo '11, pages 21–28.

Marine Carpuat and Mona Diab. 2010. Task-based evaluation of multiword expressions: a pilot study in statistical machine translation. In *Human Language Technologies: The 2010 Annual Conference of the North American Chapter of the Association for Computational Linguistics*, HLT '10, pages 242–245, Stroudsburg, PA, USA.

Tanmoy Chakraborty, Santanu Pal, Tapabrata Mondal, Tanik Saikh, and Sivaju Bandyopadhyay. 2011. Shared task system description: Measuring the compositionality of bigrams using statistical methodologies. In *Proceedings of the Workshop on Distributional Semantics and Compositionality*, pages 38–42, Portland, Oregon, USA.

Scott C. Deerwester, Susan T. Dumais, Thomas K. Landauer, George W. Furnas, and Richard A. Harshman.

WSM	Measure	wAvg(of ρ)	ρAN-VO-SV	ρAN	ρVO	ρSV	ρNN
VSM$_1$	SU$_1$	0.31	0.11	-0.03	0.36	**0.31**	**0.75**
VSM$_2$	EN$_1$	0.36	0.32	**0.41**	0.30	0.10	**0.61**
VSM$_3$	CO$_1$	0.40	0.34	**0.40**	0.26	**0.39**	**0.64**
VSM$_1$	NE$_1$	0.34	0.26	0.20	**0.48**	0.07	**0.60**
LSA$_1$	SU$_2$	0.34	0.19	-0.05	**0.46**	**0.42**	**0.71**
LSA$_2$	EN$_2$	0.56	**0.53**	**0.54**	**0.51**	**0.59**	**0.65**
LSA$_3$	CO$_1$	0.55	**0.53**	**0.49**	**0.56**	**0.63**	**0.58**
LSA$_2$	NE$_2$	0.50	**0.45**	**0.46**	0.37	**0.64**	**0.62**
HAL$_1$	SU$_3$	0.45	0.36	0.28	**0.50**	**0.40**	**0.67**
HAL$_2$	EN$_3$	0.36	0.35	**0.47**	0.28	0.27	0.38
HAL$_3$	CO$_1$	0.23	0.15	0.28	0.12	-0.01	**0.54**
HAL$_4$	NE$_3$	0.27	0.25	0.31	0.21	0.17	0.39
COALS$_1$	SU$_4$	0.48	**0.41**	0.28	**0.56**	**0.49**	**0.68**
COALS$_2$	EN$_2$	0.58	**0.54**	**0.6**	**0.63**	**0.37**	**0.68**
COALS$_2$	CO$_1$	0.59	**0.54**	**0.6**	**0.64**	**0.37**	**0.70**
COALS$_2$	NE$_4$	0.58	**0.56**	**0.61**	**0.58**	**0.46**	**0.67**
RI$_1$	SU$_5$	0.52	**0.44**	**0.45**	**0.51**	**0.52**	**0.68**
RI$_2$	EN$_3$	0.45	**0.44**	**0.41**	**0.57**	**0.33**	0.45
RI$_3$	CO$_1$	0.21	0.13	0.13	0.16	0.11	**0.54**
RI$_2$	NE$_5$	0.43	**0.43**	**0.43**	**0.53**	0.21	**0.49**

Table 3: The Spearman correlations ρ of the best performing (wAvg) combinations of particular WSMs and Measures from all the tested Setups applied to TrValD. The highest correlation values in the particular columns and the correlation values which are not statistically different from them ($p < 0.05$) are in bold (yet we do not know how to calculate the stat. significance for the wAvg(of ρ) column). The parameters of WSMs and Measures corresponding to the indexes are depicted in Tables 5 and 6, respectively.

1990. Indexing by latent semantic analysis. *Journal of the American Society of Information Science*, 41(6):391–407.

Stefan Evert. 2005. *The statistics of word cooccurrences : word pairs and collocations*. Ph.D. thesis, Universität Stuttgart, Holzgartenstr. 16, 70174 Stuttgart.

Zellig Harris. 1954. Distributional structure. *Word*, 10(23):146–162.

Anders Johannsen, Hector Martinez Alonso, Christian Rishøj, and Anders Søgaard. 2011. Shared task system description: frustratingly hard compositionality prediction. In *Proceedings of the Workshop on Distributional Semantics and Compositionality*, DiSCo '11, pages 29–32, Stroudsburg, PA, USA.

David Jurgens and Keith Stevens. 2010. The s-space package: an open source package for word space models. In *Proceedings of the ACL 2010 System Demonstrations*, ACLDemos '10, pages 30–35, Stroudsburg, PA, USA.

Lubomír Krčmář, Karel Ježek, and Massimo Poesio. 2012. Detection of semantic compositionality using semantic spaces. *Lecture Notes in Computer Science*, 7499 LNAI:353–361.

Lubomír Krčmář, Karel Ježek, and Pavel Pecina. 2013. Determining compositionality of word expressions using word space models. In *Proceedings of the 9th Workshop on Multiword Expressions*, pages 42–50, Atlanta, Georgia, USA.

Thomas K. Landauer and Susan T. Dumais. 1997. A solution to Plato's problem: The latent semantic analysis theory of acquisition, induction, and representation of knowledge. *Psychological Review*, 104(2):211–240.

Dekang Lin. 1999. Automatic identification of non-compositional phrases. In *Proceedings of the 37th annual meeting of the Association for Computational Linguistics on Computational Linguistics*, ACL '99, pages 317–324, Stroudsburg, PA, USA.

Kevin Lund and Curt Burgess. 1996. Producing high-dimensional semantic spaces from lexical co-occurrence. *Behavior Research Methods*, 28(2):203–208.

Diana McCarthy, Bill Keller, and John Carroll. 2003. Detecting a continuum of compositionality in phrasal verbs. In *Proceedings of the ACL 2003 workshop on Multiword expressions analysis acquisition and treatment*, volume 18 of *MWE '03*, pages 73–80.

WSM	Measure	wAvg(of ρ)	ρAN-VO-SV	ρAN	ρVO	ρSV	ρNN
VSM_1	SU_1	0.28	0.03	0.01	**0.51**	**0.04**	**0.62**
VSM_2	EN_1	0.26	0.19	0.08	0.29	**0.04**	**0.69**
VSM_3	CO_1	0.32	0.26	0.24	0.23	**0.25**	**0.65**
VSM_1	NE_1	0.32	0.19	**0.36**	0.25	-0.13	**0.73**
LSA_1	SU_2	0.31	0.06	0.05	**0.50**	**0.20**	**0.59**
LSA_2	EN_2	0.50	**0.40**	**0.39**	**0.55**	**0.32**	**0.78**
LSA_3	CO_1	0.48	**0.36**	**0.29**	**0.60**	**0.42**	**0.69**
LSA_2	NE_2	0.44	**0.33**	**0.34**	0.40	**0.44**	**0.67**
HAL_1	SU_3	0.29	0.16	0.09	0.32	**0.34**	**0.56**
HAL_2	EN_3	0.36	0.28	**0.33**	0.35	**0.26**	**0.53**
HAL_3	CO_1	0.24	0.22	0.25	0.16	**0.15**	0.42
HAL_4	NE_3	0.21	0.14	0.02	0.33	**0.06**	0.47
$COALS_1$	SU_4	0.42	0.28	0.28	**0.54**	**0.30**	**0.59**
$COALS_2$	EN_2	0.49	**0.44**	**0.52**	**0.51**	**0.07**	**0.72**
$COALS_2$	CO_1	0.47	**0.40**	**0.47**	**0.51**	**0.07**	**0.74**
$COALS_2$	NE_4	0.52	**0.48**	**0.55**	**0.50**	**0.21**	**0.74**
RI_1	SU_5	0.30	0.14	0.14	0.29	**0.12**	**0.72**
RI_2	EN_3	0.44	**0.34**	**0.37**	**0.54**	**0.20**	**0.63**
RI_3	CO_1	0.23	0.23	**0.29**	0.17	**0.17**	0.26
RI_2	NE_5	0.31	0.26	0.26	0.42	**0.04**	0.44
Reddy-WSM		-	**0.35**	-	-	-	-
StatMix		-	**0.33**	-	-	-	-
Krcmar-COALS		-	**0.42**	**0.42**	**0.69**	**0.24**	-
Krcmar-LSA		-	**0.50**	**0.50**	**0.56**	**0.41**	-

Table 4: The Spearman correlations ρ of the best performing (wAvg) combinations of particular WSMs and Measures trained in TranValD applied to TestD. The highest correlation values in the particular columns and the correlation values which are not statistically different from them ($p < 0.05$) are in bold (yet we do not know how to calculate the stat. significance for the wAvg(of ρ) column). Reddy-WSM and StatMix stand for the best performing system based on WSMs and association measures, respectively, applied to the DISCO task (Biemann and Giesbrecht, 2011). Krcmar-COALS and Krcmar-LSA stand for the best published results achieved upon the dataset presented in Krčmář et al. (2012) and Krčmář et al. (2013), respectively. The parameters of WSMs and Measures corresponding to the indexes are depicted in Tables 5 and 6, respectively.

Jeff Mitchell and Mirella Lapata. 2008. Vector-based models of semantic composition. In *Proceedings of ACL-08: HLT*, pages 236–244, Columbus, Ohio.

Preslav Nakov, Antonia Popova, and Plamen Mateev. 2001. Weight functions impact on lsa performance. In *Proceedings of the EuroConference Recent Advances in Natural Language Processing (RANLP'01)*, pages 187–193.

Athanasios Papoulis. 1990. *Probability & statistics*. Prentice Hall.

Darren Pearce. 2002. A Comparative Evaluation of Collocation Extraction Techniques. In *Proceedings of the Third International Conference on Language Resources and Evaluation, LREC*.

Pavel Pecina. 2008. Reference data for Czech collocation extraction. In *Proceedings of the LREC 2008 Workshop Towards a Shared Task for Multiword Expressions*, pages 11–14, Marrakech, Morocco. European Language Resources Association.

Siva Reddy, Diana McCarthy, and Suresh Manandhar. 2011a. An empirical study on compositionality in compound nouns. In *Proceedings of 5th International Joint Conference on Natural Language Processing*, pages 210–218, Chiang Mai, Thailand, November. Asian Federation of Natural Language Processing.

Siva Reddy, Diana McCarthy, Suresh Manandhar, and Spandana Gella. 2011b. Exemplar-based word-space model for compositionality detection: Shared task system description. In *Proceedings of the Workshop on Distributional Semantics and Compositionality*, pages 54–60, Portland, Oregon, USA.

WSM	parameters			
VSM	**tags**	**trans.**		
VSM_1	*noT*	*noNo*		
VSM_2	*yesT*	*noNo*		
VSM_3	*yesT*	*noIdf*		
LSA	**tags**	**trans.**	**dim.**	
LSA_1	*noT*	*logEnt*	900	
LSA_2	*yesT*	*noNo*	300	
LSA_3	*noT*	*noIdf*	300	
HAL	**tags**	**win s.**	**ret. c.**	
HAL_1	*noT*	5	20000	
HAL_2	*yesT*	5	20000	
HAL_3	*noT*	2	10000	
HAL_4	*yesT*	5	all	
COALS	**tags**	**ret. c.**		
$COALS_1$	*noT*	7000		
$COALS_2$	*yesT*	7000		
RI	**tags**	**win. s.**	**vec. s.**	**perm.**
RI_1	*noT*	2	4000	*no*
RI_2	*noT*	4	4000	*no*
RI_3	*noT*	2	4000	*yes*

Table 5: Parameters of WSMs (Section 2) which, combined with particular Measures, achieved the highest average correlation in TrValD.

Measure	parameters				
SU	**sim.**	$*$	**W**	**H**	**M**
SU_1	*cos*	*plus*	*log*	30	3
SU_2	*cos*	*plus*	*log*	100	5
SU_3	*cos*	*mult*	*log*	12	2
SU_4	*cos*	*mult*	*log*	80	4
SU_5	*cos*	*mult*	*log*	4	3
EN	**sim.**	**func.**	**x**		
EN_1	*cos*	*min*	*sim*		
EN_2	*cos*	*avg*	*sim*		
EN_3	*cos*	*min*	*–dist*		
CO	**sim.**	$*$			
CO_1	*cos*	$\oplus$			
NE	**sim.**	**O**			
NE_1	*cos*	1000			
NE_2	*cos*	500			
NE_3	*cos*	50			
NE_4	*cor*	500			
NE_5	*cos*	20			

Table 6: Parameters of Measures (Section 3) which, combined with particular WSMs, achieved the highest average correlation in TrValD.

Douglas L. Rohde, Laura M. Gonnerman, and David C. Plaut. 2005. An improved model of semantic similarity based on lexical co-occurrence. *Unpublished manuscript*.

Magnus Sahlgren, Anders Holst, and Pentti Kanerva. 2008. Permutations as a means to encode order in word space. In V. Sloutsky, B. Love, and K. Mcrae, editors, *Proceedings of the 30th Annual Conference of the Cognitive Science Society*, pages 1300–1305. Cognitive Science Society, Austin, TX.

Magnus Sahlgren. 2005. An introduction to random indexing. In *Methods and Applications of Semantic Indexing Workshop at the 7th International Conference on Terminology and Knowledge Engineering*, Leipzig, Germany.

Magnus Sahlgren. 2006. *The Word-Space Model: Using distributional analysis to represent syntagmatic and paradigmatic relations between words in highdimensional vector spaces*. Ph.D. thesis, Stockholm University.

Gerard Salton. 1971. *The SMART Retrieval System; Experiments in Automatic Document Processing*. Prentice-Hall, Inc., Upper Saddle River, NJ, USA.

Dawei Song, Peter Bruza, and Richard Cole. 2004. Concept learning and information inferencing on a highdimensional semantic space. In *ACM SIGIR 2004 Workshop on Mathematical/Formal Methods in Information Retrieval*.

Peter D. Turney and Patrick Pantel. 2010. From frequency to meaning: vector space models of semantics. *J. Artif. Int. Res.*, 37(1):141–188.

"Not not bad" is not "bad": A distributional account of negation

Karl Moritz Hermann **Edward Grefenstette** **Phil Blunsom**
University of Oxford Department of Computer Science
Wolfson Building, Parks Road
Oxford OX1 3QD, United Kingdom
firstname.lastname@cs.ox.ac.uk

Abstract

With the increasing empirical success of distributional models of compositional semantics, it is timely to consider the types of textual logic that such models are capable of capturing. In this paper, we address shortcomings in the ability of current models to capture logical operations such as negation. As a solution we propose a tripartite formulation for a continuous vector space representation of semantics and subsequently use this representation to develop a formal compositional notion of negation within such models.

1 Introduction

Distributional models of semantics characterize the meanings of words as a function of the words they co-occur with (Firth, 1957). These models, mathematically instantiated as sets of vectors in high dimensional vector spaces, have been applied to tasks such as thesaurus extraction (Grefenstette, 1994; Curran, 2004), word-sense discrimination (Schütze, 1998), automated essay marking (Landauer and Dumais, 1997), and so on.

During the past few years, research has shifted from using distributional methods for modelling the semantics of words to using them for modelling the semantics of larger linguistic units such as phrases or entire sentences. This move from word to sentence has yielded models applied to tasks such as paraphrase detection (Mitchell and Lapata, 2008; Mitchell and Lapata, 2010; Grefenstette and Sadrzadeh, 2011; Blacoe and Lapata, 2012), sentiment analysis (Socher et al., 2012; Hermann and Blunsom, 2013), and semantic relation classification (*ibid.*). Most efforts approach the problem of modelling phrase meaning through vector composition using linear algebraic vector operations (Mitchell and Lapata, 2008; Mitchell and Lapata, 2010; Zanzotto et al., 2010), matrix or tensor-based approaches (Baroni and Zamparelli, 2010; Coecke et al., 2010; Grefenstette et al., 2013; Kartsaklis et al., 2012), or through the use of recursive auto-encoding (Socher et al., 2011; Hermann and Blunsom, 2013) or neural-networks (Socher et al., 2012). On the non-compositional front, Erk and Padó (2008) keep word vectors separate, using syntactic information from sentences to disambiguate words in context; likewise Turney (2012) treats the compositional aspect of phrases and sentences as a matter of similarity measure composition rather than vector composition.

These compositional distributional approaches often portray themselves as attempts to reconcile the empirical aspects of distributional semantics with the structured aspects of formal semantics. However, they in fact only principally co-opt the syntax-sensitivity of formal semantics, while mostly eschewing the logical aspects.

Expressing the effect of logical operations in high dimensional distributional semantic models is a very different task than in boolean logic. For example, whereas predicates such as 'red' are seen in predicate calculi as functions mapping elements of some set M_{red} to $\top$ (and all other domain elements to $\bot$), in compositional distributional models we give the meaning of 'red' a vector-like representation, and devise some combination operation with noun representations to obtain the representation for an adjective-noun pair. Under the logical view, negation of a predicate therefore yields a new truth-function mapping elements of the complement of M_{red} to $\top$ (and all other domain elements to $\bot$), but the effect of negation and other logical operations in distributional models is not so sharp: we expect the representation for "not red" to remain close to other objects of the same domain of discourse (i.e. other colours) while being sufficiently different from the representation of 'red' in some manner. Exactly how textual logic would best be represented in a continuous vector space model remains an open problem.

In this paper we propose one possible formulation for a continuous vector space based representation of semantics. We use this formulation as the basis for providing an account of logical operations for distributional models. In particular, we focus on the case of negation and how it might work in higher dimensional distributional models. Our formulation separates domain, value and functional representation in such a way as to allow negation to be handled naturally. We explain the linguistic and model-related impacts of this mode of representation and discuss how this approach could be generalised to other semantic functions.

In Section 2, we provide an overview of work relating to that presented in this paper, covering the integration of logical elements in distributional models, and the integration of distributional elements in logical models. In Section 3, we introduce and argue for a tripartite representation in distributional semantics, and discuss the issues relating to providing a linguistically sensible notion of negation for such representations. In Section 4, we present matrix-vector models similar to that of Socher et al. (2012) as a good candidate for expressing this tripartite representation. We argue for the elimination of non-linearities from such models, and thus show that negation cannot adequately be captured. In Section 5, we present a short analysis of the limitation of these matrix-vector models with regard to the task of modelling non-boolean logical operations, and present an improved model bypassing these limitations in Section 6. Finally, in Section 7, we conclude by suggesting future work which will extend and build upon the theoretical foundations presented in this paper.

2 Motivation and Related Work

The various approaches to combining logic with distributional semantics can broadly be put into three categories: those approaches which use distributional models to enhance existing logical tools; those which seek to replicate logic with the mathematical constructs of distributional models; and those which provide new mathematical definitions of logical operations within distributional semantics. The work presented in this paper is in the third category, but in this section we will also provide a brief overview of related work in the other two in order to better situate the work this paper will describe in the literature.

Vector-assisted logic The first class of approaches seeks to use distributional models of word semantics to enhance logic-based models of textual inference. The work which best exemplifies this strand of research is found in the efforts of Garrette et al. (2011) and, more recently, Beltagy et al. (2013). This line of research converts logical representations obtained from syntactic parses using Bos' Boxer (Bos, 2008) into Markov Logic Networks (Richardson and Domingos, 2006), and uses distributional semantics-based models such as that of Erk and Padó (2008) to deal with issues polysemy and ambiguity.

As this class of approaches deals with improving logic-based models rather than giving a distributional account of logical function words, we view such models as orthogonal to the effort presented in this paper.

Logic with vectors The second class of approaches seeks to integrate boolean-like logical operations into distributional semantic models using existing mechanisms for representing and composing semantic vectors. Coecke et al. (2010) postulate a mathematical framework generalising the syntax-semantic passage of Montague Grammar (Montague, 1974) to other forms of syntactic and semantic representation. They show that the parses yielded by syntactic calculi satisfying certain structural constraints can be canonically mapped to vector combination operations in distributional semantic models. They illustrate their framework by demonstrating how the truth-value of sentences can be obtained from the combination of vector representations of words and multilinear maps standing for logical predicates and relations. They furthermore give a matrix interpretation of negation as a 'swap' matrix which inverts the truth-value of vectorial sentence representations, and show how it can be embedded in sentence structure.

Recently, Grefenstette (2013) showed that the examples from this framework could be extended to model a full quantifier-free predicate logic using tensors of rank 3 or lower. In parallel, Socher et al. (2012) showed that propositional logic can be learned using tensors of rank 2 or lower (i.e. only matrices and vectors) through the use of non-linear activation functions in recursive neural networks.

The work of Coecke et al. (2010) and Grefenstette (2013) limits itself to defining, rather than learning, distributional representations of logical operators for distributional models that simulate logic, and makes no pretense to the provision of operations which generalise to higher-dimensional distributional semantic representations. As for the non-linear approach of Socher et al. (2012), we will discuss, in Section 4 below, the limitations with this model with regard to the task of modelling logic for higher dimensional representations.

Logic for vectors The third and final class of approaches is the one the work presented here belongs to. This class includes attempts to define representations for logical operators in high dimensional semantic vector spaces. Such approaches do not seek to retrieve boolean logic and truth values, but to define what logical operators *mean* when applied to distributional representations. The seminal work in this area is found in the work of Widdows and Peters (2003), who define negation and other logical operators algebraically for high dimensional semantic vectors. Negation, under this approach, is effectively a binary relation rather than a unary relation: it expresses the semantics of statements such as 'A NOT B' rather than merely 'NOT B', and does so by projecting the vector for A into the orthogonal subspace of the vector for B. This approach to negation is useful for vector-based information retrieval models, but does not necessarily capture all the aspects of negation we wish to take into consideration, as will be discussed in Section 3.

3 Logic in text

In order to model logical operations over semantic vectors, we propose a tripartite meaning representation, which combines the separate and distinct treatment of domain-related and value-related aspects of semantic vectors with a domain-driven syntactic functional representation. This is a unification of various recent approaches to the problem of semantic representation in continuous distributional semantic modelling (Socher et al., 2012; Turney, 2012; Hermann and Blunsom, 2013).

We borrow from Socher et al. (2012) and others (Baroni and Zamparelli, 2010; Coecke et al., 2010) the idea that the information words refer to is of two sorts: first the semantic content of the word, which can be seen as the sense or reference to the concept the word stands for, and is typically modelled as a semantic vector; and second, the *function* the word has, which models the effect the word has on other words it combines with in phrases and sentences, and is typically modelled as a matrix or higher-order tensor. We borrow from Turney (2012) the idea that the semantic aspect of a word should not be modelled as a single vector where everything is equally important, but ideally as two or more vectors (or, as we do here, two or more *regions* of a vector) which stand for the aspects of a word relating to its *domain*, and those relating to its *value*.

We therefore effectively suggest a *tripartite representation* of the semantics of words: a word's meaning is modelled by elements representing its value, domain, and function, respectively.

The tripartite representation We argue that the tripartite representation suggested above allows us to explicitly capture several aspects of semantics. Further, while there may be additional distinct aspects of semantics, we argue that this is a minimal viable representation.

First of all, the differentiation between domain and value is useful for establishing similarity within subspaces of meaning. For instance, the words *blue* and *red* share a common domain (colours) while having very different values. We hypothesise that making this distinction explicit will allow for the definition of more sophisticated and fine-grained semantics of logical operations, as discussed below. Although we will represent domain and value as two regions of a vector, there is no reason for these not to be treated as separate vectors at the time of comparison, as done by Turney (2012).

Through the third part, the functional representation, we capture the compositional aspect of semantics: the functional representation governs how a term interacts with its environment. Inspired by the distributional interpretation (Baroni and Zamparelli, 2010; Coecke et al., 2010) of syntactically-paramatrized semantic composition functions from Montogovian semantics (Montague, 1974), we will also assume the function part of our representation to be parametrized principally by syntax and domain rather than value. The intuition behind taking domain into account in addition to syntactic class being that all members of a domain largely interact with their environment in the same fashion.

Modeling negation The tripartite representation proposed above allows us to define logical operations in more detail than competing approaches. To exemplify this, we focus on the case of negation.

We define negation for semantic vectors to be the absolute complement of a term in its domain. This implies that negation will not affect the domain of a term but only its value. Thus, *blue* and *not blue* are assumed to share a common domain. We call this naive form of negation the inversion of a term A, which we idealise as the partial inversion A^{inv} of the region associated with the value of the word in its vector representation A.

$$\begin{array}{ccc} \begin{bmatrix} d \\ v \\ v \end{bmatrix} & \begin{bmatrix} d \\ v \\ -v \end{bmatrix} & \begin{bmatrix} d \\ v \\ -\mu v \end{bmatrix} \\ \begin{bmatrix} f \end{bmatrix} & \begin{bmatrix} f \end{bmatrix} & \begin{bmatrix} f \end{bmatrix} \\ \mathrm{W} & \mathrm{W}^{inv} & \neg\mathrm{W} \end{array}$$

Figure 1: The semantic representations of a word W, its inverse W^{inv} and its negation $\neg W$. The domain part of the representation remains unchanged, while the value part will partially be inverted (inverse), or inverted and scaled (negation) with $0 < \mu < 1$. The (separate) functional representation also remains unchanged.

Additionally, we expect negation to have a diminutive effect. This diminutive effect is best exemplified in the case of sentiment: *good* is more positive than *not bad*, even though *good* and *bad* are antonyms of each other. By extension *not not good* and *not not not bad* end up somewhere in the middle—qualitative statements still, but void of any significant polarity. To reflect this diminutive effect of negation and double negation commonly found in language, we define the idealised diminutive negation $\neg A$ of a semantic vector A as a scalar inversion over a segment of the value region of its representation with the scalar $\mu : 0 < \mu < 1$, as shown in Figure 1.

As we defined the functional part of our representation to be predominately parametrized by syntax and domain, it will remain constant under negation and inversion.

4 A general matrix-vector model

Having discussed, above, how the vector component of a word can be partitioned into domain and value, we now turn to the partition between semantic content and function. A good candidate for modelling this partition would be a dual-space representation similar to that of Socher et al. (2012). In this section, we show that this sort of representation is not well adapted to the modelling of negation.

Models using dual-space representations have been proposed in several recent publications, notably in Turney (2012) and Socher et al. (2012). We use the class of recursive matrix-vector models as the basis for our investigation; for a detailed introduction see the MV-RNN model described in Socher et al. (2012).

We begin by describing composition for a general dual-space model, and apply this model to the notion of compositional logic in a tripartite representation discussed earlier. We identify the shortcomings of the general model and subsequently discuss alternative composition models and modifications that allow us to better capture logic in vector space models of meaning.

Assume a basic model of compositionality for such a tripartite representation as follows. Each term is encoded by a semantic vector v capturing its domain and value, as well as a matrix M capturing its function. Thus, composition consists of two separate operations to learn semantics and function of the composed term:

$$\begin{aligned} \mathbf{v}_p &= f_v(\mathbf{v}_a, \mathbf{v}_b, M_a, M_b) \\ M_p &= f_M(M_a, M_b) \end{aligned} \tag{1}$$

As we defined the functional representation to be parametrized by syntax and domain, its composition function does not require $\mathbf{v}_a$ and $\mathbf{v}_b$ as inputs, with all relevant information already being contained in M_a, M_b. In the case of Socher et al. (2012) these functions are as follows:

$$M_p = W_M \begin{bmatrix} M_a \\ M_b \end{bmatrix} \tag{2}$$

$$\mathbf{v}_p = g\left(W_v \begin{bmatrix} M_a \mathbf{v}_b \\ M_b \mathbf{v}_a \end{bmatrix}\right) \tag{3}$$

where g is a non-linearity.

4.1 The question of non-linearities

While the non-linearity g could be equipped with greater expressive power, such as in the boolean logic experiment in Socher et al. (2012)), the aim of this paper is to place the burden of compositionality on the atomic representations instead. For this reason we treat g as an identity function, and W_M, W_v as simple additive matrices in this investigation, by setting

$$g = I \quad W_v = W_M = [I\ I]$$

where I is an identity matrix. This simplification is justified for several reasons.

A simple non-linearity such as the commonly used hyperbolic tangent or sigmoid function will not add sufficient power to overcome the issues outlined in this paper. Only a highly complex non-linear function would be able to satisfy the requirements for vector space based logic as discussed above. Such a function would defeat the point however, by pushing the "heavy-lifting" from the model structure into a separate function.

Furthermore, a non-linearity effectively encodes a scattergun approach: While it may have the power to learn a desired behaviour, it similarly has a lot of power to learn undesired behaviours and side effects. From a formal perspective it would therefore seem more prudent to explicitly encode desired behaviour in a model's structure rather than relying on a non-linearity.

4.2 Negation

We have outlined our formal requirements for negation in the previous section. From these requirements we can deduce four equalities, concerning the effect of negation and double negation on the semantic representation and function of a term. The matrices J_μ and J_ν (illustrated in Figure 2) describe a partially scaled and inverted identity matrix, where $0 < \mu, \nu < 1$.

$$\begin{pmatrix} 1 & & & & & \\ & \ddots & & & \mathbf{0} & \\ & & 1 & & & \\ & & & -\mu & & \\ & \mathbf{0} & & & \ddots & \\ & & & & & -\mu \end{pmatrix}$$

Figure 2: A partially scaled and inverted identity matrix J_μ. Such a matrix can be used to transform a vector storing a domain and value representation into one containing the same domain but a partially inverted value, such as W and $\neg W$ described in Figure 1.

$$f_v(\text{not}, a) = J_\mu \mathbf{v}_a \quad (4)$$

$$f_M(\text{not}, a) \approx M_a \quad (5)$$

$$f_v(\text{not}, f_v(\text{not}, a)) = J_\nu J_\mu \mathbf{v}_a \quad (6)$$

$$f_M(\text{not}, f_M(\text{not}, a)) \approx M_a \quad (7)$$

Based on our assumption about the constant domain and interaction across negation, we can replace the approximate equality with a strict equality in Equations 5 and 7. Further, we assume that both $M_a \neq I$ and $M_a \neq 0$, i.e. that A has a specific and non-zero functional representation. We make a similar assumption for the semantic representation $\mathbf{v}_a \neq 0$.

Thus, to satisfy the equalities in Equations 4 through 7, we can deduce the values of $\mathbf{v}_{not}$ and M_{not} as discussed below.

Value and Domain in Negation Under the simplifications of the model explained earlier, we know that the following is true:

$$\begin{aligned} f_v(a,b) &= g\left(W_v \begin{bmatrix} M_a \mathbf{v}_b \\ M_b \mathbf{v}_a \end{bmatrix}\right) \\ &= I\left([I\ I] \begin{bmatrix} M_a \mathbf{v}_b \\ M_b \mathbf{v}_a \end{bmatrix}\right) \\ &= M_a \mathbf{v}_b + M_b \mathbf{v}_a \end{aligned}$$

I.e. the domain and value representation of a parent is the sum of the two Mv multiplications of its children. The matrix W_v could re-weight this addition, but that would not affect the rest of this analysis.

Given the idea that the domain stays constant under negation and that a part of the value is inverted and scaled, we further know that these two equations hold:

$$\forall a \in A : f_v(\text{not}, a) = J_\mu \mathbf{v}_a$$

$$\forall a \in A : f_v(\text{not}, f_v(\text{not}, a)) = J_\nu J_\mu \mathbf{v}_a$$

Assuming that both semantic and functional representation across all A varies and is non-zero, these equalities imply the following conditions for the representation of *not*:

$$M_{not} = J_\mu = J_\nu$$

$$\mathbf{v}_{not} = 0$$

These two equations suggest that the term not has no inherent value ($\mathbf{v}_{not} = 0$), but merely acts as a function, inverting part of another terms semantic representation ($M_{not} = J_\mu$).

Functional Representation in Negation We can apply the same method to the functional representation. Here, we know that:

$$
\begin{aligned}
f_M(a,b) &= W_M \begin{bmatrix} M_a \\ M_b \end{bmatrix} \\
&= \begin{bmatrix} I \ I \end{bmatrix} \begin{bmatrix} M_a \\ M_b \end{bmatrix} \\
&= M_a + M_b
\end{aligned}
$$

Further, as defined in our discussion of negation, we require the functional representation to remain unchanged under negation:

$$
\begin{aligned}
\forall a \in A : f_M(\text{not}, a) &= M_a \\
\forall a \in A : f_M(\text{not}, f_M(\text{not}, a)) &= M_a
\end{aligned}
$$

These requirements combined leave us to conclude that $M_{not} = 0$. Combined with the result from the first part of the analysis, this causes a contradiction:

$$
\begin{aligned}
M_{not} &= 0 \\
M_{not} &= J_\mu \\
\implies J_\mu &= 0 \lightning
\end{aligned}
$$

This demonstrates that the MV-RNN as described in this paper is not capable of modelling semantic logic according to the principles we outlined. The fact that we would require $M_{not} = 0$ further supports the points made earlier about the non-linearities and setting W_M to $\begin{bmatrix} I \ I \end{bmatrix}$. Even a specific W_M and non-linearity would not be able to ensure that the functional representation stays constant under negation given a non-zero M_{not}.

Clearly, any other complex semantic representation would suffer from the same issue here—the failure of double-negation to revert a representation to its (diminutive) original.

5 Analysis

The issue identified with the MV-RNN style models described above extends to a number of other models of vector spaced compositionality. It can be viewed as a problem of uninformed composition caused by a composition function that fails to account for syntax and thus for scope.

Of course, identifying the scope of negation is a hard problem in its own right—see e.g. the *SEM 2012 shared task (Morante and Blanco, 2012). However, at least for simple cases, we can deduce scope by considering the parse tree of a sentence:

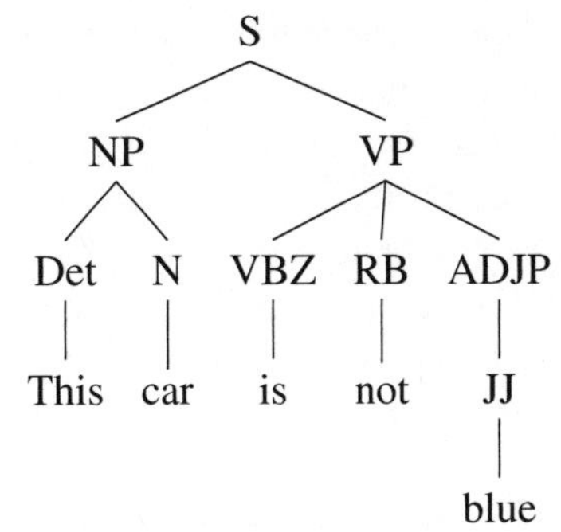

Figure 3: The parse tree for *This car is not blue*, highlighting the limited scope of the negation.

If we consider the parse tree for *this car is not blue*, it is clear that the scope of the negation expressed includes the colour but not the car (Figure 3).

While the MV-RNN model in Socher et al. (2012) incorporates parse trees to guide the order of its composition steps, it uses a single composition function across all steps. Thus, the functional representation of *not* will to some extent propagate outside of its scope, leading to a vector capturing something that is not blue, but also not quite a car.

There are several possibilities for addressing this issue. One possibility is to give greater weight to syntax, for instance by parametrizing the composition functions f_v and f_M on the parse structure. This could be achieved by using specific weight matrices W_v and W_M for each possible tag. While the power of this approach is limited by the complexity of the parse structure, it would be better able to capture effects such as the scoping and propagation of functional representations.

Another approach, which we describe in greater detail in the next section, pushes the issue of propagation onto the word level. While both approaches could easily be combined, this second option is more consistent with our aim of avoiding the implicit encoding of logic into fixed model parameters in favour of the explicit encoding in model structure.

6 An improved model

As we outlined in this paper, a key requirement for a compositional model motivated by formal semantics is the ability to propagate functional representations, but also to not propagate these representations when doing so is not semantically appropriate. Here, we propose a modification of the MV-RNN class of models that can capture this distinction without the need to move the composition logic into the non-linearity.

We add a parameter α to the representation of each word, controlling the degree to which its functional representation propagates after having been applied in its own composition step.

Thus, the composition step of the new model requires three equations:

$$M_p = W_M \begin{bmatrix} \frac{\alpha_a}{\alpha_a+\alpha_b} M_a \\ \frac{\alpha_b}{\alpha_a+\alpha_b} M_b \end{bmatrix} \quad (8)$$

$$\mathbf{v}_p = g\left(W_v \begin{bmatrix} M_a \mathbf{v}_b \\ M_b \mathbf{v}_a \end{bmatrix} \right) \quad (9)$$

$$\alpha_p = max(\alpha_a, \alpha_b) \quad (10)$$

Going back to the discussion of negation, this model has the clear advantage of being able to capture negation in the way we defined it. As $f_v(a, b)$ is unchanged, these two equations still hold:

$$M_{not} = J_\mu = J_\nu$$
$$\mathbf{v}_{not} = 0$$

However, as $f_M(a, b)$ is changed, the second set of equations changes. We use Z as the α-denominator ($Z = \alpha_a + \alpha_B$) for simplification:

$$\begin{aligned} f_M(a, b) &= W_M \begin{bmatrix} \frac{\alpha_a}{Z} M_a \\ \frac{\alpha_b}{Z} M_b \end{bmatrix} \\ &= \begin{bmatrix} I \\ I \end{bmatrix} \begin{bmatrix} \frac{\alpha_a}{Z} M_a \\ \frac{\alpha_b}{Z} M_b \end{bmatrix} \\ &= \frac{\alpha_a}{Z} M_a + \frac{\alpha_b}{Z} M_b \end{aligned}$$

Further, we still require the functional representation to remain constant under negation:

$$\forall a \in A : f_M(\text{not}, a) = M_a$$
$$\forall a \in A : f_M(\text{not}, f_M(\text{not}, a)) = M_a$$

Thus, we can infer the following two conditions on the new model:

$$\frac{\alpha_{not}}{Z} M_{not} \approx 0$$
$$\frac{\alpha_a}{Z} M_a \approx M_a$$

From our previous investigation we already know that $M_{not} = J_\mu \neq 0$, i.e. that *not* has a non-zero functional representation. While this caused a contradiction for the original MV-RNN model, the design of the improved model can resolve this issue through the α-parameter:

$$\alpha_{not} = 0$$

Thus, we can use this modified MV-RNN model to represent negation according to the principles outlined in this paper. The result $\alpha_{not} = 0$ is in accordance with our intuition about the propagation of functional aspects of a term: We commonly expect negation to directly affect the things under its scope (*not blue*) by choosing their semantic complement. However, this behaviour should not propagate outside of the scope of the negation. A *not blue car* is still very much a car, and when a film is not good, it is still very much a film.

7 Discussion and Further Work

In this paper, we investigated the capability of continuous vector space models to capture the semantics of logical operations in non-boolean cases. Recursive and recurrent vector models of meaning have enjoyed a considerable amount of success in recent years, and have been shown to work well on a number of tasks. However, the complexity and subsequent power of these models comes at the price that it can be difficult to establish which aspect of a model is responsible for what behaviour. This issue was recently highlighted by an investigation into recursive autoencoders for sentiment analysis (Scheible and Schütze, 2013). Thus, one of the key challenges in this area of research is the question of how to control the power of these models. This challenge motivated the work in this paper. By removing non-linearities and other parameters that could disguise model weaknesses, we focused our work on the basic model design. While such features enhance model power, they should not be used to compensate for inherently flawed model designs.

As a prerequisite for our investigation we established a suitable encoding of textual logic. Distributional representations have been well explained on the word level, but less clarity exists as to the semantic content of compositional vectors. With the tripartite meaning representation we proposed one possible approach in that direction, which we subsequently expanded by discussing how negation should be captured in this representation.

Having established a suitable and rigorous system for encoding meaning in compositional vectors, we were thus able to investigate the representative power of the MV-RNN model. We focused this paper on the case of negation, which has the advantage that it does not require many additional assumptions about the underlying semantics. Our investigation showed that the basic MV-RNN model is incompatible with our notion of negation and thus with any textual logic building on this proposal.

Subsequently, we analysed the reasons for this failure. We explained how the issue of negation affects the general class of MV-RNN models. Through the issue of double-negation we further showed how this issue is largely independent on the particular semantic encoding used. Based on this analysis we proposed an improved model that is able to capture such textual logic.

In summary, this paper has two key contributions. First, we developed a tripartite representation for vector space based models of semantics, incorporating multiple previous approaches to this topic. Based on this representation, the second contribution of this paper was a modified MV-RNN model that can capture effects such as negation in its inherent structure.

In future work, we would like to build on the proposals in this paper, both by extending our work on textual logic to include formulations for e.g. function words, quantifiers, or locative words. Similarly, we plan to experimentally validate these ideas. Possible tasks for this include sentiment analysis and relation extraction tasks such as in Socher et al. (2012) but also more specific tasks such as the *SEM shared task on negation scope and reversal (Morante and Blanco, 2012).

Acknowledgements

The first author is supported by the UK Engineering and Physical Sciences Research Council (EPSRC). The second author is supported by EPSRC Grant `EP/I03808X/1`.

References

M. Baroni and R. Zamparelli. 2010. Nouns are vectors, adjectives are matrices: Representing adjective-noun constructions in semantic space. In *Proceedings of the 2010 Conference on Empirical Methods in Natural Language Processing*, pages 1183–1193. Association for Computational Linguistics.

I. Beltagy, C. Chau, G. Boleda, D. Garrette, E. Erk, and R. Mooney. 2013. Montague meets markov: Deep semantics with probabilistic logical form. June.

W. Blacoe and M. Lapata. 2012. A comparison of vector-based representations for semantic composition. *Proceedings of the 2012 Conference on Empirical Methods in Natural Language Processing*.

J. Bos. 2008. Wide-coverage semantic analysis with boxer. In *Proceedings of the 2008 Conference on Semantics in Text Processing*, pages 277–286. Association for Computational Linguistics.

B. Coecke, M. Sadrzadeh, and S. Clark. 2010. Mathematical Foundations for a Compositional Distributional Model of Meaning. March.

J. R. Curran. 2004. *From distributional to semantic similarity*. Ph.D. thesis.

K. Erk and S. Padó. 2008. A structured vector space model for word meaning in context. *Proceedings of the Conference on Empirical Methods in Natural Language Processing - EMNLP '08*, (October):897.

J. R. Firth. 1957. A synopsis of linguistic theory 1930-1955. *Studies in linguistic analysis*.

D. Garrette, K. Erk, and R. Mooney. 2011. Integrating logical representations with probabilistic information using markov logic. In *Proceedings of the Ninth International Conference on Computational Semantics*, pages 105–114. Association for Computational Linguistics.

E. Grefenstette and M. Sadrzadeh. 2011. Experimental support for a categorical compositional distributional model of meaning. In *Proceedings of EMNLP*, pages 1394–1404.

E. Grefenstette, G. Dinu, Y. Zhang, M. Sadrzadeh, and M. Baroni. 2013. Multi-step regression learning for compositional distributional semantics. In *Proceedings of the Tenth International Conference on Computational Semantics*. Association for Computational Linguistics.

E. Grefenstette. 2013. Towards a formal distributional semantics: Simulating logical calculi with tensors. *Proceedings of the Second Joint Conference on Lexical and Computational Semantics*.

G. Grefenstette. 1994. *Explorations in automatic thesaurus discovery*.

K. M. Hermann and P. Blunsom. 2013. The role of syntax in vector space models of compositional semantics. In *Proceedings of ACL*, Sofia, Bulgaria, August. Association for Computational Linguistics.

D. Kartsaklis, M. Sadrzadeh, and S. Pulman. 2012. A unified sentence space for categorical distributional-compositional semantics: Theory and experiments. In *Proceedings of 24th International Conference on Computational Linguistics (COLING 2012): Posters*, pages 549–558, Mumbai, India, December.

T. K. Landauer and S. T. Dumais. 1997. A solution to Plato's problem: The latent semantic analysis theory of acquisition, induction, and representation of knowledge. *Psychological review*.

J. Mitchell and M. Lapata. 2008. Vector-based models of semantic composition. In *Proceedings of ACL*, volume 8.

J. Mitchell and M. Lapata. 2010. Composition in Distributional Models of Semantics. *Cognitive Science*.

R. Montague. 1974. English as a Formal Language. *Formal Semantics: The Essential Readings*.

R. Morante and E. Blanco. 2012. *SEM 2012 shared task: resolving the scope and focus of negation. In *Proceedings of the First Joint Conference on Lexical and Computational Semantics - Volume 1: Proceedings of the main conference and the shared task, and Volume 2: Proceedings of the Sixth International Workshop on Semantic Evaluation*, SemEval '12, pages 265–274, Stroudsburg, PA, USA. Association for Computational Linguistics.

M. Richardson and P. Domingos. 2006. Markov logic networks. *Machine learning*, 62(1-2):107–136.

C. Scheible and H. Schütze. 2013. Cutting recursive autoencoder trees. In *Proceedings of the International Conference on Learning Representations*.

H. Schütze. 1998. Automatic word sense discrimination. *Computational linguistics*, 24(1):97–123.

R. Socher, E. H. Huang, J. Pennington, A. Y. Ng, and C. D. Manning. 2011. Dynamic pooling and unfolding recursive autoencoders for paraphrase detection. *Advances in Neural Information Processing Systems*, 24:801–809.

R. Socher, B. Huval, C. D. Manning, and A. Y. Ng. 2012. Semantic compositionality through recursive matrix-vector spaces. *Proceedings of the 2012 Conference on Empirical Methods in Natural Language Processing*, pages 1201–1211.

P. D. Turney. 2012. Domain and function: A dual-space model of semantic relations and compositions. *Journal of Artificial Intelligence Research*, 44:533–585.

D. Widdows and S. Peters. 2003. Word vectors and quantum logic: Experiments with negation and disjunction. *Mathematics of language*, 8(141-154).

F. M. Zanzotto, I. Korkontzelos, F. Fallucchi, and S. Manandhar. 2010. Estimating linear models for compositional distributional semantics. In *Proceedings of the 23rd International Conference on Computational Linguistics*, pages 1263–1271. Association for Computational Linguistics.

Towards Dynamic Word Sense Discrimination with Random Indexing

Hans Moen, Erwin Marsi, Björn Gambäck
Norwegian University of Science and Technology
Department of Computer and Information and Science
Sem Sælands vei 7-9
NO-7491 Trondheim, Norway
{hansmoe,emarsi,gamback}@idi.ntnu.no

Abstract

Most distributional models of word similarity represent a word type by a single vector of contextual features, even though, words commonly have more than one sense. The multiple senses can be captured by employing several vectors per word in a multi-prototype distributional model, prototypes that can be obtained by first constructing all the context vectors for the word and then clustering similar vectors to create sense vectors. Storing and clustering context vectors can be expensive though. As an alternative, we introduce Multi-Sense Random Indexing, which performs on-the-fly (incremental) clustering. To evaluate the method, a number of measures for word similarity are proposed, both contextual and non-contextual, including new measures based on optimal alignment of word senses. Experimental results on the task of predicting semantic textual similarity do, however, not show a systematic difference between single-prototype and multi-prototype models.

1 Introduction

Many terms have more than one meaning, or sense. Some of these senses are static and can be listed in dictionaries and thesauri, while other senses are dynamic and determined by the contexts the terms occur in. Work in *Word Sense Disambiguation* often concentrate on the static word senses, making the task of distinguishing between them one of classification into a predefined set of classes (i.e., the given word senses); see, e.g., Erk et al. (2013; Navigli (2009) for overviews of current work in the area. The idea of fixed generic word senses has received a fair amount of criticism in the literature (Kilgarriff, 2000).

This paper instead primarily investigates dynamically appearing word senses, word senses that depend on the actual usage of a term in a corpus or a domain. This task is often referred to as Word Sense Induction or *Word Sense Discrimination* (Schütze, 1998). This is, in contrast, essentially a categorisation problem, distinguished by different senses being more or less similar to each other at a given time, given some input data. The dividing line between Word Sense Disambiguation and Discrimination is not necessarily razor sharp though: also different senses of a term listed in a dictionary tend to have some level of overlap.

In recent years, distributional models have been widely used to infer word similarity. Most such models represent a word type by a single vector of contextual features obtained from co-occurrence counts in large textual corpora. By assigning a single vector to each term in the corpus, the resulting model assumes that each term has a fixed semantic meaning (relative to all the other terms). However, due to homonomy and polysemy, word semantics cannot be adequately represented by a single-prototype vector.

Multi-prototype distributional models in contrast employ different vectors to represent different senses of a word (Reisinger and Mooney, 2010). Multiple prototypes can be obtained by first constructing context vectors for all words and then clustering similar context vectors to create a sense vector. This may be expensive, as vectors need to stored and clustered. As an alternative, we propose a new method called Multi-Sense Random Indexing (MSRI), which is based on Random Indexing (Kanerva et al., 2000) and performs an on-the-fly (incremental) clustering.

MSRI is a method for building a multi-prototype / multi-sense vector space model, which attempts to capture one or more senses per unique term in an unsupervised manner, where each sense is represented as a separate vector in the model.

This differs from the classical Random Indexing (RI) method which assumes a static sense inventory by restricting each term to have only one vector (sense) per term, as described in Section 2. The MSRI method is introduced in Section 3.

Since the induced dynamic senses do not necessarily correspond to the traditional senses distinguished by humans, we perform an extrinsic evaluation by applying the resulting models to data from the Semantic Textual Similarity shared task (Agirre et al., 2013), in order to compare MSRI to the classical RI method. The experimental set-up is the topic of Section 4, while the results of the experiments are given in Section 5. Section 6 then sums up the discussion and points to ways in which the present work could be continued.

2 Vector Space Models

With the introduction of LSA, Latent Semantic Analysis (Deerwester et al., 1990), distributed models of lexical semantics, built from unlabelled free text data, became a popular sub-field within the language processing research community. Methods for building such semantic models rely primarily on term co-occurrence information, and attempt to capture latent relations from analysing large amounts of text. Most of these methods represent semantic models as multi-dimensional vectors in a vector space model.

After LSA, other methods for building semantic models have been proposed, one of them being Random Indexing (Kanerva et al., 2000). Common to these methods is that they generate a *context vector* for each unique term in the training data which represents the term's "contextual" meaning in the vector space. By assigning a single context vector to each term in the corpus, the resulting model assumes that each term has a fixed semantic meaning (relative to all other terms).

Random Indexing incrementally builds a co-occurrence matrix of reduced dimensionality, by first assigning *index vectors* to each unique term. The vectors are of a predefined size (typically around 1000), and consist of a few randomly placed 1s and -1s. Context vectors of the same size are also assigned to each term, initially consisting of only zeros. When traversing a document corpus using a sliding window of a fixed size, the context vectors are continuously updated: the term in the centre of the window (the target term), has the index vectors of its neighbouring terms (the ones in the window) added to its context vector using vector summation. Then the *cosine similarity measure* can be used on term pairs to calculate their similarity (or "contextual similarity").

Random Indexing has achieved promising results in various experiments, for example, on the TOEFL test ("Test of English as a Foreign Language") (Kanerva et al., 2000). However, it is evident that many terms have more than one meaning or sense, some being static and some dynamic, that is, determined by the contexts the terms occur in. Schütze (1998) proposed a method for clustering the contextual occurrences of terms into individual "prototype" vectors, where one term can have multiple prototype vectors representing separate senses of the term. Others have adopted the same underlying idea, using alternative methods and techniques (Reisinger and Mooney, 2010; Huang et al., 2012; Van de Cruys et al., 2011; Dinu and Lapata, 2010).

3 Multi-Sense Random Indexing, MSRI

Inspired by the work of Schütze (1998) and Reisinger and Mooney (2010), this paper introduces a novel variant of Random Indexing, which we have called "Multi-Sense Random Indexing". MSRI attempts to capture one or more senses per unique term in an unsupervised and incremental manner, each sense represented as an separate vector in the model. The method is similar to classical sliding window RI, but each term can have multiple context vectors (referred to as *sense vectors* here) which are updated separately.

When updating a term vector, instead of directly adding the index vectors of the neighbouring terms in the window to its context vector, the system first computes a separate *window vector* consisting of the sum of the index vectors. The similarity between the window vector and each of the term's sense vectors is calculated. Each similarity score is then compared to a pre-set *similarity threshold*:

- if no score exceeds the threshold, the window vector becomes a new separate sense vector for the term,
- if exactly one score is above the threshold, the window vector is added to that sense vector, and
- if multiple scores are above the threshold, all the involved senses are merged into one sense vector, together with the window vector.

Algorithm 1 MSRI training

for all terms t in a document D **do**
  generate window vector $\vec{win}$ from the neighbouring words' index vectors
  for all sense vectors $\vec{s}_i$ of t **do**
    $sim(s_i) = CosSim(\vec{win}, \vec{s}_i)$
  end for
  if $sim(s_{i..k}) \geq \tau$ **then**
    Merge $\vec{s}_{i..k}$ and $\vec{win}$ through summing
  else
    if $sim(s_i) \geq \tau$ **then**
      $\vec{s}_i + = \vec{win}$
    end if
  else
    if $sim(s_{i..n}) < \tau$ **then**
      Assign $\vec{win}$ as new sense vector of t
    end if
  end if
end for

See Algorithm 1 for a pseudo code version. Here τ represents the similarity threshold.

This accomplishes an incremental (on-line) clustering of senses in an unsupervised manner, while retaining the other properties of classical RI. Even though the algorithm has a slightly higher complexity than classical RI, this is mainly a matter of optimisation, which is not the focus of this paper. The incremental clustering that we apply is somewhat similar to what is used by Lughofer (2008), although we are storing in memory only one element (i.e., vector) for each "cluster" (i.e., sense) at any given time.

When looking up a term in the vector space, a pre-set *sense-frequency threshold* is applied to filter out "noisy" senses. Hence, senses that have occurred less than the threshold are not included when looking up a term and its senses for, for example, similarity calculations.

As an example of what the resulting models contain in terms of senses, Table 1 shows four different senses of the term 'round' produced by the MSRI model. Note that these senses do not necessarily correspond to human-determined senses. The idea is only that using multiple prototype vectors facilitates better modelling of a term's meaning than a single prototype (Reisinger and Mooney, 2010).

round$_1$	**round**$_2$	**round**$_3$	**round**$_4$
finish	camping	inch	launcher
final	restricted	bundt	grenade
match	budget	dough	propel
half	fare	thick	antitank
third	adventure	cake	antiaircraft

Table 1: Top-5 most similar terms for four different senses of 'round' using the *Max* similarity measure to the other terms in the model.

3.1 Term Similarity Measures

Unlike classical RI, which only has a single context vector per term and thus calculates similarity between two terms directly using cosine similarity, there are multiple ways of calculating the similarity between two terms in MSRI. Some alternatives are described in Reisinger and Mooney (2010). In the experiment in this paper, we test four ways of calculating similarity between two terms t and t' in isolation, with the Average and Max methods stemming from Reisinger and Mooney (2010).

Let $\vec{s}_{i..n}$ and $\vec{s'}_{j..m}$ be the sets of sense vectors corresponding to the terms t and t' respectively. Term similarity measures are then defined as:

Centroid

For term t, compute its centroid vector by summing its sense vectors $\vec{s}_{i..n}$. The same is done for t' with its sense vectors $\vec{s'}_{j..m}$. These centroids are in turn used to calculate the cosine similarity between t and t'.

Average

For all $\vec{s_{i..n}}$ in t, find the pair $\vec{s}_i, \vec{s'}_j$ with highest cosine similarity:

$$\frac{1}{n}\sum_{i=1}^{n} CosSim_{max}(\vec{s}_i, \vec{s'}_j)$$

Then do the same for all $\vec{s'}_{j..m}$ in t':

$$\frac{1}{m}\sum_{j=1}^{m} CosSim_{max}(\vec{s'}_j, \vec{s}_i)$$

The similarity between t and t' is computed as the average of these two similarity scores.

Max

The similarity between t_i and t'_i equals the similarity of their most similar sense:

$$Sim(t, t') = CosSim_{max_{ij}}(\vec{s}_i, \vec{s'}_i)$$

Hungarian Algorithm

First cosine similarity is computed for each possible pair of sense vectors $\vec{s}_{i..n}$ and $\vec{s'}_{j..m}$, resulting in a matrix of similarity scores. Finding the optimal matching from senses $\vec{s}_i$ to $\vec{s'}_j$ that maximises the sum of similarities is known as the *assignment problem*. This combinatorial optimisation problem can be solved in polynomial time through the Hungarian Algorithm (Kuhn, 1955). The overall similarity between terms t and t' is then defined as the average of the similarities between their aligned senses.

All measures defined so far calculate similarity between terms in isolation. In many applications, however, terms occur in a particular context that can be exploited to determine their most likely sense. Narrowing down their possible meaning to a subset of senses, or a single sense, can be expected to yield a more adequate estimation of their similarity. Hence a context-sensitive measure of term similarity is defined as:

Contextual similarity

Let $\vec{C}$ and $\vec{C'}$ be vectors representing the contexts of terms t and t' respectively. These context vectors are constructed by summing the index vectors of the neighbouring terms within a window, following the same procedure as used when training the MSRI model. We then find $\hat{s}$ and $\hat{s}\,'$ as the sense vectors best matching the context vectors:

$$\hat{s} = \arg\max_i \ CosSim(\vec{s}_i, \vec{C})$$

$$\hat{s}\,' = \arg\max_j \ CosSim(\vec{s}_j, \vec{C'})$$

Finally, contextual similarity is defined as the similarity between these sense vectors:

$$Sim_{context}(t, t') = CosSim(\hat{s}, \hat{s}\,')$$

3.2 Sentence Similarity Features

In the experiments reported on below, a range of different ways to represent sentences were tested. Sentence similarity was generally calculated by the average of the maximum similarity between pairs of terms from both sentences, respectively. The different ways of representing the data in combination with some sentence similarity measure will here be referred to as similarity *features*.

1. `MSRI-TermCentroid`:
   In each sentence, each term is represented as the sum of its sense vectors. This is similar to having one context vector, as in classical RI, but due to the sense-frequency filtering, potentially "noisy" senses are not included.

2. `MSRI-TermMaxSense`:
   For each bipartite term pair in the two sentences, their sense-pairs with maximum cosine similarity are used, one sense per term.

3. `MSRI-TermInContext`:
   A $5+5$ window around each (target) term is used as context for selecting one sense of the term. A window vector is calculated by summing the index vectors of the other terms in the window (i.e., except for the target term itself). The sense of the target term which is most similar to the window vector is used as the representation of the term.

4. `MSRI-TermHASenses`:
   Calculating similarity between two terms is done by applying the Hungarian Algorithm to all their bipartite sense pairs.

5. `RI-TermAvg`:
   Classical Random Indexing — each term is represented as a single context vector.

6. `RI-TermHA`:
   Similarity between two sentences is calculated by applying the Hungarian Algorithm to the context vectors of each constituent term.

The parameters were selected based on a combination of surveying previous work on RI (e.g., Sokolov (2012)), and by analysing how sense counts evolved during training. For MSRI, we used a similarity threshold of 0.2, a vector dimensionality of 800, a non-zero count of 6, and a window size of $5+5$. Sense vectors resulting from less than 50 observations were removed. For classical RI, we used the same parameters as for MSRI (except for a similarity threshold).

4 Experimental Setup

In order to explore the potential of the MSRI model and the textual similarity measures proposed here, experiments were carried out on data from the Semantic Textual Similarity (STS) shared task (Agirre et al., 2012; Agirre et al., 2013).

Given a pair of sentences, systems participating in this task shall compute how semantically similar the two sentences are, returning a similarity score between zero (completely unrelated) and five (completely semantically equivalent). Gold standard scores are obtained by averaging multiple scores obtained from human annotators. System performance is then evaluated using the Pearson product-moment correlation coefficient (ρ) between the system scores and the human scores.

The goal of the experiments reported here was not to build a competitive STS system, but rather to investigate whether MSRI can outperform classical Random Indexing on a concrete task such as computing textual similarity, as well as to identify which similarity measures and meaning representations appear to be most suitable for such a task. The system is therefore quite rudimentary: a simple linear regression model is fitted on the training data, using a single sentence similarity measure as input and the similarity score as the dependent variable. The implementations of RI and MSRI are based on JavaSDM (Hassel, 2004).

As data for training random indexing models, we used the CLEF 2004–2008 English corpus, consisting of approximately 130M words of newspaper articles (Peters et al., 2004). All text was tokenized and lemmatized using the TreeTagger for English (Schmid, 1994). Stopwords were removed using a customized version of the stoplist provided by the Lucene project (Apache, 2005).

Data for fitting and evaluating the linear regression models came from the STS development and test data, consisting of sentence pairs with a gold standard similarity score. The STS 2012 development data stems from the Microsoft Research Paraphrase corpus (`MSRpar`, 750 pairs), the Microsoft Research Video Description corpus (`MSvid`, 750 pairs), and statistical machine translation output based on the Europarl corpus (`SMTeuroparl`, 734 pairs). Test data for STS 2012 consists of more data from the same sources: `MSRpar` (750 pairs), `MSRvid` (750 pairs) and `SMTeuroparl` (459 pairs). In addition, different test data comes from translation data in the news domain (`SMTnews`, 399 pairs) and ontology mappings between OntoNotes and WordNet (`OnWN`, 750 pairs). When testing on the STS 2012 data, we used the corresponding development data from the same domain for training, except for `OnWN` where we used all development data combined.

The development data for STS 2013 consisted of all development and test data from STS 2012 combined, whereas test data comprised machine translation output (`SMT`, 750 pairs), ontology mappings both between WordNet and OntoNotes (`OnWN`, 561 pairs) and between WordNet and FrameNet (`FNWN`, 189 pairs), as well as news article headlines (`HeadLine`, 750 pairs). For simplicity, all development data combined were used for fitting the linear regression model, even though careful matching of development and test data sets may improve performance.

5 Results and Discussion

Table 2 shows Pearson correlation scores per feature on the STS 2012 test data using simple linear regression. The most useful features for each data set are marked in bold. For reference, the scores of the best performing STS systems for each data set are also shown, as well as baseline scores obtained with a simple normalized token overlap measure.

There is large variation in correlation scores, ranging from 0.77 down to 0.27. Part of this variation is due to the different nature of the data sets. For example, sentence similarity in the SMT domain seems harder to predict than in the video domain. Yet there is no single measure that obtains the highest score on all data sets. There is also no consistent difference in performance between the RI and MSRI measures, which seem to yield about equal scores on average. The `MSRI-TermInContext` measure has the lowest score on average, suggesting that word sense disambiguation in context is not beneficial in its current implementation.

The corresponding results on the STS 2013 test data are shown in Table 3. The same observations as for the STS 2012 data set can be made: again there was no consistent difference between the RI and MSRI features, and no single best measure.

All in all, these results do not provide any evidence that MSRI improves on standard RI for this particular task (sentence semantic similarity). Multi-sense distributional models have, however, been found to outperform single-sense models on other tasks. For example, Reisinger and Mooney (2010) report that multi-sense models significantly increase the correlation with human similarity judgements. Other multi-prototype distributional models may yield better results than their single-prototype counterparts on the STS task.

Features:	MSRpar	MSRvid	SMTeuroparl	SMTnews	OnWN	Mean
Best systems	0.73	0.88	0.57	0.61	0.71	0.70
Baseline	0.43	0.30	0.45	0.39	0.59	0.43
RI-TermAvg	0.44	0.71	**0.50**	**0.42**	0.65	**0.54**
RI-TermHA	0.41	0.72	0.44	0.35	0.56	0.49
MSRI-TermCentroid	**0.45**	0.73	**0.50**	0.33	0.64	0.53
MSRI-TermHASenses	0.40	**0.77**	0.47	0.39	**0.68**	**0.54**
MSRI-TermInContext	0.33	0.55	0.36	0.27	0.42	0.38
MSRI-TermMaxSense	0.44	0.71	**0.50**	0.32	0.64	0.52

Table 2: Pearson correlation scores per feature on STS 2012 test data using simple linear regression

Feature	Headlines	SMT	FNWN	OnWN	Mean
Best systems	0.78	0.40	0.58	0.84	0.65
Baseline	0.54	0.29	0.21	0.28	0.33
RI-TermAvg	0.60	**0.37**	0.21	0.52	0.42
RI-TermHA	**0.65**	0.36	0.27	0.52	0.45
MSRI-TermCentroid	0.60	0.35	**0.37**	0.45	0.44
MSRI-TermHASenses	0.63	0.35	0.33	**0.54**	**0.46**
MSRI-TermInContext	0.20	0.29	0.19	0.36	0.26
MSRI-TermMaxSense	0.58	0.35	0.31	0.45	0.42

Table 3: Pearson correlation scores per feature on STS 2013 test data using simple linear regression

Notably, the more advanced features used in our experiment, such as `MSRI-TermInContext`, gave very clearly inferior results when compared to `MSRI-TermHASenses`. This suggests that more research on MSRI is needed to understand how both training and retrieval can be fully utilized and optimized.

6 Conclusion and Future Work

The paper introduced a new method called Multi-Sense Random Indexing (MSRI), which is based on Random Indexing and performs on-the-fly clustering, as an efficient way to construct multi-prototype distributional models for word similarity. A number of alternative measures for word similarity were proposed, both context-dependent and context-independent, including new measures based on optimal alignment of word senses using the Hungarian algorithm. An extrinsic evaluation was carried out by applying the resulting models to the Semantic Textual Similarity task. Initial experimental results did not show a systematic difference between single-prototype and multi-prototype models in this task.

There are many questions left for future work. One of them is how the number of senses per word evolves during training and how the distribution of senses in the final model looks like. So far we only know that on average the number of senses keeps growing with more training material, currently resulting in about 5 senses per word at the end of training (after removing senses with frequency below the sense-frequency threshold). It is worth noting that this depends heavily on the similarity threshold for merging senses, as well as on the weighting schema used.

In addition there are a number of model parameters that have so far only been manually tuned on the development data, such as window size, number of non-zeros, vector dimensionality, and the sense frequency filtering threshold. A systematic exploration of the parameter space is clearly desirable. Another thing that would be worth looking into, is how to compose sentence vectors and document vectors from the multi-sense vector space in a proper way, focusing on how to pick the right senses and how to weight these. It would also be interesting to explore the possibilities for combining the MSRI method with the Reflective Random Indexing method by Cohen et al. (2010) in an attempt to model higher order co-occurrence relations on sense level.

The fact that the induced dynamic word senses do not necessarily correspond to human-created senses makes evaluation in traditional word sense disambiguation tasks difficult. However, correlation to human word similarity judgement may provide a way of intrinsic evaluation of the models (Reisinger and Mooney, 2010). The *Usim* bench mark data look promising for evaluation of word similarity in context (Erk et al., 2013).

It is also worth exploring ways to optimise the algorithm, as this has not been the focus of our work so far. This would also allow faster training and experimentation on larger text corpora, such as Wikipedia. In addition to the JavaSDM package (Hassel, 2004), Lucene (Apache, 2005) with the Semantic Vectors package (Widdows and Ferraro, 2008) would be an alternative framework for implementing the proposed MSRI algorithm.

Acknowledgements

This work was partly supported by the Research Council of Norway through the EviCare project (NFR project no. 193022) and by the European Community's Seventh Framework Programme (FP7/20072013) under grant agreement nr. 248307 (PRESEMT). Part of this work has been briefly described in our contribution to the STS shared task (Marsi et al., 2013).

References

Eneko Agirre, Daniel Cer, Mona Diab, and Aitor Gonzalez-Agirre. 2012. SemEval 2012 Task 6: A pilot on semantic textual similarity. In *Proceedings of the First Joint Conference on Lexical and Computational Semantics (*SEM)*, volume 2: Proceedings of the Sixth International Workshop on Semantic Evaluation, pages 385–393, Montreal, Canada, June. Association for Computational Linguistics.

Eneko Agirre, Daniel Cer, Mona Diab, Aitor Gonzalez-Agirre, and Weiwei Guo. 2013. *SEM 2013 shared task: Semantic textual similarity. In *Second Joint Conference on Lexical and Computational Semantics (*SEM)*, volume 1: Proceedings of the Main Conference and the Shared Task: Semantic Textual Similarity, pages 32–43, Atlanta, Georgia, June. Association for Computational Linguistics.

Apache. 2005. Apache Lucene open source package. `http://lucene.apache.org/`.

Trevor Cohen, Roger Schvaneveldt, and Dominic Widdows. 2010. Reflective random indexing and indirect inference: A scalable method for discovery of implicit connections. *Journal of Biomedical Informatics*, 43(2):240–256, April.

Scott Deerwester, Susan T. Dumais, George W. Furnas, Thomas K. Landauer, and Richard Harshman. 1990. Indexing by latent semantic analysis. *Journal of the American Society for Information Science*, 41(6):391–407.

Georgiana Dinu and Mirella Lapata. 2010. Measuring distributional similarity in context. In *Proceedings of the 2010 Conference on Empirical Methods in Natural Language Processing*, pages 1162–1172, Cambridge, Massachusetts, October. Association for Computational Linguistics.

Katrin Erk, Diana McCarthy, and Nicholas Gaylord. 2013. Measuring word meaning in context. *Computational Linguistics*, 39(3):501–544.

Martin Hassel. 2004. JavaSDM package. `http://www.nada.kth.se/~xmartin/java/`. School of Computer Science and Communication; Royal Institute of Technology (KTH); Stockholm, Sweden.

Eric H. Huang, Richard Socher, Christopher D. Manning, and Andrew Y. Ng. 2012. Improving word representations via global context and multiple word prototypes. In *Proceedings of the 50th Annual Meeting of the Association for Computational Linguistics: Long Papers - Volume 1*, ACL '12, pages 873–882, Jeju Island, Korea. Association for Computational Linguistics.

Pentti Kanerva, Jan Kristoferson, and Anders Holst. 2000. Random indexing of text samples for latent semantic analysis. In *Proceedings of the 22nd Annual Conference of the Cognitive Science Society*, page 1036, Philadelphia, Pennsylvania. Erlbaum.

Adam Kilgarriff. 2000. I don't believe in word senses. *Computers and the Humanities*, 31(2):91–113.

Harold W. Kuhn. 1955. The Hungarian method for the assignment problem. *Naval Research Logistics Quarterly*, 2:83–97.

Edwin Lughofer. 2008. Extensions of vector quantization for incremental clustering. *Pattern Recognition*, 41(3):995–1011, March.

Erwin Marsi, Hans Moen, Lars Bungum, Gleb Sizov, Björn Gambäck, and André Lynum. 2013. NTNU-CORE: Combining strong features for semantic similarity. In *Second Joint Conference on Lexical and Computational Semantics (*SEM)*, volume 1: Proceedings of the Main Conference and the Shared Task: Semantic Textual Similarity, pages 66–73, Atlanta, Georgia, June. Association for Computational Linguistics.

Roberto Navigli. 2009. Word Sense Disambiguation: a survey. *ACM Computing Surveys*, 41(2):1–69.

Carol Peters, Paul Clough, Julio Gonzalo, Gareth J.F. Jones, Michael Kluck, and Bernardo Magnini, editors. 2004. *Multilingual Information Access for Text, Speech and Images, 5th Workshop of the Cross-Language Evaluation Forum, CLEF 2004*, volume 3491 of *Lecture Notes in Computer Science*. Springer-Verlag, Bath, England.

Joseph Reisinger and Raymond J. Mooney. 2010. Multi-prototype vector-space models of word meaning. In *Human Language Technologies: The 2010 Annual Conference of the North American Chapter of the Association for Computational Linguistics*, pages 109–117, Los Angeles, California, June.

Helmut Schmid. 1994. Probabilistic part-of-speech tagging using decision trees. In *Proceedings of the 1st International Conference on New Methods in Natural Language Processing*, pages 44–49, University of Manchester Institute of Science and Technology, Manchester, England, September.

Hinrich Schütze. 1998. Automatic word sense discrimination. *Computational Linguistics*, 24(1):97–123, March.

Artem Sokolov. 2012. LIMSI: learning semantic similarity by selecting random word subsets. In *Proceedings of the First Joint Conference on Lexical and Computational Semantics (*SEM)*, volume 2: Proceedings of the Sixth International Workshop on Semantic Evaluation, pages 543–546, Montreal, Canada, June. Association for Computational Linguistics.

Tim Van de Cruys, Thierry Poibeau, and Anna Korhonen. 2011. Latent vector weighting for word meaning in context. In *Proceedings of the 2011 Conference on Empirical Methods in Natural Language Processing*, pages 1012–1022, Edinburgh, Scotland, July. Association for Computational Linguistics.

Dominic Widdows and Kathleen Ferraro. 2008. Semantic vectors: a scalable open source package and online technology management application. In *Proceedings of the Sixth International Language Resources and Evaluation (LREC'08)*, pages 1183–1190, Marrakech, Morocco.

A Generative Model of Vector Space Semantics

Jacob Andreas
Computer Laboratory
University of Cambridge
jda33@cam.ac.uk

Zoubin Ghahramani
Department of Engineering
University of Cambridge
zoubin@eng.cam.ac.uk

Abstract

We present a novel compositional, generative model for vector space representations of meaning. This model reformulates earlier tensor-based approaches to vector space semantics as a top-down process, and provides efficient algorithms for transformation from natural language to vectors and from vectors to natural language. We describe procedures for estimating the parameters of the model from positive examples of similar phrases, and from distributional representations, then use these procedures to obtain similarity judgments for a set of adjective-noun pairs. The model's estimation of the similarity of these pairs correlates well with human annotations, demonstrating a substantial improvement over several existing compositional approaches in both settings.

1 Introduction

Vector-based word representations have gained enormous popularity in recent years as a basic tool for natural language processing. Various models of linguistic phenomena benefit from the ability to represent words as vectors, and vector space word representations allow many problems in NLP to be reformulated as standard machine learning tasks (Blei et al., 2003; Deerwester et al., 1990).

Most research to date has focused on only one means of obtaining vectorial representations of words: namely, by representing them *distributionally*. The meaning of a word is assumed to be fully specified by "the company it keeps" (Firth, 1957), and word co-occurrence (or occasionally term-document) matrices are taken to encode this context adequately. Distributional representations have been shown to work well for a variety of different tasks (Schütze and Pedersen, 1993; Baker and McCallum, 1998).

The problem becomes more complicated when we attempt represent larger linguistic structures—multiword constituents or entire sentences—within the same vector space model. The most basic issue is one of sparsity: the larger a phrase, the less frequently we expect it to occur in a corpus, and the less data we will have from which to estimate a distributional representation. To resolve this problem, recent work has focused on *compositional* vector space models of semantics. Based on the Fregean observation that the meaning of a sentence is composed from the individual meanings of its parts (Frege, 1892), research in compositional distributional semantics focuses on describing procedures for combining vectors for individual words in order to obtain an appropriate representation of larger syntactic constituents.

But various aspects of this account remain unsatisfying. We have a continuous semantic space in which finitely many vectors are associated with words, but no way (other than crude approximations like nearest-neighbor) to interpret the "meaning" of all the other points in the space. More generally, it's not clear that it even makes sense to talk about the meaning of sentences or large phrases in distributional terms, when there is no natural context to represent.

We can begin to address these concerns by turning the conventional account of composition in vector space semantics on its head, and describing a model for generating language from vectors in semantic space. Our approach is still compositional, in the sense that a sentence's meaning can be inferred from the meanings of its parts, but we relax the requirement that lexical items correspond to single vectors by allowing any vector. In the process, we acquire algorithms for both meaning inference and natural language generation.

Our contributions in this paper are as follows:

- A new generative, compositional model of

phrase meaning in vector space.

- A convex optimization procedure for mapping words onto their vector representations.
- A training algorithm which requires only positive examples of phrases with the same meaning.
- Another training algorithm which requires only distributional representations of phrases.
- A set of preliminary experimental results indicating that the model performs well on real-world data in both training settings.

2 Model overview

2.1 Motivations

The most basic requirement for a vector space model of meaning is that whatever distance metric it is equipped with accurately model human judgments of semantic similarity. That is: sequences of words which are judged to "mean the same thing" should cluster close together in the semantic space, and totally unrelated sequences of words should be spread far apart.

Beyond this, of course, inference of vector space representations should be tractable: we require efficient algorithms for analyzing natural language strings into their corresponding vectors, and for estimating the parameters of the model that does the mapping. For some tasks, it is also useful to have an algorithm for the opposite problem—given a vector in the semantic space, it should be possible to produce a natural-language string encoding the meaning of that vector; and, in keeping with our earlier requirements, if we choose a vector close to the vector corresponding to a known string, the resulting interpretation should be judged by a human to mean the same thing, and perhaps with some probability be exactly the same.

It is these three requirements—the use of human similarity judgments as the measure of the semantic space's quality, and the existence of efficient algorithms for both generation and inference—that motivate the remainder of this work.

We take as our starting point the general program of Coecke et al. (2010) which suggests that the task of analyzing into a vector space should be driven by syntax. In this framework, the compositional process consists of repeatedly combining vector space word representations according to linguistic rules, in a *bottom-up* process for translating a natural language string to a vector in space.

But our requirement that all vectors be translatable into meanings—that we have both analysis and generation algorithms—suggests that we should take the opposite approach, working with a *top down* model of vector space semantics.

For simplicity, our initial presentation of this model, and the accompanying experiments, will be restricted to the case of adjective-noun pairs. Section 5 will then describe how this framework can be extended to full sentences.

2.2 Preliminaries

We want to specify a procedure for mapping a natural language noun-adjective pair (a, n) into a vector space which we will take to be $\mathbb{R}^p$. We assume that our input sentence has already been assigned a single CCG parse (Steedman and Baldridge, 2011), which for noun-adjective pairs has the form

$$\dfrac{\dfrac{\textit{blue}}{\mathrm{N/N}} \quad \dfrac{\textit{orangutans}}{\mathrm{N}}}{\mathrm{N}}> \qquad (1)$$

Here, the parser has assigned each token a *category* of the form N, N/N, etc. Categories are either *simple*, drawn from a set of base types (here just N for "noun"), or *complex*, formed by combining simple categories. A category of the form X/Y "looks right" for a category of the form Y, and can combine with other constituents by application (we write $\mathrm{X/Y \;\; Y \Rightarrow X}$) or composition ($\mathrm{X/Y \;\; Y/Z \Rightarrow X/Z}$) to form higher-level constituents.

To this model we add a vector space semantics. We begin with a brief review the work of Coecke et al. (2010). Having assigned simple categories to vector spaces (in this case, N to $\mathbb{R}^p$), complex categories correspond to spaces of *tensors*. A category of the form X/Y is recursively associated with $\mathbb{S}_X \otimes \mathbb{S}_Y$, where $\mathbb{S}_X$ and $\mathbb{S}_Y$ are the tensor spaces associated with the categories X and Y respectively. So the space of adjectives (of type N/N) is just $\mathbb{R}^q \otimes \mathbb{R}^q$, understood as the set of $q \times q$ matrices. To find the meaning of a adjective-noun pair, we simply multiply the adjective matrix and noun vector as specified by the CCG derivation. The result is another vector in the same semantic space as the noun, as desired.

To turn this into a top-down process, we need to describe a procedure for splitting meanings and their associated categories.

2.3 Generation

Our goal in this subsection is to describe a probabilistic generative process by which a vector in a semantic space is realized in natural language.

Given a constituent of category X, and a corresponding vector x residing in some $\mathbb{S}_X$, we can either generate a lexical item of the appropriate type or probabilistically draw a CCG derivation rooted in X, then independently generate the leaves. For noun-adjective pairs, this can only be done in one way, namely as in (1) (for a detailed account of generative models for CCG see Hockenmaier and Steedman (2002)). We will assume that this CCG derivation tree is observed, and concern ourselves with filling in the appropriate vectors and lexical items. This is a strong independence assumption! It effectively says "the grammatical realization of a concept is independent of its meaning". We will return to it in Section 6.

The adjective-noun model has four groups of parameters: (1) a collection $\Theta_{\text{N/N}}$ of weight vectors θ_a for adjectives a, (2) a collection Θ_{N} of weight vectors θ_n for nouns n, (3) a collection $\mathcal{E}_{\text{N/N}}$ of adjective matrices E_a for adjectives a, and finally (4) a noise parameter σ^2. For compactness of notation we will denote this complete set of parameters $\boldsymbol{\Theta}$.

Now we can describe how to generate an adjective-noun pair from a vector x. The CCG derivation tells us to produce a noun and an adjective, and the type information further informs us that the adjective acts as a functor (here a matrix) and the noun as an argument. We begin by choosing an adjective a conditional on x. Having made our lexical choice, we deterministically select the corresponding matrix E_a from $\mathcal{E}_{\text{N/N}}$. Next we noisily generate a new vector $y = E_a x + \varepsilon$, a vector in the same space as x, corresponding to the meaning of x *without* the semantic content of a. Finally, we select a noun n conditional on y, and output the noun-adjective pair (a, n). To use the previous example, suppose x means *blue orangutans*. First we choose an adjective $a =$ "blue" (or with some probability "azure" or "ultramarine"), and select a corresponding adjective E_a. Then the vector $y = E_a x$ should mean *orangutan*, and when we generate a noun conditional on y we should have $n =$ "orangutan" (or perhaps "monkey", "primate", etc.).

This process can be summarized with the graphical model in Figure 1. In particular, we draw a

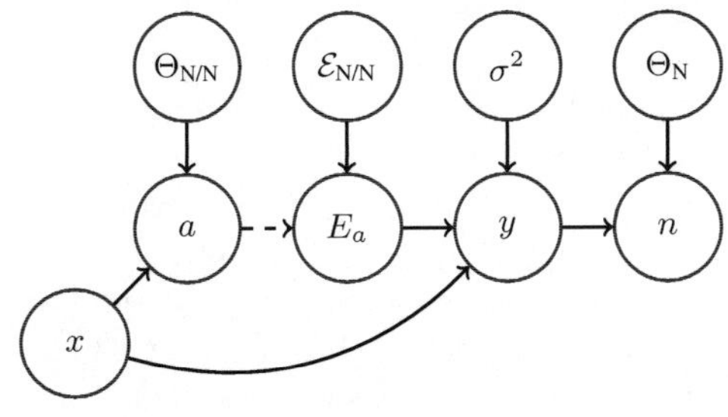

Figure 1: Graphical model of the generative process.

from a log-linear distribution over all words of the appropriate category, and use the corresponding E_a with Gaussian noise to map x onto y:

$$p(a|x; \Theta_{\text{N/N}}) = \frac{\exp(\theta_a^\top x)}{\sum_{\theta' \in \Theta_{\text{N/N}}} \exp(\theta'^\top x)} \quad (2)$$

$$p(y|x, E_a; \sigma^2) = \mathcal{N}(E_a x, \sigma^2)(y) \quad (3)$$

Last we choose n as

$$p(n|y; \Theta_{\text{N}}) = \frac{\exp(\theta_n^\top y)}{\sum_{\theta' \in \Theta_{\text{N}}} \exp(\theta'^\top z)} \quad (4)$$

Some high-level intuition about this model: in the bottom-up account, operators (drawn from tensor spaces associated with complex categories) can be thought of as acting on simple objects and "adding" information to them. (Suppose, for example, that the dimensions of the vector space correspond to actual perceptual dimensions; in the bottom-up account the matrix corresponding to the adjective "red" should increase the component of an input vector that lies in dimension corresponding to redness.) In our account, by contrast, matrices *remove* information, and the "red" matrix should act to reduce the vector component corresponding to redness.

2.4 Analysis

Now we must solve the opposite problem: given an input pair (a, n), we wish to map it to an appropriate vector in $\mathbb{R}^p$. We assume, as before, that we already have a CCG parse of the input. Then, analysis corresponds to solving the following optimization problem:

$$\arg\min_x \quad -\log p(x|a, n; \boldsymbol{\Theta})$$

By Bayes' rule,

$$p(x|a,n;\mathbf{\Theta}) \propto p(a,n|x;\mathbf{\Theta})p(x)$$

so it suffices to minimize

$$-\log p(x) - \log p(a,n|x;\mathbf{\Theta})$$

To find the single best complete derivation of an input pair (equivalent to the Viterbi parse tree in syntactic parsing), we can rewrite this as

$$\operatorname*{arg\,min}_{x,y} \quad -\log p(x) - \log p(a,b,y|x;\mathbf{\Theta}) \quad (5)$$

where, as before, y corresponds to the vector space semantics representation of the noun alone. We take our prior $\log p(x)$ to be a standard normal. We have:

$$\begin{aligned} &-\log p(a,n,y|x) \\ &\quad = -\log p(a|x;\mathbf{\Theta}) - \log p(y|a,x;\mathbf{\Theta}) \\ &\qquad - \log p(n|y;\mathbf{\Theta}) \\ &\quad \propto -\theta_a^\top x + \log \sum_{\theta' \in \Theta_{N/N}} \exp \theta'^\top x \\ &\qquad + \frac{1}{\sigma^2}||E_a x - y||^2 \\ &\qquad - \theta_n^\top y + \log \sum_{\theta' \in \Theta_N} \exp \theta'^\top y \end{aligned}$$

Observe that this probability is convex: it consists of a sum of linear terms, Euclidean norms, and log-normalizers, all convex functions. Consequently, Equation 5 can be solved exactly and efficiently using standard convex optimization tools (Boyd and Vandenberghe, 2004).

3 Relation to existing work

The approach perhaps most closely related to the present work is the bottom-up account given by Coecke et al. (2010), which has already been discussed in some detail in the preceding section. A regression-based training procedure for a similar model is given by Grefenstette et al. (2013). Other work which takes as its starting point the decision to endow some (or all) lexical items with matrix-like operator semantics include that of Socher et al. (2012) and Baroni and Zamparelli (2010). Indeed, it is possible to think of the model in Baroni and Zamparelli's paper as corresponding to a training procedure for a special case of this model, in which the positions of both nouns and noun-adjective vectors are fixed in advance, and in which no lexical generation step takes place. The adjective matrices learned in that paper correspond to the inverses of the E matrices used above.

Also relevant here is the work of Mitchell and Lapata (2008) and Zanzotto et al. (2010), which provide several alternative procedures for composing distributional representations of words, and Wu et al. (2011), which describes a compositional vector space semantics with an integrated syntactic model. Our work differs from these approaches in requiring only positive examples for training, and in providing a mechanism for generation as well as parsing. Other *generative* work on vector space semantics includes that of Hermann et al. (2012), which models the distribution of noun-noun compounds. This work differs from the model that paper in attempting to generate complete natural language strings, rather than simply recover distributional representations.

In training settings where we allow all positional vectors to be free parameters, it's possible to view this work as a kind of linear relational embedding (Paccanaro and Hinton, 2002). It differs from that work, obviously, in that we are interested in modeling natural language syntax and semantics rather than arbitrary hierarchical models, and provide a mechanism for realization of the embedded structures as natural language sentences.

4 Experiments

Since our goal is to ensure that the distance between natural language expressions in the vector space correlates with human judgments of their relatedness, it makes sense to validate this model by measuring precisely that correlation. In the remainder of this section, we provide evidence of the usefulness of our approach by focusing on measurements of the similarity of adjective-noun pairs (ANs). We describe two different parameter estimation procedures for different kinds of training data.

4.1 Learning from matching pairs

We begin by training the model on *matching pairs*. In this setting, we start with a collection N sets of up to M adjective-noun pairs $(a_{i1}, n_{i1}), (a_{i2}, n_{i2}), \ldots$ which mean the same thing. We fix the vector space representation y_i of each noun n_i distributionally, as described below, and find optimal settings for the lexical choice parameters $\Theta_{\mathrm{N/N}}$ and Θ_{N}, matrices (here all $q \times q$)

$\mathcal{E}_{\text{N/N}}$, and, for each group of adjective-noun pairs in the training set, a latent representation x_i. The fact that the vectors y_i are tied to their distributional vectors does not mean we have committed to the distributional representation of the corresponding nouns! The final model represents lexical choice only with the weight vectors Θ—fixing the vectors just reduces the dimensionality of the parameter estimation problem and helps steer the training algorithm toward a good solution. The noise parameter then acts as a kind of slack variable, modeling the fact that there may be no parameter setting which reproduces these fixed distributional representations through exact linear operations alone.

We find a maximum-likelihood estimate for these parameters by minimizing

$$\mathcal{L}(\mathbf{\Theta}, x) = -\sum_{i=1}^{N}\sum_{i=1}^{M} \log p(a_{ij}, n_{ij}|x_i; \mathbf{\Theta}) \quad (6)$$

The latent vectors x_i are initialized to one of their corresponding nouns, adjective matrices E are initialized to the identity. The components of Θ_{N} are initialized identically to the nouns they select, and the components of $\Theta_{\text{N/N}}$ initialized randomly. We additionally place an L_2 regularization penalty on the scoring vectors in both Θ (to prevent weights from going to infinity) and $\mathcal{E}$ (to encourage adjectives to behave roughly like the identity). These penalties, as well as the noise parameter, are initially set to 0.1.

Note that the training objective, unlike the analysis objective, is non-convex. We use L-BFGS (Liu and Nocedal, 1989) on the likelihood function described above with ten such random restarts, and choose the parameter setting which assigns the best score to a held-out cross-validation set. Computation of the objective and its gradient at each step is linear in the number of training examples and quadratic in the dimensionality of the vector space.

Final evaluation is performed by taking a set of pairs of ANs which have been assigned a similarity score from 1–6 by human annotators. For each pair, we map it into the vector space as described in Section 2.4 above. and finally compute the cosine similarity of the two pair vectors. Performance is measured in the correlation (Spearman's ρ) between these cosine similarity scores and the human similarity judgments.

4.1.1 Setup details

Noun vectors y_i are estimated distributionally from a corpus of approximately 10 million tokens of English-language Wikipedia data (Wikimedia Foundation, 2013). A training set of adjective-noun pairs are collected automatically from a collection of reference translations originally prepared for a machine translation task. For each foreign sentence we have four reference translations produced by different translators. We assign POS tags to each reference (Loper and Bird, 2002) then add to the training data any adjective that appears exactly once in multiple reference translations, with all the nouns that follow it (e.g. "great success", "great victory", "great accomplishment"). We then do the same for repeated nouns and the adjectives that precede them (e.g. "great success", "huge success", "tremendous success"). This approach is crude, and the data collected are noisy, featuring such "synonym pairs" as ("incomplete myths", "incomplete autumns") and ("similar training", "province-level training"), as well as occasional pairs which are not adjective-noun pairs at all (e.g. "first parliamentary"). Nevertheless, as results below suggest, they appear to be good enough for purposes of learning an appropriate representation.

For the experiments described in this section, we use 500 sets of such adjective-noun pairs, corresponding to 1104 total training examples. Testing data consists of the subset of entries in the dataset from (Mitchell and Lapata, 2010) for which both the adjective and noun appear at least once (not necessarily together) in the training set, a total of 396 pairs. None of the pairs in this test set appears in training. We additionally withhold from this set the ten pairs assigned a score of 6 (indicating exact similarity), setting these aside for cross-validation.

In addition to the model discussed in the first section of this paper (referred to here as "GEN"), we consider a model in which there is only one adjective matrix E used regardless of the lexical item (referred to as "GEN-1").

The NP space is taken to be $\mathbb{R}^{20}$, and we reduce distributional vectors to 20 dimensions using a singular value decomposition.

4.2 Learning from distributional representations

While the model does not require distributional representations of latent vectors, it's useful to consider whether it can also provide a generative analog to recent models aimed explicitly at producing vectorial representations of phrases given only distributional representations of their constituent words. To do this, we take as our training data a set of N single ANs, paired with a distributional representation of each AN. In the new model, the meaning vectors x are no longer free parameters, but fully determined by these distributional representations. We must still obtain estimates for each Θ and $\mathcal{E}_{\text{N/N}}$, which we do by minimizing

$$\mathcal{L}(\mathbf{\Theta}) = -\sum_{i=1}^{N} \log p(a_{i,j}, n_{i,j} | x_i; \mathbf{\Theta}) \quad (7)$$

4.2.1 Experimental setup

Experimental setup is similar to the previous section; however, instead of same-meaning pairs collected from a reference corpus, our training data is a set of distributional vectors. We use the same noun vectors, and obtain these new latent pair vectors by estimating them in the same fashion from the same corpus.

In order to facilitate comparison with the other experiment, we collect all pairs (a_i, n_i) such that both a_i and n_i appear in the training set used in Section 4.1 (although, once again, not necessarily together). Initialization of Θ and $\mathcal{E}$, regularization and noise parameters, as well as the cross-validation procedure, all proceed as in the previous section. We also use the same restricted evaluation set, again to allow the results of the two experiments to be compared. We evaluate by measuring the correlation of cosine similarities in the learned model with human similarity judgments, and as before consider a variant of the model in which a single adjective matrix is shared.

4.3 Results

Experimental results are displayed in Table 1. For comparison, we also provide results for a baseline which uses a distributional representation of the noun only, the Adjective-Specific Linear Map (ALM) model of Baroni and Zamparelli (2010) and two vector-based compositional models discussed in (Mitchell and Lapata, 2008): $\odot$, which takes the Hadamard (elementwise) product of the distributional representations of the adjective and noun, and $+$, which adds the distributions. As before, we use SVD to project these distributional representations onto a 20-dimensional subspace.

We observe that in both matrix-based learning settings, the GEN model or its parameter-tied variant achieves the highest score (though the distributionally-trained GEN-1 doesn't perform as well as the summing approach). The pair-trained model performs best overall. All correlations except $\odot$ and the distributionally-trained GEN are statistically significant ($p < 0.05$), as are the differences in correlation between the matching-pairs-trained GEN and all other models, and between the distributionally-trained GEN-1 and ALM. Readers familiar with other papers employing the similarity-judgment evaluation will note that scores here are uniformly lower than reported elsewhere; we attribute this to the comparatively small training set (with hundreds, instead of thousands or tens of thousands of examples). This is particularly notable in the case of the ALM model, which Baroni and Zamparelli report outperforms the noun baseline when given a training set of sufficient size.

Training data	Model	ρ
Word distributions	*Noun*	.185
	$+$	.239
	$\odot$	.000
Matching pairs	GEN-1	.130
	GEN	**.365**
Word and phrase distributions	ALM	.136
	GEN-1	.201
	GEN	.097

Table 1: Results for the similarity judgment experiment.

We also give a brief demonstration of the generation capability of this model as shown in Figure 2. We demonstrate generation from three different vectors: one inferred as the latent representation of "basic principles" during training, one obtained by computing a vectorial representation of "economic development" as described in Section 2.4 and one selected randomly from within vector space. We observe that the model correctly identifies the adjectives "fundamental" and "main" as synonymous with "basic" (at least when applied to "principles"). It is also able to correctly map the vector associated with "economic

Input	Realization
Training vector ("basic principles")	tyrannical principles fundamental principles main principles
Test vector ("economic development")	economic development economic development economic development
Random vector	vital turning further obligations bad negotiations

Figure 2: Generation examples using the GEN model trained with matching pairs.

development" back onto the correct lexical realization. Words generated from the random vector appear completely unrelated; this suggests that we are sampling a portion of the space which does not correspond to any well-defined concept.

4.4 Discussion

These experimental results demonstrate, first and foremost, the usefulness of a model that is not tied to distributional representations of meaning vectors: as the comparatively poor performance of the distribution-trained models shows, with only a small number of training examples it is better to let the model invent its own latent representations of the adjective-noun pairs.

It is somewhat surprising, in the experiments with distributional training data, that the single-adjective model outperforms the multiple-adjective model by so much. We hypothesize that this is due to a search error—the significantly expanded parameter space of the multiple-adjective model makes it considerably harder to estimate parameters; in the case of the distribution-only model it is evidently so hard the model is unable to identify an adequate solution even over multiple training runs.

5 Extending the model

Having described and demonstrated the usefulness of this model for capturing noun-adjective similarity, we now describe how to extend it to capture arbitrary syntax. While appropriate experimental evaluation is reserved for future work, we outline the formal properties of the model here. We'll take as our example the following CCG derivation:

```
sister   Cecilia      has      blue   orangutans
 N/N       N        (S\N)/N    N/N        N
 ------------->               ------------------>
       N                              N
                    ------------------------------>
                                 S\N
 ---------------------------------------------------<
                       S
```

Observe that "blue orangutans" is generated according to the noun-adjective model already described.

5.1 Generation

To handle general syntax, we must first extend the set $\mathcal{E}_{\text{N/N}}$ of adjective matrices to sets $\mathcal{E}_{\text{X}}$ for all functor categories X, and create an additional set of weight vectors Θ_{X} for every category X.

When describing how to generate one split in the CCG derivation (e.g. a constituent of type S into constituents of type NP and S\NP), we can identify three cases. The first, "fully-lexicalized" case is the one already described, and is the generative process by which the a vector meaning *blue orangutans* is transformed into "blue" and "orangutans", or *sister Cecilia* into "sister" and "Cecilia". But how do we get from the top-level sentence meaning to a pair of vectors meaning *sister Cecilia* and *has blue orangutans* (an "unlexicalized" split), and from *has blue orangutans* to the word "has" and a vector meaning *blue orangutans* (a "half-lexicalized" split)?

Unlexicalized split We have a vector x with category X, from which we wish to obtain a vector y with category Y, and z with category Z. For this we further augment the sets $\mathcal{E}$ with matrices indexed by category rather than lexical item. Then we produce $y = E_{\text{Y}}x + \varepsilon$, $z = E_{\text{Z}} + \varepsilon$ where, as in the previous case, ε is Gaussian noise with variance σ^2. We then recursively generate subtrees from y and z.

Half-lexicalized split This proceeds much as in the fully lexicalized case. We have a vector x from which we wish to obtain a vector y with category Y, and a lexical item w with category Z.

We choose w according to Equation 2, select a matrix E_w and produce $y = E_w x + \varepsilon$ as before, and then recursively generate a subtree from y without immediately generating another lexical item for y.

5.2 Analysis

As before, it suffices to minimize $-\log p(x) - \log p(W, P|x)$ for a sentence

$W = (w_1, w_2, \cdots, w_n)$ and a set of internal vectors P. We select our prior $p(x)$ exactly as before, and can define $p(W, P|x)$ recursively. The fully-lexicalized case is exactly as above. For the remaining cases, we have:

Unlexicalized split Given a subsequence $W_{i:j} = (w_i, \cdots, w_j)$, if the CCG parse splits $W_{i:j}$ into constituents $W_{i:k}$ and $W_{k:j}$, with categories Y and Z, we have:

$$\begin{aligned} -\log p(W_{i:j}|x) = &-\log p(W_{i:k}, P|E_Y x) \\ &-\log p(W_{k:j}, P|E_Z x) \end{aligned}$$

Half-lexicalized split If the parse splits $W_{i:j}$ into w_i and $W_{i+1:j}$ with categories Y and Z, and $y \in P$ is the intermediate vector used at this step of the derivation, we have:

$$\begin{aligned} &-\log p(W_{i:j}, y|x) \\ &\quad = -\log p(w_i|x) - \log p(y|x, w_i) \\ &\qquad - \log p(W_{i+1:j}|y) \\ &\quad \propto -\theta_{w_i}^T x + \log \sum_{w' \in L_Y} \exp \theta_{w'}^T x \\ &\qquad + \frac{1}{\sigma^2} ||E_{w_i} x - y||^2 \\ &\qquad - \log p(W_{i+1:j}, P|y) \end{aligned}$$

Finally, observe that the complete expression of the log probability of any derivation is, as before, a sum of linear and convex terms, so the optimization problem remains convex for general parse trees.

6 Future work

Various extensions to the model proposed in this paper are possible. The fact that relaxing the distributional requirement for phrases led to performance gains suggests that something similar might be gained from nouns. If a reliable training procedure could be devised with noun vectors as free parameters, it might learn an even better model of phrase similarity—and, in the process, simultaneously perform unsupervised word sense disambiguation on the training corpus.

Unlike the work of Coecke et al. (2010), the structure of the types appearing in the CCG derivations used here are neither necessary nor sufficient to specify the form of the matrices used in this paper. Instead, the function of the CCG derivation is simply to determine which words should be assigned matrices, and which nouns. While CCG provides a very natural way to do this, it is by no means the only way, and future work might focus on providing an analog using a different grammar—all we need is a binary-branching grammar with a natural functor-argument distinction.

Finally, as mentioned in Section 2.3, we have made a significant independence assumption in requiring that the entire CCG derivation be generated in advance. This assumption was necessary to ensure that the probability of a vector in meaning space given its natural language representation would be a convex program. We suspect, however, that it is possible to express a similar probability for an entire packed forest of derivations, and optimize it globally by means of a CKY-like dynamic programming approach. This would make it possible to optimize simultaneously over all possible derivations of a sentence, and allow positions in meaning space to influence the form of those derivations.

7 Conclusion

We have introduced a new model for vector space representations of word and phrase meaning, by providing an explicit probabilistic process by which natural language expressions are generated from vectors in a continuous space of meanings. We've given efficient algorithms for both analysis into and generation out of this meaning space, and described two different training procedures for estimating the parameters of the model. Experimental results demonstrate that these algorithms are capable of modeling graded human judgments of phrase similarity given only positive examples of matching pairs, or distributional representations of pairs as training data; when trained in this fashion, the model outperforms several other compositional approaches to vector space semantics. We have concluded by suggesting how syntactic information might be more closely integrated into this model. While the results presented here are preliminary, we believe they present compelling evidence of representational power, and motivate further study of related models for this problem.

Acknowledgments

We would like to thank Stephen Clark and Andreas Vlachos for feedback on a draft of this paper.

References

L Douglas Baker and Andrew Kachites McCallum. 1998. Distributional clustering of words for text classification. In *Proceedings of the 21st annual international ACM SIGIR conference on Research and development in information retrieval*, pages 96–103. ACM.

Marco Baroni and Roberto Zamparelli. 2010. Nouns are vectors, adjectives are matrices: Representing adjective-noun constructions in semantic space. In *Proceedings of the 2010 Conference on Empirical Methods in Natural Language Processing*, pages 1183–1193. Association for Computational Linguistics.

David M Blei, Andrew Y Ng, and Michael I Jordan. 2003. Latent dirichlet allocation. *the Journal of Machine Learning Research*, 3:993–1022.

Stephen Boyd and Lieven Vandenberghe. 2004. *Convex optimization*. Cambridge university press.

Bob Coecke, Mehrnoosh Sadrzadeh, and Stephen Clark. 2010. Mathematical foundations for a compositional distributional model of meaning. *arXiv preprint arXiv:1003.4394*.

Scott Deerwester, Susan T. Dumais, George W Furnas, Thomas K Landauer, and Richard Harshman. 1990. Indexing by latent semantic analysis. *Journal of the American society for information science*, 41(6):391–407.

John Rupert Firth. 1957. *A synopsis of linguistic theory, 1930-1955*.

Gottlob Frege. 1892. Uber Sinn und Bedeutung. *Zeitschrift fur Philosophie und philosophische Kritik*, pages 25–50. English Translation: em On Sense and Meaning, in Brian McGuinness (ed), em Frege: collected works, pp. 157–177, Basil Blackwell, Oxford.

Edward Grefenstette, Georgiana Dinu, Yao-Zhong Zhang, Mehrnoosh Sadrzadeh, and Marco Baroni. 2013. Multi-step regression learning for compositional distributional semantics. *Proceedings of the 10th International Conference on Computational Semantics (IWCS 2013)*.

Karl Moritz Hermann, Phil Blunsom, and Stephen Pulman. 2012. An unsupervised ranking model for noun-noun compositionality. In *Proceedings of the First Joint Conference on Lexical and Computational Semantics-Volume 1: Proceedings of the main conference and the shared task, and Volume 2: Proceedings of the Sixth International Workshop on Semantic Evaluation*, pages 132–141. Association for Computational Linguistics.

Julia Hockenmaier and Mark Steedman. 2002. Generative models for statistical parsing with combinatory categorial grammar. In *Proceedings of the 40th Annual Meeting on Association for Computational Linguistics*, pages 335–342. Association for Computational Linguistics.

Dong C Liu and Jorge Nocedal. 1989. On the limited memory bfgs method for large scale optimization. *Mathematical programming*, 45(1-3):503–528.

Edward Loper and Steven Bird. 2002. Nltk: the natural language toolkit. In *Proceedings of the ACL-02 Workshop on Effective tools and methodologies for teaching natural language processing and computational linguistics - Volume 1*, ETMTNLP '02, pages 63–70, Stroudsburg, PA, USA. Association for Computational Linguistics.

Jeff Mitchell and Mirella Lapata. 2008. Vector-based models of semantic composition. *proceedings of ACL-08: HLT*, pages 236–244.

Jeff Mitchell and Mirella Lapata. 2010. Composition in distributional models of semantics. *Cognitive Science*, 34(8):1388–1429.

Alberto Paccanaro and Jefferey Hinton. 2002. Learning hierarchical structures with linear relational embedding. In *Advances in Neural Information Processing Systems 14: Proceedings of the 2001 Neural Information Processing Systems (NIPS) Conference*, volume 14, page 857. MIT Press.

Hinrich Schütze and Jan Pedersen. 1993. A vector model for syntagmatic and paradigmatic relatedness. *Making sense of words*, pages 104–113.

Richard Socher, Brody Huval, Christopher D Manning, and Andrew Y Ng. 2012. Semantic compositionality through recursive matrix-vector spaces. In *Proceedings of the 2012 Joint Conference on Empirical Methods in Natural Language Processing and Computational Natural Language Learning*, pages 1201–1211. Association for Computational Linguistics.

Mark Steedman and Jason Baldridge. 2011. Combinatory categorial grammar. *Non-Transformational Syntax Oxford: Blackwell*, pages 181–224.

Wikimedia Foundation. 2013. Wikipedia. http://dumps.wikimedia.org/enwiki/. Accessed: 2013-04-20.

Stephen Wu, William Schuler, et al. 2011. Structured composition of semantic vectors. In *Proceedings of the Ninth International Conference on Computational Semantics (IWCS 2011)*, pages 295–304. Citeseer.

Fabio Massimo Zanzotto, Ioannis Korkontzelos, Francesca Fallucchi, and Suresh Manandhar. 2010. Estimating linear models for compositional distributional semantics. In *Proceedings of the 23rd International Conference on Computational Linguistics*, pages 1263–1271. Association for Computational Linguistics.

Aggregating Continuous Word Embeddings for Information Retrieval

Stéphane Clinchant
Xerox Research Centre Europe
stephane.clinchant@xrce.xerox.com

Florent Perronnin
Xerox Research Centre Europe
florent.perronnin@xrce.xerox.com

Abstract

While words in documents are generally treated as discrete entities, they can be embedded in a Euclidean space which reflects an *a priori* notion of similarity between them. In such a case, a text document can be viewed as a bag-of-embedded-words (BoEW): a set of real-valued vectors. We propose a novel document representation based on such continuous word embeddings. It consists in non-linearly mapping the word-embeddings in a higher-dimensional space and in aggregating them into a document-level representation. We report retrieval and clustering experiments in the case where the word-embeddings are computed from standard topic models showing significant improvements with respect to the original topic models.

1 Introduction

For many tasks such as information retrieval (IR) or clustering, a text document is represented by a vector, where each dimension corresponds to a given word and where each value encodes the word importance in the document (Salton and McGill, 1983). This Vector Space Model (VSM) or bag-of-words (BoW) representation is at the root of topic models such as Latent Semantic Indexing (LSI) (Deerwester, 1988), Probablistic Latent Semantic Analysis (PLSA) (Hofmann, 1999) or Latent Dirichlet Allocation (LDA) (Blei et al., 2003). All these topic models consist in "projecting" documents on a set of topics generally learned in an unsupervised manner. During the learning stage, as a by-product of the projection of the training documents, one also obtains an embedding of the words in a typically small-dimensional continuous space. The distance between two words in this space translates the measure of similarity between words which is captured by the topic models. For LSI, PLSA or LDA, the implicit measure is the number of co-occurrences in the training corpus.

In this paper, we raise the following question: if we were provided with an embedding of words in a continuous space, how could we best use it in IR/clustering tasks? Especially, could we develop probabilistic models which would be able to benefit from this *a priori* information on the similarity between words? When the words are embedded in a continuous space, one can view a document as a Bag-of-Embedded-Words (BoEW). We therefore draw inspiration from the computer vision community where it is common practice to represent an image as a bag-of-features (BoF) where each real-valued feature describes local properties of the image (such as its color, texture or shape). We model the generative process of embedded words using a mixture model where each mixture component can be loosely thought of as a "topic". To transform the variable-cardinality BoEW into a fixed-length representation which is more amenable to comparison, we make use of the Fisher kernel framework of Jaakkola and Haussler (Jaakkola and Haussler, 1999). We will show that this induces a non-linear mapping of the embedded words in a higher-dimensional space where their contributions are aggregated.

We underline that our contribution is **not** the application of the FK to text analysis (see (Hofmann, 2000) for such an attempt). Knowing that words can be embedded in a continuous space, our main contribution is to show that we can *consequently represent a document as a bag-of-embedded-words*. The FK is just *one possible way* to subsequently transform this bag representation into a fixed-length vector which is more amenable to large-scale processing.

The remainder of the article is organized as follows. In the next section, we review related works. In section 3, we describe the proposed framework based on embedded words, GMM topic models and the Fisher kernel. In section 4, we report and discuss experimental results on clustering and retrieval tasks before concluding in section 5.

2 Related Works

We provide a short review of the literature on those topics which are most related to our work: topic models, word embeddings and bag-of-patches representations in computer vision.

Topic models. Statistical topic models build on the idea of Latent Semantic Indexing (LSI) in a probabilistic way. The PLSA model proposed by Hoffman (Hofmann, 1999) can be thought of as a constrained matrix factorization problem equivalent to NMF (Lee and Seung, 1999; Gaussier and Goutte, 2005). Latent Dirichlet Allocation (LDA) (Blei et al., 2003) , the generative counterpart of PLSA, has played a major role in the development of probabilistic models for textual data. As a result, it has been extended or refined in a countless studies (Griffiths et al., 2004; Eisenstein et al., 2011; Hoffman et al., 2010). Statistical topic models are often evaluated with the perplexity measure on a held-out dataset but it has been shown that perplexity only correlates weakly with human preference (Chang et al., 2009). Moreover, several studies reported that LDA does not generally outperform LSI in IR or sentiment analysis tasks (Wang et al., 2011; Maas et al., 2011).

Nevertheless, LSI has known a resurging interest. Supervised Semantic Indexing (SSI) (Bai et al., 2009) learns low-rank projection matrices on query-document pairs so as to minimize a ranking loss. Similarly, (Wang et al., 2011) studies the influence of ℓ_1 and ℓ_2 regularization on the projection matrices and shows how to distribute the algorithm using Map-Reduce.

Word embeddings. Parrallel to the large development of statistical topic models, there has been an increasing amount of literature on word embeddings where it has been proposed to include higher-level dependencies between words, either syntactic or semantic. We note that topic models such as LSI, PLSA or LDA implicitly perform such an embedding (jointly with the embedding of documents) and that the measure of similarity is the co-occurrence of words in the training corpus.

A seminal work in this field is the one by Collobert and Weston (Collobert and Weston, 2008) where a neural network is trained by stochastic gradient descent in order to minimize a loss function on the observed n-grams. This work has later then been refined in (Bengio et al., 2009). Probabilistic methods have also been proposed to learn language models such as the HLBL embedding (Mnih and Hinton, 2007).

Similarly, (Maas et al., 2011) parametrizes a probabilistic model in order to capture word representations, instead of modeling individually latent topics, which lead to significant improvements over LDA in sentiment analysis. Furthermore, (Dhillon et al., 2011) uses the Canonical Correlation Analysis technique between the left and right context vectors of a word to learn word embeddings. Lastly, (Turian et al., 2010) proposes an empirical comparison of several word embedding techniques in a named entity recognition task and provides an excellent state-of-the-art of word representation. Except (Maas et al., 2011) , there has been very little work to your knowledge bridging the statistical topic models with the word embedding techniques.

Computer vision. In modern computer vision, an image is usually described by a set of local descriptors extracted from small image patches such as SIFT. This local representation provides some invariance to changes in viewpoint, lighting or occlusion. The local descriptors characterize the low-level properties of the image such as its color, texture or shape. Since it is computationally intensive to handle (e.g. to match) sets of descriptors of variable cardinality, it has been proposed to aggregate the local descriptors into a global vector which is more amenable to retrieval and classification.

The most popular aggregation mechanism was directly inspired by the work in text analysis. It makes use of an intermediate representation – the *visual vocabulary* – which is a set of prototypical descriptors – the *visual words* – obtained through a clustering algorithm such as k-means (Leung and Malik, 1999; Sivic and Zisserman, 2003; Csurka et al., 2004). Given an image, each of its descriptors is assigned to its closest visual word and the image is described by the histogram of visual words frequencies. This representation is referred to as the *Bag-of-Visual-words* (BoV).

Some works pushed the analogy with text analysis even further. For instance, in large-scale retrieval, Sivic and Zisserman proposed to use a tf-idf weighting of the BoV vector and an inverted file for efficient matching (Sivic and Zisserman, 2003). As another example, pLSA, LDA and their many variations have been extensively applied to problems such as image classification (Quelhas et al., 2005) or object discovery (Russell et al., 2006). However, it has been noted that the quantization process mentioned above incurs a loss of information since a *continuous descriptor* is transformed into a *discrete value* (the index of the closest visual word). To overcome this limitation, several improvements have been proposed which depart from the pure discrete model. These improvements include the soft assignment of descriptors to visual words (Farquhar et al., 2005; Philbin et al., 2008; Gemert et al., 2008) or the use of more advanced coding techniques than vector quantization such as sparse coding (Yang et al., 2009) or locality-constrained linear coding (Wang et al., 2010).

All the previous techniques can be understood (with some simplifications) as simple counting mechanisms (computation of 0-order statistics). It has been proposed to take into account higher-order statistics (first and second order for instance) which encode more descriptor-level information and therefore incur a lower loss of information. This includes the Fisher vector (Perronnin and Dance, 2007; Perronnin et al., 2010), which was directly inspired by the Fisher kernel of Jaakkola and Haussler (Jaakkola and Haussler, 1999). In a nutshell, the Fisher vector consists in modeling the distribution of patches in any image with a Gaussian mixture model (GMM) and then in describing an image by its deviation from this average probability distribution. In a recent evaluation (Chatfield et al., 2011), it has been shown experimentally that the Fisher vector was the state-of-the-art representation for image classification. However, in this work *we question the treatment of words as discrete entities*. Indeed, intuitvely some words are closer to each other from a semantic standpoint and words can be embedded in a continuous space as is done for instance in LSA.

3 The Bag-of-Embedded-Words (BoEW)

In this work, we draw inspiration from the work in the computer vision community: we model the generation process of words with continuous mixture models and use the FK for aggregation.

The proposed bag-of-embedded-words proceeds as follows: **Learning phase.** Given an unlabeled training set of documents:

1. Learn an embedding of words in a low-dimensional space, *i.e.* lower-dimensional than the VSM. After this operation, each word w is then represented by a vector of size e:
$$w \rightarrow E_w = [E_{w,1}, \ldots, E_{w,e}]. \quad (1)$$
2. Fit a probabilistic model – *e.g.* a mixture model – on the continuous word embeddings.

Document representation. Given a document whose BoW representation is $\{w_1, \ldots, w_T\}$:

1. Transform the BoW representation into a BoEW:
$$\{w_1, \ldots, w_T\} \rightarrow \{E_{w_1}, \ldots, E_{w_T}\} \quad (2)$$
2. Aggregate the continuous word embeddings E_{w_t} using the FK framework.

Since the proposed framework is independent of the particular embedding technique, we will first focus on the modeling of the generation process and on the FK-based aggregation. We will then compare the proposed continuous topic model to the traditional LSI, PLSA and LDA topic models.

3.1 Probabilistic modeling and FK aggregation

We assume that the continuous word embeddings in a document have been generated by a "universal" (i.e. document-independent) probability density function (pdf). As is common practice for continuous features, we choose this pdf to be a Gaussian mixture model (GMM) since any continuous distribution can be approximated with arbitrary precision by a mixture of Gaussians. In what follows, the pdf is denoted u_λ where $\lambda = \{\theta_i, \mu_i, \Sigma_i, i = 1 \ldots K\}$ is the set of parameters of the GMM. θ_i, μ_i and Σ_i denote respectively the mixture weight, mean vector and covariance matrix of Gaussian i. For computational reasons, we assume that the covariance matrices are diagonal and denote σ_i^2 the variance vector of Gaussian i, i.e. $\sigma_i^2 = \text{diag}(\Sigma_i)$. In practice, the GMM is estimated offline with a set of continuous word embeddings extracted from a representative set of documents. The parameters λ are estimated through the optimization of a Maximum

Likelihood (ML) criterion using the Expectation-Maximization (EM) algorithm.

Let us assume that a document contains T words and let us denote by $X = \{x_1, \ldots, x_T\}$ the set of continuous word embeddings extracted from the document. We wish to derive a fixed-length representation (i.e. a vector whose dimensionality is independent of T) that characterizes X with respect to u_λ. A natural framework to achieve this goal is the FK (Jaakkola and Haussler, 1999). In what follows, we use the notation of (Perronnin et al., 2010).

Given u_λ one can characterize the sample X using the score function:

$$G_\lambda^X = \nabla_\lambda^T \log u_\lambda(X). \quad (3)$$

This is a vector whose size depends only on the number of parameters in λ. Intuitively, it describes in which direction the parameters λ of the model should be modified so that the model u_λ better fits the data. Assuming that the word embeddings x_t are iid (a simplifying assumption), we get:

$$G_\lambda^X = \sum_{t=1}^{T} \nabla_\lambda \log u_\lambda(x_t). \quad (4)$$

Jaakkola and Haussler proposed to measure the similarity between two samples X and Y using the FK:

$$K(X,Y) = G_\lambda^{X'} F_\lambda^{-1} G_\lambda^Y \quad (5)$$

where F_λ is the Fisher Information Matrix (FIM) of u_λ:

$$F_\lambda = E_{x\sim u_\lambda}\left[\nabla_\lambda \log u_\lambda(x) \nabla_\lambda \log u_\lambda(x)'\right]. \quad (6)$$

As F_λ is symmetric and positive definite, it has a Cholesky decomposition $F_\lambda = L_\lambda' L_\lambda$ and $K(X,Y)$ can be rewritten as a dot-product between normalized vectors $\mathcal{G}_\lambda$ with:

$$\mathcal{G}_\lambda^X = L_\lambda G_\lambda^X. \quad (7)$$

(Perronnin et al., 2010) refers to $\mathcal{G}_\lambda^X$ as the *Fisher Vector* (FV) of X. Using a diagonal approximation of the FIM, we obtain the following formula for the gradient with respect to μ_i [1]:

$$\mathcal{G}_i^X = \frac{1}{\sqrt{\theta_i}} \sum_{t=1}^{T} \gamma_t(i) \left(\frac{x_t - \mu_i}{\sigma_i}\right). \quad (8)$$

where the division by the vector σ_i should be understood as a term-by-term operation and $\gamma_t(i) = p(i|x_t, \lambda)$ is the soft assignment of x_t to Gaussian i (*i.e.* the probability that x_t was generated by Gaussian i) which can be computed using Bayes' formula. The FV $\mathcal{G}_\lambda^X$ is the concatenation of the $\mathcal{G}_i^X$, $\forall i$. Let e be the dimensionality of the continuous word descriptors and K be the number of Gaussians. The resulting vector is $e \times K$ dimensional.

3.2 Relationship with LSI, PLSA, LDA

Relationship with LSI. Let n be the number of documents in the collection and t be the number of indexing terms. Let A be the $t \times n$ document matrix. In LSI (or NMF), A decomposes as:

$$A \approx U\Sigma V' \quad (9)$$

where $U \in \mathbb{R}^{txe}$, $\Sigma \in \mathbb{R}^{exe}$ is diagonal, $V \in \mathbb{R}^{nxe}$ and e is the size of the embedding space. If we choose $V\Sigma$ as the LSI document embedding matrix – which makes sense if we accept the dot-product as a measure of similarity between documents since $A'A \approx (V\Sigma)(V\Sigma)'$ – then we have $V\Sigma \approx A'U$. This means that the LSI embedding of a document is approximately the sum of the embedding of the words, weighted by the number of occurrences of each word.

Similarly, from equations (4) and (7), it is clear that the FV $\mathcal{G}_\lambda^X$ is a sum of non-linear mappings:

$$x_t \rightarrow L_\lambda \nabla_\lambda \log u_\lambda(x_t) = \left[\frac{\gamma_t(1)}{\sqrt{\theta_1}} \frac{x_t - \mu_1}{\sigma_1}, \ldots, \frac{\gamma_t(K)}{\sqrt{\theta_K}} \frac{x_t - \mu_K}{\sigma_K}\right] \quad (10)$$

computed for each embedded-word x_t. When the number of Gaussians $K = 1$, the mapping simplifies to a linear one:

$$x_t \rightarrow \frac{x_t - \mu_1}{\sigma_1} \quad (11)$$

and the FV is simply a whitened version of the sum of word-embeddings. Therefore, if we choose LSI to perform word-embeddings in our framework, the Fisher-based representation is similar to the LSI document embedding in the one Gaussian case. This does not come as a surprise in the case of LSI since Singular Value Decomposition (SVD) can be viewed as a the limite case of a probabilistic model with a Gaussian noise assumption (Salakhutdinov and Mnih, 2007). Hence, the proposed framework enables to model documents when the word embeddings are non-Gaussian.

[1] we only consider the partial derivatives with respect to the mean vectors since the partial derivatives with respect to the mixture weights and variance parameters carry little additional information (we confirmed this fact in preliminary experiments).

Another advantage is that the proposed framework is rotation and scale invariant. Indeed, while it "makes sense" to use $V\Sigma$ as the document embedding, in practice better results can be obtained when using simply V. Our framework is independent of such an arbitrary choice.

Relationship with PLSA and LDA. There is also a strong parallel between topic models on discrete word occurrences such as PLSA/LDA and the proposed model for continuous word embeddings. Indeed, both generative models include a latent variable which indicates which mixture generates which words. In the LDA case, each topic is modeled by a multinomial distribution which indicates the frequency of each word for the particular topic. In the mixture model case, each mixture component can be loosely understood as a "topic".

Therefore, one could wonder if the proposed framework is not somehow equivalent to topic models such PLSA/LDA. The major difference is that PLSA, LDA and other topic models on word counts *jointly* perform the embedding of words and the learning of the topics. A major deficiency of such approaches is that they cannot deal with words which have not been seen at training time. In the proposed framework, these two steps are *decoupled*. Hence, we can cope with words which have not been seen during the training of the probabilistic model. We will see in section 4.3.1 that this yields a major benefit: the mixture model can be trained efficiently on a small subset of the corpus and yet generalize to unseen words.

In the same manner, our work is significantly different from previous attempts at applying the FK framework to topic models such as PLSA (Hofmann, 2000; Chappelier and Eckard, 2009) or LDA (Chandalia and Beal, 2006) (we will refer to such combinations as FKPLSA and FKLDA). Indeed, while FKPLSA and FKLDA can improve over PLSA and LDA respectively, they inherit the deficiencies of the original PLSA and LDA approaches, especially their unability to deal with words unseen at training time. We note also that FKPLSA is extremely computationally intensive: in the recent (Chappelier and Eckard, 2009), the largest corpus which could be handled contained barely 7,466 documents. In contrast, we can easily handle on a single machine corpora containing hundreds of thousands of documents (see section 4.2).

Collection	#docs	#terms	#classes
20NG	19,995	32,902	20
TDT	4,214	8,978	18

(a) Clustering

Collection	#docs	#terms	#queries
ROBUST	490,779	87,223	250
TREC1&-3	741,856	108,294	150
CLEF03	166,754	79,008	60

(b) IR

Table 1: Characteristics of the clustering and IR collections

4 Experiments

The experiments aim at demonstrating that the proposed *continuous* model is competitive with existing topic models on *discrete* words. We focus our experiments on the case where the embedding of the continuous words is obtained by LSI as it enables us to compare the quality of the document representation obtained originally by LSI and the one derived by our framework on top of LSI. In what follows, we will refer to the FV on the LSI embedding simply as the FV.

We assessed the performance of the FV on clustering and ad-hoc IR tasks. We used two datasets for clustering and three for IR. Using the Lemur toolkit (Ogilvie and Callan, 2001), we applied a standard processing pipeline on all these datasets including stopword removal, stemming or lemmatization and the filtering of rare words to speed up computations. The GMMs were trained on 1,000,000 word occurences, which represents roughly 5,000 documents for the collections we have used. In what follows, the cosine similarity was used to compare FVs and LSI document vectors.

4.1 Clustering

We used two well-known and publicly available datasets which are 20 NewsGroup (20NG) and a subset of one TDT dataset (http://www.ldc.upenn.edu/ProjectsTDT2004, 2004). The 20NG is a classical dataset when evaluating classifiers or clustering methods. For the TDT dataset we retain only topics with more than one hundred documents, which resulted in 18 classes. After preprocessing, the 20NG collection has approximately 20,000 documents and 33,000 unique words and the TDT has approximately 4,000 documents and 9,000 unique words. Table

Collection	Model	ARI	NMI
20NG	PLSA	41.0	57.4
	LDA	40.7	57.9
	LSI	41.0	59.5
	FV	45.2	60.7
TDT	PLSA	64.2	84.5
	LDA	69.4	86.4
	LSI	72.1	88.5
	FV	70.4	88.2

Table 2: Clustering experiments on 20NG and the WebKB TDT Corpus: Mean performance over 20 runs (in %).

1 (a) gives the general statistics of the two datasets after preprocessing.

We use 2 standard evaluation metrics to assess the quality of the clusters, which are the Adjusted Rand Index (ARI) (Hubert and Arabie, 1985) and Normalized Mutual Information (NMI) (Manning and Schütze, 1999). These measures compare the clusters with respect to the partition induced by the category information. The ARI and NMI range between 0 and 1 where 1 indicates a perfect match with the categories. For all the clustering methods, the number of clusters is set to the true number of classes of the collections and the performances were averaged over 20 runs.

We compared spherical k-means on the FV document representations to topic models such as PLSA and LDA[2]. We choose a priori an embedding of size $e = 20$ for both datasets for LSI and therefore for the FV. LDA and PLSA were trained on the whole dataset. For the FV, we varied the number of Gaussians (K) to analyze the evolution of performances. Table 2 shows the best results for the FV and compares them to LSI, PLSA and LDA. First, LDA has lower performance than LSI in our experiments as reported by several studies which showed that LDA does not necessarily outperform LSI (Wang et al., 2011; Maas et al., 2011). Overall, the FV outperforms all the other models on 20NG and probabilistic topic models on TDT.

4.2 Retrieval

We used three IR collections, from two evaluation campaigns: TREC[3] and CLEF[4]: Table 1 (b) gives the statistics of the collections we retained: (i) ROBUST (TREC), (ii) the English subpart of CLEF03 AdHoc Task and (iii) the TREC 1&2 collection, with 150 queries corresponding to topics 51 to 200. For the ROBUST and TREC 1&2 collections, we used standard Porter stemming. For CLEF, words were lemmatized. We removed rare words to speed up the computation of LSI. Performances were measured with the Mean Average Precision (MAP) over the top 1,000 retrieved documents. All the collections have more than 80,000 unique words and approximately 166,000 documents for CLEF, 500,000 for ROBUST and 741,000 for TREC. LSI was computed on the whole dataset and the GMMs were trained on a random subset of 5,000 documents. We then computed the FVs for all documents in the collection. Note that we did not compute topic models with LDA on these datasets as LSI provides similar performances to LDA (Wang et al., 2011; Bai et al., 2009).

Table 3 shows the evolution of the MAP for the LSI baseline with respect to the size of the latent space. Note that we use Matlab to compute singular valued decompositions and that some numbers are missing in this table because of the memory limitations of our machine. Figure 1 shows the evolution of the MAP for different numbers of Gaussians (K) for respectively the CLEF, TREC and ROBUST datasets. For all these plots, FV performances are displayed with a circle and LSI with crosses. We tested an embedding of size $e = 50$ and $e = 200$ for the CLEF dataset, an embedding of size $e = 100$ and $e = 200$ for the TREC dataset and $e = 100$ and $e = 300$ for ROBUST. All these figures show the same trend: a) the performance of the FV increases up to 16 Gaussians and then reaches a plateau and b) the FV significantly outperforms LSI (since it is able to double LSI's performance in several cases). In addition, the LSI results in table 3 (a) indicate that LSI with more dimensions will not reach the level of performance obtained by the FV.

[2]We use Blei's implementation available at http://www.cs.princeton.edu/ blei/lda-c/

[3]trec.nist.gov

[4]www.clef-campaign.org

e	50	100	200	300	400	500
CLEF	4.0	6.7	9.2	11.0	13.0	13.9
TREC-1 &2	2.2	4.3	6.5	8.3	-	-
ROBUST	1.3	2.4	3.6	4.5	-	-

Table 3: LSI MAP (%) for the IR datasets for several sizes of the latent subspace.

4.3 Discussion

In the previous section we validated the good behavior of the proposed continuous document representation. In the following parts, we conduct additional experiments to further show the strengths and weaknesses of the proposed approach.

IR Baselines. If the FV based on LSI word embeddings significantly outperforms LSI, it is outperformed by strong IR baselines such as Divergence From Randomness (DFR) models (Amati and Rijsbergen, 2002) or Language Models (Ponte and Croft, 1998). This is what we show in table 4 with the PL2 DFR model compared to standard TFIDF, the best FV and LSI.

Collection	PL2	TFIDF	FV	LSI
CLEF'03	35.7	16.4	23.7	9.2
TREC-1&2	22.6	12.4	10.8	6.5
ROBUST	24.8	12.6	10.5	4.5

Table 4: Mean Average Precision(%) for the PL2 and TFIDF model on the three IR Collections compared to Fisher Vector and LSI

These results are not surprising as it has been shown experimentally in many studies that latent-based approaches such as LSI are generally outperformed by state-of-the-art IR models in Ad-Hoc tasks. There are a significant gap in performances between LSI and TFIDF and between TFIDF and the PL2 model. The first gap is due to the change in representation, from a vector space model to latent based representation, while the second one is only due to a 'better' similarity as both methods operate in a similar space. In a way, the FV approach offers a better similarity for latent representations even if several improvements could be further proposed (pivoted document length normalization, combination with exact representation).

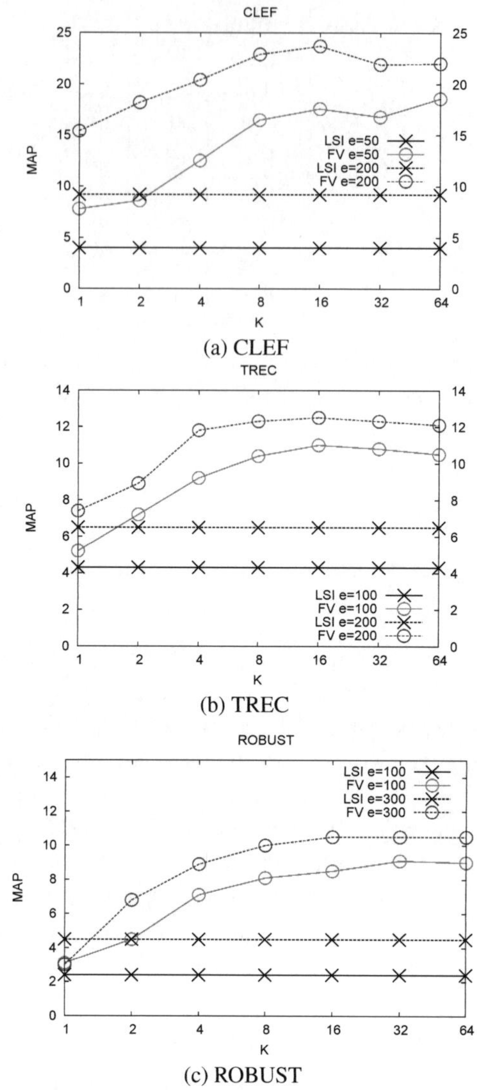

Figure 1: MAP(%) for the FV with different numbers of Gaussians against LSI on the CLEF, TREC and ROBUST datasets

4.3.1 Influence of Training Set Size and Unseen Words.

One of the main benefits of our method is its ability to cope with unseen words: our framework allows to assign probabilities for words unseen while training the topic model assuming that they can be embedded in the Euclidean space. Thus, one can train the probabilistic model on a subpart of the collection without having to discard unseen words at test time. Therefore, we can easily address large-scale collections as we can restrict the GMM learning step on a subset of a collection of documents. This is something that LDA cannot cope with as the vocabulary is frozen at training

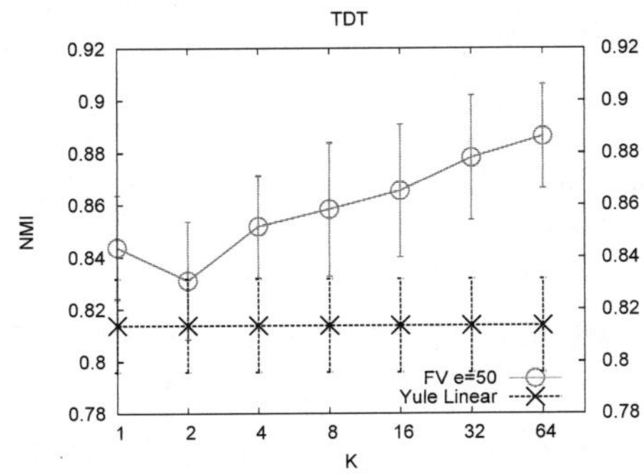

Figure 2: NMI for the FV with different Number of Gaussians against averaging word embeddings on TDT with the Yule measure

M	# docs	MAP TREC
0.5M	$\approx 2{,}700$	11.0
1M	$\approx 5{,}400$	11.0
5M	$\approx 27{,}000$	10.6
10M	$\approx 54{,}000$	10.6

Table 5: Model performance for different subsets used to train the GMM. M refers to a million word occurences

time. We show in figure 5 that our model is robust to the number of word occurences used for training the GMM. We illustrate this point using the TREC 1-&2 collection with an embedding of size $e = 100$. We varied the number of documents to train the GMM. Figure 5 shows that increasing the number of documents does not lead to improvements and the performance remains stable. Therefore, these empirical results indeed confirm that we can adress large-scale collections as we can restrict the learning step on a small subset of a collection of documents.

4.3.2 Beyond LSI Embedding

While we focused in the experimental section on word embeddings obtained with LSI, we now show that the proposed framework can be applied to other word embeddings. To do so, we use a word embedding based on the Yule association measure (Jagarlamudi et al., 2011) which is closely related to the Mutual Information but relies on the raw frequencies rather than on probabilities. We use this measure to compute a similarity matrix between words. Then, we applied a spherical kmeans on this matrix to find $e = 50$ word clusters and used the cluster centroids as the word embedding matrix. A simple baseline is to use as document representation the average word embedding as is the case of LSI. The baseline gets 82% NMI wherease the FV with 32 Gaussians reaches 88%. The non-linear mapping induced by the FV always outperforms the simple averaging. Therefore, it is worthwhile to learn non-linear mappings.

5 Conclusion

In this work, we proposed to treat documents as bags-of-embedded-words (BoEW) and to learn probabilistic mixture models *once* words were embedded in a Euclidean space. This is a significant departure from the vast majority of the works in the machine learning and information retrieval communities which deal with words as discrete entities. We assessed our framework on several clustering and ad-hoc IR collections and the experiments showed that our model is able to yield effective descriptors of textual documents. In particular, the FV based on LSI embedding was shown to significantly outperform LSI for retrieval tasks.

There are many possible applications and generalizations of our framework. In this study, we focused on the LSI embedding and showed preliminary results with the Yule embedding. Since we believe that the word embedding technique is of crucial importance, we would like to experiment with recent embedding techniques such as the Collobert and Weston embedding (Collobert and Weston, 2008) which has been shown to scale well in several NLP tasks.

Moreover, another significant advantage of the proposed framework is that we could deal seamlessly with collections of multilingual documents. This requires the ability to embedd the words of different languages and techniques exist to perform such an embedding including Canonical Correlation Analysis. Finally, the GMM still has several theoretical limitations to model textual documents appropriately so that one could design a better statistical model for bags-of-embedded-words.

References

Gianni Amati and Cornelis Joost Van Rijsbergen. 2002. Probabilistic models of information retrieval based on measuring the divergence from randomness. *ACM Trans. Inf. Syst.*, 20(4):357–389.

B. Bai, J. Weston, D. Grangier, R. Collobert, K. Sadamasa, Y. Qi, O. Chapelle, and K. Weinberger. 2009. Supervised semantic indexing. In *Proceeding of the 18th ACM CIKM*.

Y. Bengio, J. Louradour, R. Collobert, and J. Weston. 2009. Curriculum learning. In *ICML*.

David M. Blei, Andrew Y. Ng, and Michael I. Jordan. 2003. Latent dirichlet allocation. *JMLR*.

Gaurav Chandalia and Matthew J. Beal. 2006. Using fisher kernels from topic models for dimensionality reduction.

Jonathan Chang, Jordan Boyd-graber, Sean Gerrish, Chong Wang, and David M. Blei. 2009. Reading tea leaves: How humans interpret topic models. In *NIPS*.

Jean-Cédric Chappelier and Emmanuel Eckard. 2009. Plsi: The true fisher kernel and beyond. In *ECML/PKDD (1)*.

K. Chatfield, V. Lempitsky, A. Vedaldi, and A. Zisserman. 2011. The devil is in the details: an evaluation of recent feature encoding methods. In *BMVC*.

R. Collobert and J. Weston. 2008. A unified architecture for natural language processing: Deep neural networks with multitask learning. In *ICML*.

G. Csurka, C. Dance, L Fan, J. Willamowski, and C. Bray. 2004. Visual categorization with bags of keypoints. In *Proc. of ECCV Workshop on Statistical Learning for Computer Vision*.

Scott Deerwester. 1988. Improving Information Retrieval with Latent Semantic Indexing. In *Proceedings of (ASIS '88)*.

Paramveer S. Dhillon, Dean Foster, and Lyle Ungar. 2011. Multi-view learning of word embeddings via cca. In *NIPS*, volume 24.

Jacob Eisenstein, Amr Ahmed, and Eric P. Xing. 2011. Sparse additive generative models of text. In Lise Getoor and Tobias Scheffer, editors, *ICML*, pages 1041–1048. Omnipress.

Jason Farquhar, Sandor Szedmak, Hongying Meng, and John Shawe-Taylor. 2005. Improving "bag-of-keypoints" image categorisation: Generative models and pdf-kernels. Technical report, University of Southampton.

Éric Gaussier and Cyril Goutte. 2005. Relation between PLSA and NMF and implications. In *SIGIR*.

Jan Van Gemert, Jan-Mark Geusebroek, Cor Veenman, and Arnold Smeulders. 2008. Kernel codebooks for scene categorization. In *European Conference on Computer Vision (ECCV)*.

Thomas L. Griffiths, Mark Steyvers, David M. Blei, and Joshua B. Tenenbaum. 2004. Integrating topics and syntax. In *NIPS*.

Matthew D. Hoffman, David M. Blei, and Francis Bach. 2010. Online learning for latent dirichlet allocation. In *In NIPS*.

Thomas Hofmann. 1999. Probabilistic latent semantic indexing. In *SIGIR*. ACM.

T. Hofmann. 2000. Learning the similarity of documents: An information geometric approach to document retrieval and categorization. In *Neural Information Processing Systems*.

http://www.ldc.upenn.edu/ProjectsTDT2004. 2004. TDT: Annotation manual - version 1.2.

Lawrence Hubert and Phipps Arabie. 1985. Comparing partitions. *Journal of Classification*.

Tommi S. Jaakkola and David Haussler. 1999. Exploiting generative models in discriminative classifiers. In *NIPS*, Cambridge, MA, USA. MIT Press.

Jagadeesh Jagarlamudi, Raghavendra Udupa, Hal Daumé III, and Abhijit Bhole. 2011. Improving bilingual projections via sparse covariance matrices. In *EMNLP*, pages 930–940.

D. D. Lee and H. S. Seung. 1999. Learning the parts of objects by non-negative matrix factorization. *Nature*, 401(6755):788–791, October.

T. Leung and J. Malik. 1999. Recognizing surfaces using three-dimensional textons. In *IEEE International Conference on Computer Vision (ICCV)*.

Andrew L. Maas, Raymond E. Daly, Peter T. Pham, Dan Huang, Andrew Y. Ng, and Christopher Potts. 2011. Learning word vectors for sentiment analysis. In *ACL*, pages 142–150.

Christopher D. Manning and Hinrich Schütze. 1999. *Foundations of statistical natural language processing*. MIT Press, Cambridge, MA, USA.

Andriy Mnih and Geoffrey E. Hinton. 2007. Three new graphical models for statistical language modelling. In Zoubin Ghahramani, editor, *ICML*, volume 227 of *ACM International Conference Proceeding Series*, pages 641–648. ACM.

Paul Ogilvie and James P. Callan. 2001. Experiments Using the Lemur Toolkit. In *TREC*.

Florent Perronnin and Christopher R. Dance. 2007. Fisher kernels on visual vocabularies for image categorization. In *CVPR*.

Florent Perronnin, Yan Liu, , Jorge Sánchez, and Hervé Poirier. 2010. Large-scale image retrieval with compressed fisher vectors. In *CVPR*.

James Philbin, Ondrej Chum, Michael Isard, Josef Sivic, and Andrew Zisserman. 2008. Lost in quantization: Improving particular object retrieval in large scale image databases. In *IEEE International Conference on Computer Vision and Pattern Recognition (CVPR)*.

Jay M. Ponte and W. Bruce Croft. 1998. A language modeling approach to information retrieval. In *SIGIR*, pages 275–281. ACM.

P. Quelhas, F. Monay, J.-M. Odobez, D. Gatica-Perez, T. Tuytelaars, and L. Van Gool. 2005. Modeling scenes with local descriptors and latent aspects. In *IEEE International Conference on Computer Vision (ICCV)*.

B. Russell, A. Efros, J. Sivic, W. Freeman, and A. Zisserman. 2006. Using multiple segmentations to discover objects and their extent in image collections. In *IEEE International Conference on Computer Vision and Pattern Recognition (CVPR)*.

R. Salakhutdinov and A. Mnih. 2007. Probabilistic matrix factorization. In *NIPS*.

G. Salton and M. J. McGill. 1983. *Introduction to Modern Information Retrieval*. McGraw-Hill, Inc., New York, NY, USA.

J. Sivic and A. Zisserman. 2003. Video google: A text retrieval approach to object matching in videos. In *IEEE International Conference on Computer Vision (ICCV)*.

Joseph P. Turian, Lev-Arie Ratinov, and Yoshua Bengio. 2010. Word representations: A simple and general method for semi-supervised learning. In *ACL*, pages 384–394.

J. Wang, J. Yang, K. Yu, F. Lv, T. Huang, and Y. Gong. 2010. Locality-constrained linear coding for image classification. In *IEEE International Conference on Computer Vision and Pattern Recognition (CVPR)*.

Quan Wang, Jun Xu, Hang Li, and Nick Craswell. 2011. Regularized latent semantic indexing. In *SIGIR'11*.

J. Yang, K. Yu, Y. Gong, and T. Huang. 2009. Linear spatial pyramid matching using sparse coding for image classification. In *IEEE International Conference on Computer Vision and Pattern Recognition (CVPR)*.

Answer Extraction by Recursive Parse Tree Descent

Christopher Malon
NEC Laboratories America
4 Independence Way
Princeton, NJ 08540
malon@nec-labs.com

Bing Bai
NEC Laboratories America
4 Independence Way
Princeton, NJ 08540
bbai@nec-labs.com

Abstract

We develop a recursive neural network (RNN) to extract answers to arbitrary natural language questions from supporting sentences, by training on a crowdsourced data set (to be released upon presentation). The RNN defines feature representations at every node of the parse trees of questions and supporting sentences, when applied recursively, starting with token vectors from a neural probabilistic language model. In contrast to prior work, we fix neither the types of the questions nor the forms of the answers; the system classifies tokens to match a substring chosen by the question's author.

Our classifier decides to follow each parse tree node of a support sentence or not, by classifying its RNN embedding together with those of its siblings and the root node of the question, until reaching the tokens it selects as the answer. A novel co-training task for the RNN, on *subtree recognition*, boosts performance, along with a scheme to consistently handle words that are not well-represented in the language model. On our data set, we surpass an open source system epitomizing a classic "pattern bootstrapping" approach to question answering.

1 Introduction

The goal of this paper is to learn the syntax used to answer arbitrary natural language questions. If the kinds of questions were fixed but the supporting sentences were open, this would be a kind of relation extraction or slot-filling. If the questions were open but the supporting information was encoded in a database, this would be a kind of semantic parsing.

In spite of many evaluation sets, no suitable data set for *learning* to answer questions has existed before. Data sets such as TREC (Dang et al., 2008) do not identify supporting sentences or even answers unless a competing system submitted an answer and a human verified it. Exceeding the capabilities of current systems is difficult by training on such labels; any newly discovered answer is penalized as wrong. The Jeopardy Archive (Schmidt, 2013) offers more than 200,000 answer/question pairs, but no pointers to information that supports the solutions.

Believing that it is impossible to *learn* to answer questions, QA systems in TREC tended to *measure* syntactic similarity between question and candidate answer, or to map the question into an enumerated set of possible question types. For the pre-determined question types, learning could be achieved, not from the QA data itself, but from pattern bootstrapping (Brin, 1998) or distant supervision against an ontology like Freebase (Mintz et al., 2009). These techniques lose precision; Riedel et al. (2010) found the distant supervision assumption was violated on 31% of examples aligning Freebase relations to text from The New York Times.

We introduce a new, crowdsourced dataset, *TurkQA*, to enable question answering to be learned. TurkQA consists of single sentences, each with several crowdsourced questions. The answer to each question is given as a substring of the supporting sentence. For example,

> James Hervey (February 26, 1714 - December 25, 1758), English divine, was born at Hardingstone, near Northampton, and was educated at the grammar school of Northampton, and at Lincoln College, Oxford.

could have questions like "Where did James Hervey attend school as a boy?" with answers like "the grammar school of Northampton." Our approach has yielded almost 40,000 such questions, and easily scales to many more. Since the sentence containing the answer has already been located, the machine's output can be judged without worrying about missing labels elsewhere in the corpus. Token-level ground truth forces the classifier to isolate the relevant information.

To meet this challenge, we develop a classifier that recursively classifies nodes of the parse tree of a supporting sentence. The positively classified nodes are followed down the tree, and any positively classified terminal nodes become the tokens in the answer. Feature representations are dense vectors in a continuous feature space; for the terminal nodes, they are the word vectors in a neural probabilistic language model (like (Bengio and Ducharme, 2001)), and for interior nodes, they are derived from children by recursive application of an autoencoder.

The contributions of this paper are: a data set for learning to answer free-form questions; a top-down supervised method using continuous word features in parse trees to find the answer; and a co-training task for training a recursive neural network that preserves deep structural information.

2 Related Work

Most submissions to TREC, TAC, and CLEF (Forner et al., 2008) QA workshops rely on a large pipeline of modules, emphasizing feature development, pattern bootstrapping, and distant supervision. However, some recent work has introduced new learning techniques for question answering.

Restricting the forms of the questions, Poon and Domingos (2009) present a question-answering system for simple questions about biomedical text, by *unsupervised semantic parsing* (USP), using Markov logic. Because of its dependence on semantic role labeling (SRL), USP can only extract limited kinds of information from a sentence's syntax. Particularly, USP has been programmed to use information from just five dependencies: `NN`, `AMOD`, `PREP_OF`, `NUM`, and `APPOS`. The system handles only questions of two forms: "What VERB OBJ?" and "What does SUBJ VERB?"

Liang et al. (2011) offers a compositional focus on semantic parsing. He has implemented a question-answering system for geography and job databases, learning to transform natural language questions into SQL queries. Liang is able to take many words as verbatim analogues of table columns (*e.g.* "city" triggers a search on a *city* column), but our task requires learning such associations in natural language ("city" to a *place* named entity), and less attention to Boolean compositional semantics.

We have not seen recursive neural networks (RNN) applied to QA yet, but Socher has developed applications to paraphrase (Socher et al., 2011a) and sentiment analysis (Socher et al., 2011b). Relying either on dynamic pooling or the root feature alone, these methods do not use the full information of the input graphs.

3 TurkQA: a scalable, crowdsourced data set

The TurkQA data set consists of 13,424 problem sets. Each problem set consists of the first sentence of a Wikipedia article, which we call a *support sentence*, and four questions, written by workers from Amazon Mechanical Turk.[1] (Occasionally, due to a faulty heuristic, two or three consecutive sentences at the beginning of the article are taken.) Each of the four questions is answered by a phrase in the support sentence, or yes/no. At least two short answer questions must exist in each problem set, and their answers are selected by their authors as contiguous, non-overlapping substrings of the support sentence.

Over 600 workers contributed. The quality of the questions was ensured by rigorous constraints on the input: no pronouns could be used; all words from the question had to be in the dictionary or the support sentence; the same phrase could not be used as the answer for multiple questions. We requested that anyone who understood English should be able to understand the question just by reading the support sentence, without any background knowledge. As we took the support sentences from the start of an article, references to prior text should not occur.

At first we reviewed submissions by hand, but as we found that 96% of the problem sets were acceptable (and a higher percentage of the questions), we approved most submissions automatically. Thus we expect the data acquisition technique to be scalable with a budget.

A possible drawback of our data acquisition is so-called *back-formulation*: a tendency of question writers to closely match the syntax of the supporting sentence when writing questions. This drawback was observed in TREC 8, and caused TREC organizers to change data set construction for later conferences by starting with questions input to a search engine, and then localize supporting sentences, rather than starting with the support (Voorhees, 2000). In actuality, many TurkQA question writers introduced their own wording and asked questions with more qualifications than a typical search engine query. They even asked 100 "why" questions.

4 Recursive neural networks

In their traditional form (Pollack, 1990), autoencoders consist of two neural networks: an encoder E to compress multiple input vectors into a single output vector, and a decoder D to restore the inputs from the compressed vector. Through recursion, autoencoders allow single vectors to represent variable length data structures. Supposing each terminal node t of a rooted tree T has been assigned a feature vector $\vec{x}(t) \in \mathbb{R}^n$, the encoder E is used to define n-dimensional feature vectors at all remaining nodes. Assuming for simplicity that T is a binary tree, the encoder E takes the form $E : \mathbb{R}^n \times \mathbb{R}^n \to \mathbb{R}^n$. Given children c_1 and c_2 of a node p, the encoder assigns the representation $\vec{x}(p) = E(\vec{x}(c_1), \vec{x}(c_2))$. Applying this rule recursively defines vectors at every node of the tree.

The decoder and encoder may be trained together to minimize reconstruction error, typically Euclidean distance. Applied to a set of trees $\mathcal{T}$ with features already assigned at their terminal nodes, autoencoder training minimizes:

$$L_{ae} = \sum_{t \in \mathcal{T}} \sum_{p \in N(t)} \sum_{c_i \in C(p)} ||\vec{x}'(c_i) - \vec{x}(c_i)||, \qquad (1)$$

where $N(t)$ is the set of non-terminal nodes of tree

[1] https://www.mturk.com

Algorithm 1: Auto-encoders co-trained for subtree recognition by stochastic gradient descent

Data: $E : \mathbb{R}^n \times \mathbb{R}^n \to \mathbb{R}^n$ a neural network (encoder)
Data: $S : \mathbb{R}^n \times \mathbb{R}^n \to \mathbb{R}^2$ a neural network for binary classification (subtree or not)
Data: $D : \mathbb{R}^n \to \mathbb{R}^n \times \mathbb{R}^n$ a neural network (decoder)
Data: $\mathcal{T}$ a set of trees T with features $\vec{x}(t)$ assigned to terminal nodes $t \in T$
Result: Weights of E and D trained to minimize a combination of reconstruction and subtree recognition error

```
begin
  while stopping criterion not satisfied do
    Randomly choose T ∈ 𝒯
    for p in a postorder depth first traversal of T do
      if p is not terminal then
        Let c1, c2 be the children of p
        Compute x⃗(p) = E(x⃗(c1), x⃗(c2))
        Let (x⃗'(c1), x⃗'(c2)) = D(x⃗(p))
        Compute reconstruction loss L_R = ||x⃗'(c1) − x⃗(c1)||_2 + ||x⃗'(c2) − x⃗(c2)||_2
        Choose a random q ∈ T such that q is a descendant of p
        Let c1^q, c2^q be the children of q, if they exist
        Compute S(x⃗(p), x⃗(q)) = S(E(x⃗(c1), x⃗(c2)), E(x⃗(c1^q), x⃗(c2^q)))
        Compute cross-entropy loss L_1 = h(S(x⃗(p), x⃗(q)), 1)
        if p is not the root of T then
          Choose a random r ∈ T such that r is not a descendant of p
          Let c1^r, c2^r be the children of r, if they exist
          Compute cross-entropy loss L_2 = h(S(x⃗(p), x⃗(r)), 0)
        else
          Let L_2 = 0
        Compute gradients of L_R + L_1 + L_2 with respect to weights of E, D, and S, fixing x⃗(c1),
          x⃗(c2), x⃗(c1^q), x⃗(c2^q), x⃗(c1^r), and x⃗(c2^r).
        Update parameters of E, D, and S by backpropagation
```

t, $C(p) = c_1, c_2$ is the set of children of node p, and $(\vec{x}'(c_1), \vec{x}'(c_2)) = D(E(\vec{x}(c_1), \vec{x}(c_2)))$. This loss can be trained with stochastic gradient descent (Bottou, 2004).

However, there have been some perennial concerns about autoencoders:

1. Is information lost after repeated recursion?

2. Does low reconstruction error actually keep the information needed for classification?

Socher attempted to address the first of these concerns in his work on paraphrase with *deep unfolding recursive autoencoders* (Socher et al., 2011a), where each node is penalized for reconstruction errors many levels down an input tree, not just the reconstruction of its immediate descendants. Beyond five levels, Socher observed many word-choice errors on decoding input sentences. Socher's work on sentiment analysis (Socher et al., 2011b) focused on the second concern, by co-training on desired sentence classification, along with the usual reconstruction objective, at every level down to the terminal nodes. Of course, this had the side effect of imputing sentence-level sentiment labels to words where it was not really relevant.

As an alternative, we propose *subtree recognition* as a semi-supervised co-training task for any recurrent neural network on tree structures. This task can be defined just as generally as reconstruction error. While accepting that some information will be lost as we go up the tree, the co-training objective encourages the encoder to produce representations that can answer basic questions about the presence or absence of descendants far below.

Subtree recognition is a binary classification problem concerning two nodes x and y of a tree T; we train a neural network S to predict whether y is a descendant of x. The neural network S should produce two outputs, corresponding to log probabilities that the descendant relation is satisfied. In our experiments, we take S (as we do E and D) to have one hidden layer. We train the outputs $S(x, y) = (z_0, z_1)$ to minimize the cross-entropy function

$$h((z_0, z_1), j) = -\log\left(\frac{e^{z_j}}{e^{z_0} + e^{z_1}}\right) \text{ for } j = 0, 1. \quad (2)$$

so that z_0 and z_1 estimate log likelihoods that the descendant relation is satisfied.

Our algorithm for training the subtree classifier is presented in Algorithm 1. We use SENNA software (Collobert et al., 2011) to compute parse trees for sentences. Training on a corpus of 64,421 Wikipedia sentences and testing on 20,160, we achieve a test error rate of 3.2% on pairs of parse tree nodes that are subtrees, for 6.9% on pairs that are not subtrees ($F1 = .95$), with .02 mean squared reconstruction error.

5 Features for question and answer data

Application of the recursive neural network begins with features from the terminal nodes (the tokens). These features come from the language model of SENNA (Collobert et al., 2011), the Semantic Extraction Neural Network Architecture. Originally, neural probabilistic language models associated words with learned feature vectors so that a neural network could predict the joint probability function of word sequences (Bengio and Ducharme, 2001). SENNA's language model is co-trained on many syntactic tagging tasks, with a semi-supervised task in which valid sentences are to be ranked above sentences with random word replacements. Through the ranking and tagging tasks, this model learned embeddings of each word in a 50-dimensional space. Besides this learned representations, we encode capitalization and SENNA's predictions of named entity and part of speech tags with random vectors associated to each possible tag, as shown in Figure 1. The dimensionality of these vectors is chosen roughly as the logarithm of the number of possible tags. Thus every terminal node obtains a 61-dimensional feature vector.

We modify the basic RNN construction of Section 4 to obtain features for interior nodes. Since interior tree nodes are tagged with a node type, we encode the possible node types in a six-dimensional vector and make E and D work on triples (ParentType, Child 1, Child 2), instead of pairs (Child 1, Child 2).

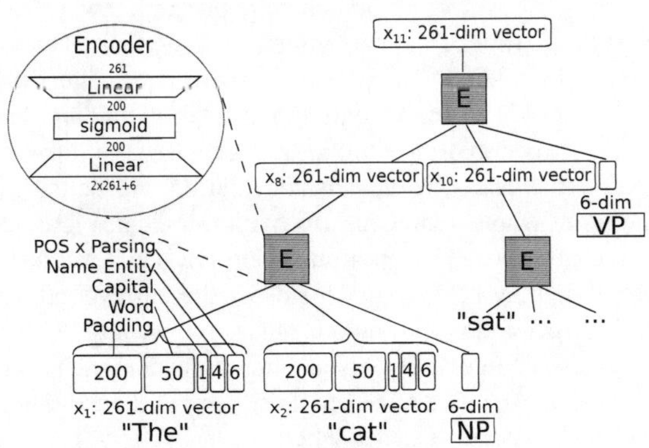

Figure 1: Recursive autoencoder to assign features to nodes of the parse tree of, "The cat sat on the mat." Note that the node types (e.g. "NP" or "VP") of internal nodes, and not just the children, are encoded.

Also, parse trees are not necessarily binary, so we binarize by right-factoring. Newly created internal nodes are labeled as "SPLIT" nodes. For example, a node with children c_1, c_2, c_3 is replaced by a new node with the same label, with left child c_1 and newly created right child, labeled "SPLIT," with children c_2 and c_3.

Vectors from terminal nodes are padded with 200 zeros before they are input to the autoencoder. We do this so that interior parse tree nodes have more room to encode the information about their children, as the original 61 dimensions may already be filled with information about just one word.

The feature construction is identical for the question and the support sentence.

5.1 Modeling unknown words

Many QA systems derive powerful features from exact word matches. In our approach, we trust that the classifier will be able to match information from autoencoder features of related parse tree branches, if it needs to. But our neural language probabilistic language model is at a great disadvantage if its features cannot characterize words outside its original training set.

Since Wikipedia is an encyclopedia, it is common for support sentences to introduce entities that do not appear in the dictionary of 100,000 most common words for which our language model has learned features. In the support sentence

> Jean-Bedel Georges Bokassa, Crown Prince of Central Africa was born on the 2nd November 1975 the son of Emperor Bokassa I of the Central African Empire and his wife Catherine Denguiade, who became Empress on Bokassa's accession to the throne.

both *Bokassa* and *Denguiade* are uncommon, and do not have learned language model embeddings. SENNA typically replaces these words with a fixed vector associated with all unknown words, and this works fine for syntactic tagging; the classifier learns to use the context around the unknown word. However, in a question-answering setting, we may need to read *Denguiade* from a question and be able to match it with *Denguiade*, not *Bokassa*, in the support.

Thus we extend the language model vectors with a random vector associated to each distinct word. The random vectors are fixed for all the words in the original language model, but a new one is generated the first time any unknown word is read. For known words, the original 50 dimensions give useful syntactic and semantic information. For unknown words, the newly introduced dimensions facilitate word matching without disrupting predictions based on the original 50.

6 Convolutions inside trees

We extract answers from support sentences by classifying each token as a word to be included in the answer or not. Essentially, this decision is a tagging problem on the support sentence, with additional features required from the question.

Convolutional neural networks efficiently classify sequential (or multi-dimensional) data, with the ability to reuse computations within a sliding frame tracking

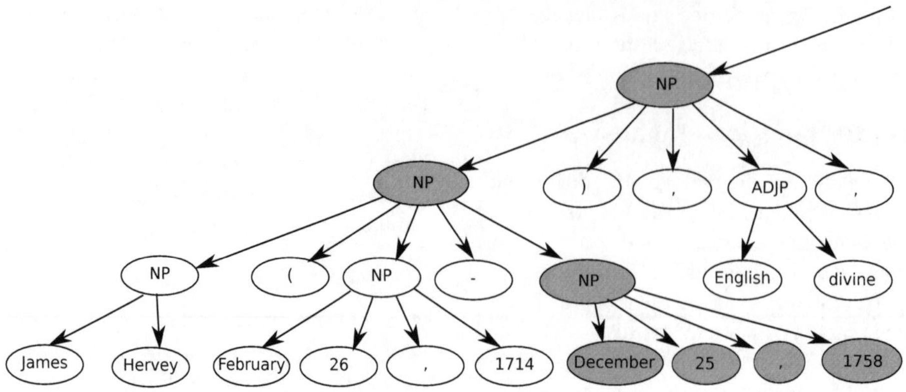

Figure 2: Labeling nodes to be followed to select "December 25, 1758."

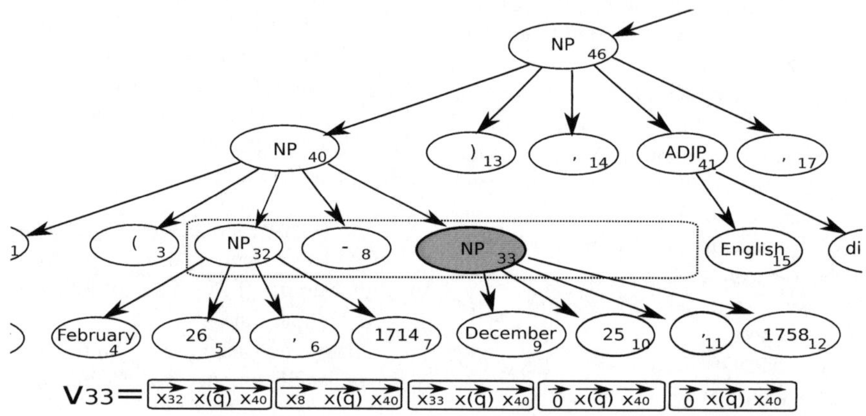

Figure 3: Assembling features from the question, the parent, and siblings, to decide whether to follow node 33

the item to be classified (Waibel et al., 1989). Convolving over token sequences has achieved state-of-the-art performance in part-of-speech tagging, named entity recognition, and chunking, and competitive performance in semantic role labeling and parsing, using one basic architecture (Collobert et al., 2011). Moreover, at classification time, the approach is 200 times faster at POS tagging than next-best systems such as (Shen et al., 2007) and 100 times faster at semantic role labeling (Koomen et al., 2005).

Classifying tokens to answer questions involves not only information from nearby tokens, but long range syntactic dependencies. In most work utilizing parse trees as input, a systematic description of the whole parse tree has not been used. Some state-of-the-art semantic role labeling systems require multiple parse trees (alternative candidates for parsing the same sentence) as input, but they measure many ad-hoc features describing path lengths, head words of prepositional phrases, clause-based path features, *etc.*, encoded in a sparse feature vector (Pradhan et al., 2005).

By using feature representations from our RNN and performing convolutions across siblings inside the tree, instead of token sequences in the text, we can utilize the parse tree information in a more principled way. We start at the root of the parse tree and select branches to follow, working down. At each step, the entire question is visible, via the representation at its root, and we decide whether or not to follow each branch of the support sentence. Ideally, irrelevant information will be cut at the point where syntactic information indicates it is no longer needed. The point at which we reach a terminal node may be too late to cut out the corresponding word; the context that indicates it is the wrong answer may have been visible only at a higher level in the parse tree. The classifier must cut words out earlier, though we do not specify exactly where.

Our classifier uses three pieces of information to decide whether to follow a node in the support sentence or not, given that its parent was followed:

1. The representation of the question at its root
2. The representation of the support sentence at the parent of the current node
3. The representations of the current node and a frame of k of its siblings on each side, in the order induced by the order of words in the sentence

Algorithm 2: Training the convolutional neural network for question answering

Data: Ξ, a set of triples (Q, S, T), with Q a parse tree of a question, S a parse tree of a support sentence, and $T \subset \mathcal{W}(S)$ a ground truth answer substring, and parse tree features $\vec{x}(p)$ attached by the recursive autoencoder for all $p \in Q$ or $p \in S$

Let $n = \dim \vec{x}(p)$

Let h be the cross-entropy loss (equation (2))

Data: $\Phi : (\mathbb{R}^{3n})^{2k+1} \to \mathbb{R}^2$ a convolutional neural network over frames of size $2k+1$, with parameters to be trained for question-answering

Result: Parameters of Φ trained

```
begin
  while stopping criterion not satisfied do
    Randomly choose (Q, S, T) ∈ Ξ
    Let q, r = root(Q), root(S)
    Let X = {r} (the set of nodes to follow)
    Let A(T) ⊂ S be the set of ancestor nodes of T in S
    while X ≠ ∅ do
      Pop an element p from X
      if p is not terminal then
        Let c_1, ..., c_m be the children of p
        Let x_j = x(c_j) for j ∈ {1, ..., m}
        Let x_j = 0 for j ∉ {1, ..., m}
        for i=1, ... m do
          Let t = 1 if c_i ∈ A(T), or 0 otherwise
          Let v_{c_i} = ⊕_{j=i-k}^{i+k} (x_j ⊕ x(p) ⊕ x(q))
          Compute the cross-entropy loss h(Φ(v_{c_i}), t)
          if exp(−h(Φ(v_{c_i}), 1)) > 1/2 then
            Let X = X ∪ {c_i} (the network predicts c_i should be followed)
          Update parameters of Φ by backpropagation
```

Each of these representations is n-dimensional. The convolutional neural network concatenates them together (denoted by $\oplus$) as a $3n$-dimensional feature at each node position, and considers a frame enclosing k siblings on each side of the current node. The CNN consists of a convolutional layer mapping the $3n$ inputs to an r-dimensional space, a sigmoid function (such as $\tanh$), a linear layer mapping the r-dimensional space to two outputs, and another sigmoid. We take $k = 2$ and $r = 30$ in the experiments.

Application of the CNN begins with the children of the root, and proceeds in breadth first order through the children of the followed nodes. Sliding the CNN's frame across siblings allows it to decide whether to follow adjacent siblings faster than a non-convolutional classifier, where the decisions would be computed without exploiting the overlapping features. A followed terminal node becomes part of the short answer of the system.

The training of the question-answering convolutional neural network is detailed in Algorithm 2. Only visited nodes, as predicted by the classifier, are used for training. For ground truth, we say that a node should be followed if it is the ancestor of some token that is part of the desired answer. For example, to select the death date "December 25, 1758" from the support sentence (displayed on page one) about James Hervey, nodes of the tree would be attached ground truth values according to the coloring in Figure 2. At classification time, some unnecessary (negatively labeled) nodes may be followed without mistaking the final answer.

For example, when deciding whether to follow the "NP" in node 33 on the third row of Figure 3, the classifier would see features of node 32 (NP) and node 8 ('-') on its left, its own features, and nothing on its right. Since there are no siblings to the right of node 33, zero vectors, used for padding, would be placed in the two empty slots. To each of these feature vectors, features from the parent and the question root would be concatenated.

The combination of recursive autoencoders with convolutions inside the tree affords flexibility and generality. The ordering of children would be immeasurable by a classifier relying on path-based features alone. For instance, our classifier may consider a branch of a parse tree as in Figure 2, in which the birth date and death date have isomorphic connections to the rest of the parse tree. It can distinguish them by the ordering of nodes in a parenthetical expression (see examples in Table 2).

System	Short Answer Precision	Short Answer Recall	Short Answer F1	MC Precision	MC Recall	MC F1
Main	58.9%	27.0%	.370	79.9%	38.8%	.523
No subtree recognition	48.9%	18.6%	.269	71.7%	27.8%	.400
No unknown word embeddings	66.8%	19.7%	.305	84.2%	29.0%	.431
Smaller training (1,333 questions)	40.6%	16.7%	.236	65.5%	20.4%	.311
OpenEphyra	52.2%	13.1%	.209	73.6%	32.0 %	.446

Table 1: Performance on TurkQA test set, for short answer and multiple choice (MC) evaluations.

7 Experiments

From the TurkQA data, we disregard the yes/no questions, and obtain 12,916 problem sets with 38,083 short answer questions for training, and 508 problem sets with 1,488 short answer questions for testing.

Because there may be several ways of stating a short answer, short answer questions in other data sets are typically judged by humans. In TurkQA, because answers must be extracted as substrings, we can approximate the machine's correctness by considering the token classification error against the substring originally chosen by the Turk worker. Of course, answer validation strategies could be used to clean up the short answers—for instance, require that they are contiguous substrings (as is guaranteed by the task)—but we did not employ them here, so as not to obfuscate the performance of the substring extraction system itself. Inevitably, some token misclassification will occur because question writers choose more or less complete answers ("in Nigeria" or just "Nigeria").

Table 6 shows the performance of our main algorithm, evaluated both as short-answer and as multiple choice. The short answer results describe the main setting, which formulates answer extraction as token classification. The multiple choice results come from considering all the short answers in the problem sets as alternative choices, and comparing the classifier's outputs averaged over the words in each response to select the best, or skip if no average is positive. (Thus, all questions in a single problem set have the same set of choices.) Although the multiple choice setting is less challenging, it helps us see how much of the short answer error may be due to finding poor answer boundaries as opposed to the classifier being totally misled. On more than half of the 1,488 test questions, no answer at all is selected, so that multiple choice precision remains high even with low recall.

As one baseline method, we took the OpenEphyra question answering system, an open source project led by Carnegie Mellon University, which evolved out of submissions to TREC question answering contests (Ko et al., 2007), bypassing its retrieval module to simply use our support sentence. In contrast to our system, OpenEphyra's question analysis module is trained to map questions to one of a fixed number of answer types, such as `PERCENTAGE`, or `PROPER_NAME.PERSON.FIRST_NAME`, and utilizes a large database of answer patterns for these types. In spite of OpenEphyra's laborious pattern coding, our system performs 17% better on a multiple choice basis, and 77% better on short answers, the latter likely because OpenEphyra's answer types cover shorter strings than the Turks' answers.

The results show the impact of several of our algorithmic contributions. If the autoencoder is trained only on reconstruction error and not subtree recognition, the F1 score for token classification drops from .370 (58.9% precision, 27.0% recall) to .269 (48.9% precision, 18.6% recall). Without extended embeddings to differentiate unknown words, F1 is only .305 (66.8% precision, 19.7% recall). We are encouraged that increasing the amount of data contributes 50% to the F1 score (from only F1=.236 training on 1,333 questions), as it suggests that the power of our algorithms is not saturated while picking up the simplest features.

Table 2 gives examples of questions in the test set, together with the classifier's selection from the support sentence.

8 Discussion

We have developed a recursive neural network architecture capable of using learned representations of words and syntax in a parse tree structure to answer free form questions about natural language text. Using meaning representations of the question and supporting sentences, our approach buys us freedom from explicit rules, question and answer types, and exact string matching.

Certainly retrieval is important in a full-fledged question answering system, whereas our classifier performs deep analysis after candidate supporting sentences have been identified. Also, multi-sentence documents would require information to be linked among coreferent entities. Despite these challenges, we present our system in the belief that strong QA technologies should begin with a mastery of the syntax of single sentences. A computer cannot be said to have a complete knowledge representation of a sentence until it can answer all the questions a human can ask about that sentence.

Question:	What is the name of the British charity based in Haringey in north London?
Support:	Based in Haringey in North London, Exposure is a British charity which enables children and young people from all backgrounds, including disadvantaged groups and those from areas of deprivation, to participate and achieve their fullest potential in the media.
Selection:	Exposure
Correct Answer:	Exposure
Question:	What was Robert Person's profession?
Support:	Robert Person was a professional baseball pitcher who played 9 seasons in Major League Baseball: two for the New York Mets, two and a half for the Toronto Blue Jays, three and a half for the Philadelphia Phillies, and only pitched 7 games for the Boston Red Sox in the last year of his career.
Selection:	baseball pitcher
Correct Answer:	baseball pitcher
Question:	How many seasons did Robert Person play in the Major League?
Support:	Robert Person was a professional baseball pitcher who played 9 seasons in Major League Baseball: two for the New York Mets, two and a half for the Toronto Blue Jays, three and a half for the Philadelphia Phillies, and only pitched 7 games for the Boston Red Sox in the last year of his career.
Selection:	9
Correct Answer:	9 seasons
Question:	What sea does Mukka have a shore on?
Support:	Mukka is suburb of Mangalore city on the shore of Arabian sea . It is located to north of NITK, Surathkal campus on National Highway 17 . There is a beach in Mukka which has escaped public attention.
Selection:	Arabian sea
Correct Answer:	Arabian sea
Question:	What genre was Lights Out?
Support:	Lights Out was an extremely popular American old-time radio program, an early example of a network series devoted mostly to horror and the supernatural, predating Suspense and Inner Sanctum.
Selection:	horror supernatural
Correct Answer:	horror and the supernatural
Question:	Where is the Arwa Group?
Support:	The Arwa Group is a set of three Himalayan peaks, named Arwa Tower, Arwa Crest, and Arwa Spire, situated in the Chamoli district of Uttarakhand state, in northern India.
Selection:	the Chamoli district Uttarakhand state northern India
Correct Answer:	the Chamoli district of Uttarakhand state
Question:	What year did Juan Bautista Segura die in?
Support:	Juan Bautista Quiros Segura (1853 - 1934) was president of Costa Rica for two weeks, from August 20 to September 2, 1919, following the resignation of Federico Tinoco.
Selection:	1934
Correct Answer:	1934
Question:	What state is the Oregon School Activities Association in?
Support:	The Oregon School Activities Association, or OSAA, is a non-profit, board-governed organization that regulates high school athletics and competitive activities in Oregon, providing equitable competition amongst its members, both public and private.
Selection:	OSAA
Correct Answer:	Oregon

Table 2: Example results of main classifier on TurkQA test set.

References

Y. Bengio and R. Ducharme. 2001. A neural probabilistic language model. In *Advances in NIPS*, volume 13.

L. Bottou. 2004. Stochastic learning. In O. Bousquet and U. von Luxburg, editors, *Advanced Lectures on Machine Learning*, Lecture Notes in Artificial Intelligence, LNAI 3176, pages 146–168. Springer.

S. Brin. 1998. Extracting patterns and relations from the World Wide Web. In *Proceedings World Wide Web and Databases International Workshop (LNCS 1590)*, pages 172–183. Springer.

R. Collobert, J. Weston, L. Bottou, M. Karlen, K. Kavukcuoglu, and P. Kuksa. 2011. Natural language processing (almost) from scratch. *Journal of Machine Learning Research*, 12:2493–2537.

H. T. Dang, D. Kelly, and J. Lin. 2008. Overview of the TREC 2007 question answering track. In *NIST Special Pub. 500-274: The Sixteenth Text Retrieval Conference (TREC 2007)*.

P. Forner, A. Penas, E. Agirre, I. Alegria, C. Forascu, N. Moreau, P. Osenova, P. Prokopidis, P. Rocha, B. Sacaleanu, R. Sutcliffe, and E. T. K. Sang. 2008. Overview of the Clef 2008 Multilingual Question Answering Track. In *CLEF*.

J. Ko, E. Nyberg, and L. Luo Si. 2007. A probabilistic graphical model for joint answer ranking in question answering. In *Proceedings of the 30th ACM SIGIR Conference*.

P. Koomen, V. Punyakanok, D. Roth, and W. Yih. 2005. Generalized inference with multiple semantic role labeling systems. In *Proceedings of CoNLL*.

P. Liang, M. I. Jordan, and D. Klein. 2011. Learning dependency-based compositional semantics. In *ACL*.

M. Mintz, S. Bills, R. Snow, and D. Jurafsky. 2009. Distant supervision for relation extraction without labeled data. In *Proceedings of ACL-IJCNLP*, pages 1003–1011.

J. B. Pollack. 1990. Recursive distributed representations. *Artficial Intelligence*, 46.

H. Poon and P. Domingos. 2009. Unsupervised semantic parsing. In *Proceedings of ACL*.

S. Pradhan, K. Hacioglu, W. Ward, J. H. Martin, and D. Jurafsky. 2005. Semantic role chunking combining complementary syntactic views. In *Conference on Computational Natural Language Learning (CoNLL)*, pages 217–220.

S. Riedel, L. Yao, and A. McCallum. 2010. Modeling relations and their mentions without labeled text. In *Proceedings of ECML-PKDD*.

R. Schmidt. 2013. The fan-created archive of Jeopardy! games and players. `http://www.j-archive.com`. Accessed: April 26, 2013.

L. Shen, G. Satta, and A. K. Joshi. 2007. Guided learning for bidirectional sequence classification. In *Proceedings of ACL*.

R. Socher, E. H. Huang, J. Pennington, A. Y. Ng, and C. D. Manning. 2011a. Dynamic pooling and unfolding recursive autoencoders for paraphrase detection. In *Advances in NIPS*.

R. Socher, J. Pennington, E. Huang, A. Y. Ng, and C. D. Manning. 2011b. Semi-supervised recursive autoencoders for predicting sentiment distributions. In *Proceedings of EMNLP*.

E. M. Voorhees. 2000. Overview of the TREC-9 Question Answering track. In *NIST Special Pub. 500-249: The Ninth Text Retrieval Conference (TREC 9)*, pages 71–79.

A. Waibel, T. Hanazawa, G. Hinton, K. Shikano, and K. J. Lang. 1989. Phoneme recognition using time-delay neural networks. *IEEE Trans. Acoustics, Speech, and Signal Processing*, 37(3):328–339.

Recurrent Convolutional Neural Networks for Discourse Compositionality

Nal Kalchbrenner
Department of Computer Science
Oxford University
nkalch@cs.ox.ac.uk

Phil Blunsom
Department of Computer Science
Oxford University
pblunsom@cs.ox.ac.uk

Abstract

The compositionality of meaning extends beyond the single sentence. Just as words combine to form the meaning of sentences, so do sentences combine to form the meaning of paragraphs, dialogues and general discourse. We introduce both a sentence model and a discourse model corresponding to the two levels of compositionality. The sentence model adopts convolution as the central operation for composing semantic vectors and is based on a novel hierarchical convolutional neural network. The discourse model extends the sentence model and is based on a recurrent neural network that is conditioned in a novel way both on the current sentence and on the current speaker. The discourse model is able to capture both the sequentiality of sentences and the interaction between different speakers. Without feature engineering or pretraining and with simple greedy decoding, the discourse model coupled to the sentence model obtains state of the art performance on a dialogue act classification experiment.

1 Introduction

There are at least two levels at which the meaning of smaller linguistic units is composed to form the meaning of larger linguistic units. The first level is that of sentential compositionality, where the meaning of words composes to form the meaning of the sentence or utterance that contains them (Frege, 1892). The second level extends beyond the first and involves general discourse compositionality, where the meaning of multiple sentences or utterances composes to form the meaning of the paragraph, document or dialogue that comprises them (Korta and Perry, 2012; Potts, 2011). The problem of discourse compositionality is the problem of modelling how the meaning of general discourse composes from the meaning of the sentences involved and, since the latter in turn stems from the meaning of the words, how the meaning of discourse composes from the words themselves.

Tackling the problem of discourse compositionality promises to be central to a number of different applications. These include sentiment or topic classification of single sentences within the context of a longer discourse, the recognition of dialogue acts within a conversation, the classification of a discourse as a whole and the attainment of general unsupervised or semi-supervised representations of a discourse for potential use in dialogue tracking and question answering systems and machine translation, among others.

To this end much work has been done on modelling the meaning of single words by way of semantic vectors (Turney and Pantel, 2010; Collobert and Weston, 2008) and the latter have found applicability in areas such as information retrieval (Jones et al., 2006). With regard to modelling the meaning of sentences and sentential compositionality, recent proposals have included simple additive and multiplicative models that do not take into account sentential features such as word order or syntactic structure (Mitchell and Lapata, 2010), matrix-vector based models that do take into account such features but are limited to phrases of a specific syntactic type (Baroni and Zamparelli, 2010) and structured models that fully capture such features (Grefenstette et al., 2011) and are embedded within a deep neural architecture (Socher et al., 2012; Hermann and Blunsom, 2013). It is notable that the additive and multiplicative models as well as simple, non-compositional bag of n-grams and word vector averaging models have equalled or outperformed the structured models at certain phrase similarity (Blacoe and Lapata, 2012) and sentiment classification tasks (Scheible and Schütze, 2013; Wang and Manning, 2012).

With regard to discourse compositionality, most of the proposals aimed at capturing semantic aspects of paragraphs or longer texts have focused on bag of n-grams or sentence vector averaging approaches (Wang and Manning, 2012; Socher et al., 2012). In addition, the recognition of dialogue acts within dialogues has largely been treated in non-compositional ways by way of language models coupled to hidden Markov sequence models (Stolcke et al., 2000). Principled approaches to discourse compositionality have largely been unexplored.

We introduce a novel model for sentential compositionality. The composition operation is based on a hierarchy of one dimensional convolutions. The convolutions are applied feature-wise, that is they are applied across each feature of the word vectors in the sentence. The weights adopted in each convolution are different for each feature, but do not depend on the different words being composed. The hierarchy of convolution operations involves a sequence of convolution kernels of increasing sizes (Fig. 1). This allows for the composition operation to be applied to sentences of any length, while keeping the model at a depth of roughly $\sqrt{2l}$ where l is the length of the sentence. The hierarchy of feature-wise convolution operations followed by sigmoid non-linear activation functions results in a hierarchical convolutional neural network (HCNN) based on a convolutional architecture (LeCun et al., 2001). The HCNN shares with the structured models the aspect that it is sensitive to word order and adopts a hierarchical architecture, although it is not based on explicit syntactic structure.

We also introduce a novel model for discourse compositionality. The discourse model is based on a recurrent neural network (RNN) architecture that is a powerful model for sequences (Sutskever et al., 2011; Mikolov et al., 2010). The model aims at capturing two central aspects of discourse and its meaning: the sequentiality of the sentences or utterances in the discourse and, where applicable, the interactions between the different speakers. The underlying RNN has its recurrent and output weights conditioned on the respective speaker, while simultaneously taking as input at every turn the sentence vector for the current sentence generated through the sentence model (Fig. 2).

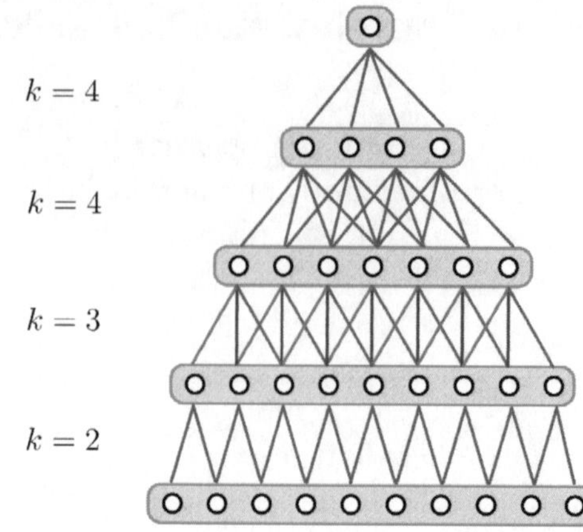

Figure 1: A hierarchical convolutional neural network for sentential compositionality. The bottom layer represents a single feature across all the word vectors in the sentence. The top layer is the value for that feature in the resulting sentence vector. Lines represent single weights and color coded lines indicate sharing of weights. The parameter k indicates the size of the convolution kernel at the corresponding layer.

We experiment with the discourse model coupled to the sentence model on the task of recognizing dialogue acts of utterances within a conversation. The dataset is given by 1134 transcribed and annotated telephone conversations amounting to about 200K utterances from the Switchboard Dialogue Act Corpus (Calhoun et al., 2010).[1] The model is trained in a supervised setting without previous pretraining; word vectors are also randomly initialised. The model learns a probability distribution over the dialogue acts at step i given the sequence of utterances up to step i, the sequence of acts up to the previous step $i-1$ and the binary sequence of agents up to the current step i. Predicting the sequence of dialogue acts is performed in a greedy fashion.[2]

We proceed as follows. In Sect. 2 we give the motivation and the definition for the HCNN sentence model. In Sect. 3 we do the same for the RCNN discourse model. In Sect. 4 we describe the dialogue act classification experiment and the training procedure. We also inspect the discourse vector representations produced by the model. We conclude in Sect. 5.

[1]The dataset is available at `compprag.christopherpotts.net/swda.html`

[2]Code and trained model available at `nal.co`

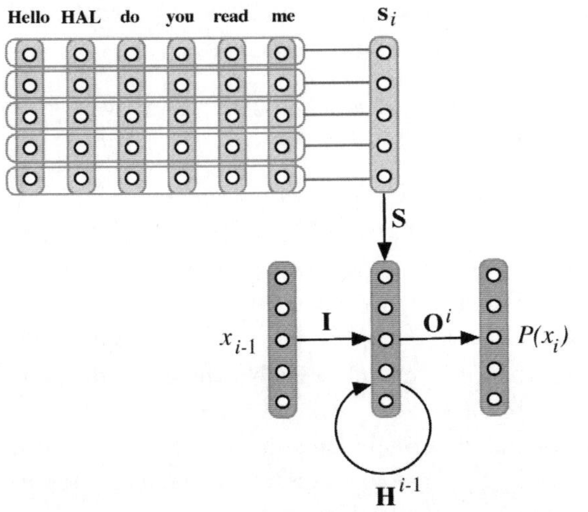

Figure 2: Recurrent convolutional neural network (RCNN) discourse model based on a RNN architecture. At each step the RCNN takes as input the current sentence vector $\mathbf{s}_i$ generated through the HCNN sentence model and the previous label x_{i-1} to predict a probability distribution over the current label $P(x_i)$. The recurrent weights $\mathbf{H}^{i-1}$ are conditioned on the previous agent a_{i-1} and the output weights are conditioned on the current agent a_i. Note also the sentence matrix $\mathbf{M}_s$ of the sentence model and the hierarchy of convolutions applied to each feature that is a row in $\mathbf{M}_s$ to produce the corresponding feature in $\mathbf{s}_i$.

2 Sentence Model

The general aim of the sentence model is to compute a vector for a sentence s given the sequence of words in s and a vector for each of the words. The computation captures certain general considerations regarding sentential compositionality. We first relate such considerations and we then proceed to give a definition of the model.

2.1 Sentential compositionality

There are three main aspects of sentential compositionality that the model aims at capturing. To relate these, it is useful to note the following basic property of the model: a sentence s is paired to the matrix $\mathbf{M}^s$ whose columns are given sequentially by the vectors of the words in s. A row in $\mathbf{M}^s$ corresponds to the values of the corresponding feature across all the word vectors. The first layer of the network in Fig. 1 represents one such row of $\mathbf{M}^s$, whereas the whole matrix $\mathbf{M}^s$ is depicted in Fig. 2. The three considerations are as follows.

First, at the initial stage of the composition, the value of a feature in the sentence vector is a function of the values of the same feature in the word vectors. That is, the m-th value in the sentence vector of s is a function of the m-th row of $\mathbf{M}^s$. This aspect is preserved in the additive and multiplicative models where the composition operations are, respectively, addition $+$ and component-wise multiplication $\odot$. The current model preserves the aspect up to the computation of the sentence vector $\mathbf{s}$ by adopting one-dimensional, feature-wise convolution operations. Subsequently, the discourse model that uses the sentence vector $\mathbf{s}$ includes transformations across the features of $\mathbf{s}$ (the transformation $\mathbf{S}$ in Fig. 2).

The second consideration concerns the hierarchical aspect of the composition operation. We take the compositionality of meaning to initially yield local effects across neighbouring words and then yield increasingly more global effects across all the words in the sentence. Composition operations like those in the structured models that are guided by the syntactic parse tree of the sentence capture this trait. The sentence model preserves this aspect not by way of syntactic structure, but by adopting convolution kernels of gradually increasing sizes that span an increasing number of words and ultimately the entire sentence.

The third aspect concerns the dependence of the composition operation. The operation is taken to depend on the different features, but not on the different words. Word specific parameters are introduced only by way of the learnt word vectors, but no word specific operations are learnt. We achieve this by using a single convolution kernel across a feature, and by utilizing different convolution kernels for different features. Given these three aspects of sentential compositionality, we now proceed to describe the sentence model in detail.

2.2 Hierarchical Convolutional Neural Network

The sentence model is taken to be a CNN where the convolution operation is applied one dimensionally across a single feature and in a hierarchical manner. To describe it in more detail, we first recall the convolution operation that is central to the model. Then we describe how we compute the sequence of kernel sizes and how we determine the hierarchy of layers in the network.

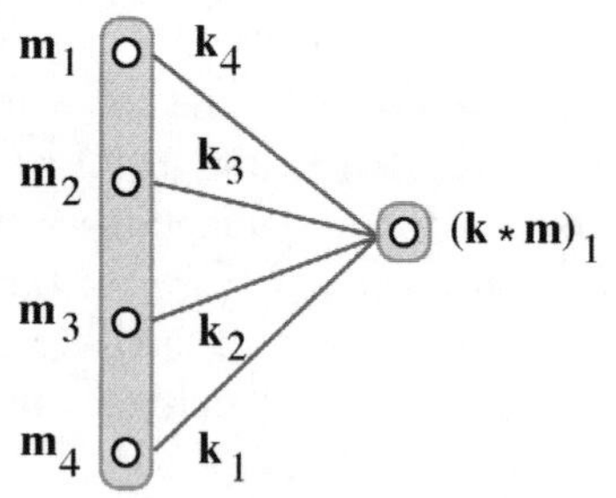

Figure 3: Convolution of a vector $\mathbf{m}$ with a kernel $\mathbf{k}$ of size 4.

2.2.1 Kernel and One-dimensional Convolution

Given a sentence s and its paired matrix $\mathbf{M}^s$, let $\mathbf{m}$ be a feature that is a row in $\mathbf{M}^s$. Before defining kernels and the convolution operation, let us consider the underlying operation of *local weighted addition*. Let $w_1, ..., w_k$ be a sequence of k weights; given the feature $\mathbf{m}$, local weighted addition over the *first* k values of $\mathbf{m}$ gives:

$$y = w_1\mathbf{m}_1 + ... + w_k\mathbf{m}_k \tag{1}$$

Then, a kernel simply defines the value of k by specifying the sequence of weights $w_1, ..., w_k$ and the one-dimensional convolution applies local weighted addition with the k weights to each subsequence of values of $\mathbf{m}$.

More precisely, let a one-dimensional *kernel* $\mathbf{k}$ be a vector of weights and assume $|\mathbf{k}| \leq |\mathbf{m}|$, where $|\cdot|$ is the number of elements in a vector. Then we define the discrete, valid, *one-dimensional convolution* $(\mathbf{k} * \mathbf{m})$ of kernel $\mathbf{k}$ and feature $\mathbf{m}$ by:

$$(\mathbf{k} * \mathbf{m})_i := \sum_{j=1}^{k} \mathbf{k}_j \cdot \mathbf{m}_{k+i-j} \tag{2}$$

where $k = |\mathbf{k}|$ and $|\mathbf{k} * \mathbf{m}| = |\mathbf{m}| - k + 1$. Each value in $\mathbf{k} * \mathbf{m}$ is a sum of k values of $\mathbf{m}$ weighted by values in $\mathbf{k}$ (Fig. 3). To define the hierarchical architecture of the model, we need to define a sequence of kernel sizes and associated weights. To this we turn next.

2.2.2 Sequence of Kernel Sizes

Let l be the number of words in the sentence s. The sequence of kernel sizes $\langle k_i^l \rangle_{i \leq t}$ depends only on the length of s and itself has length $t = \lceil \sqrt{2l} \rceil - 1$. It is given recursively by:

$$k_1^l = 2, \quad k_{i+1}^l = k_i^l + 1, \quad k_t^l = l - \sum_{j=1}^{t-1}(k_j^l - 1) \tag{3}$$

That is, kernel sizes increase by one until the resulting convolved vector is smaller or equal to the last kernel size; see for example the kernel sizes in Fig. 1. Note that, for a sentence of length l, the number of layers in the HCNN including the input layer will be $t + 1$ as convolution with the corresponding kernel is applied at every layer of the model. Let us now proceed to define the hierarchy of layers in the HCNN.

2.2.3 Composition Operation in a HCNN

Given a sentence s, its length l and a sequence of kernel sizes $\langle k_i^l \rangle_{i \leq t}$, we may now give the recursive definition that yields the hierarchy of one-dimensional convolution operations applied to each feature f that is a row in $\mathbf{M}^s$. Specifically, for each feature f, let $\mathbf{K}_i^f$ be a sequence of t kernels, where the size of the kernel $|\mathbf{K}_i^f| = k_i^l$. Then we have the hierarchy of matrices and corresponding features as follows:

$$\mathbf{M}^1_{f,:} = \mathbf{M}^s_{f,:} \tag{4}$$

$$\mathbf{M}^{i+1}_{f,:} = \sigma(\, \mathbf{K}_i^f * \mathbf{M}^i_{f,:} + b_f^i \,) \tag{5}$$

for some non-linear sigmoid function σ and bias b_f^i, where i ranges over $1, ..., t$. In sum, one-dimensional convolution is applied feature-wise to each feature of a matrix at a certain layer, where the kernel weights depend both on the layer and the feature at hand (Fig. 1). A hierarchy of matrices is thus generated with the top matrix being a single vector for the sentence.

2.2.4 Multiple merged HCNNs

Optionally one may consider multiple parallel HCNNs that are merged according to different strategies either at the top sentence vector layer or at intermediate layers. The weights in the word vectors may be tied across different HCNNs. Although potentially useful, multiple merged HCNNs are not used in the experiment below.

This concludes the description of the sentence model. Let us now proceed to the discourse model.

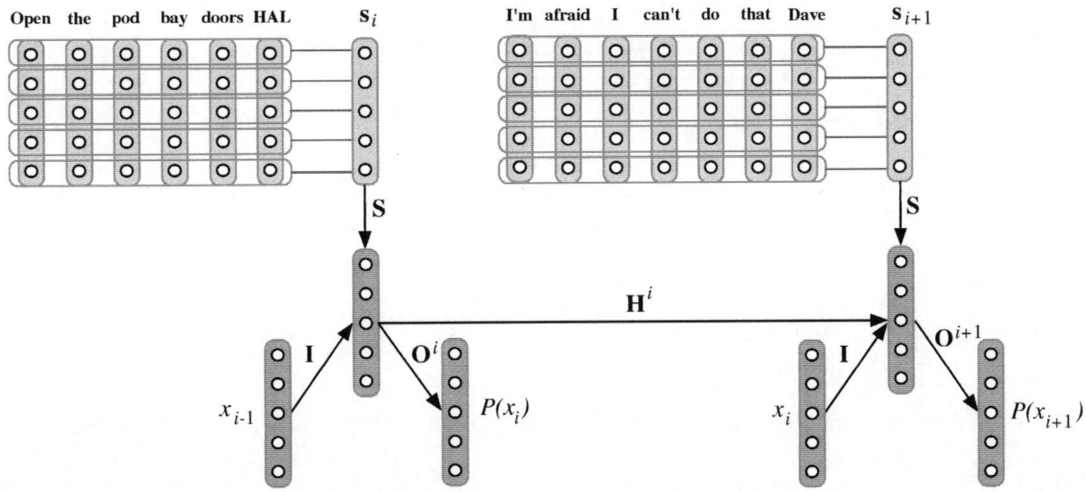

Figure 4: Unravelling of a RCNN discourse model to depth $d = 2$. The recurrent $\mathbf{H}^i$ and output $\mathbf{O}^i$ weights are conditioned on the respective agents a_i.

3 Discourse Model

The discourse model adapts a RNN architecture in order to capture central properties of discourse. We here first describe such properties and then define the model itself.

3.1 Discourse Compositionality

The meaning of discourse - and of words and utterances within it - is often a result of a rich ensemble of context, of speakers' intentions and actions and of other relevant surrounding circumstances (Korta and Perry, 2012, Potts, 2011). Far from capturing all aspects of discourse meaning, we aim at capturing in the model at least two of the most prominent ones: the sequentiality of the utterances and the interactions between the speakers.

Concerning sequentiality, just the way the meaning of a sentence generally changes if words in it are permuted, so does the meaning of a paragraph or dialogue change if one permutes the sentences or utterances within. The change of meaning is more marked the larger the shift in the order of the sentences. Especially in tasks where one is concerned with a specific sentence within the context of the previous discourse, capturing the order of the sentences preceding the one at hand may be particularly crucial.

Concerning the speakers' interactions, the meaning of a speaker's utterance within a discourse is differentially affected by the speaker's previous utterances as opposed to *other* speakers' previous utterances. Where applicable we aim at making the computed meaning vectors reflect the current speaker and the sequence of interactions with the previous speakers. With these two aims in mind, let us now proceed to define the model.

3.2 Recurrent Convolutional Neural Network

The discourse model coupled to the sentence model is based on a RNN architecture with inputs from a HCNN and with the recurrent and output weights conditioned on the respective speakers.

We take as given a sequence of sentences or utterances $s_1, ..., s_T$, each in turn being a sequence of words $s_i = y_1^i ... y_l^i$, a sequence of labels $x_1, ..., x_T$ and a sequence of speakers or agents $a_1, ..., a_T$, in such way that the i-th utterance is performed by the i-th agent and has label x_i. We denote by $\mathbf{s}_i$ the sentence vector computed by way of the sentence model for the sentence s_i. The RCNN computes probability distributions p_i for the label at step i by iterating the following equations:

$$\mathbf{h}_i = \sigma(\mathbf{I}x_{i-1} + \mathbf{H}^{i-1}\mathbf{h}_{i-1} + \mathbf{S}\mathbf{s}_i + b_h) \quad (6)$$

$$p_i = softmax(\mathbf{O}^i\mathbf{h}_i + b_o) \quad (7)$$

where $\mathbf{I}, \mathbf{H}^i, \mathbf{O}^i$ are corresponding weight matrices for each agent a_i and $softmax(y)_k = \frac{e^{y_k}}{\sum_j e^{y_j}}$ returns a probability distribution. Thus p_i is taken to model the following predictive distribution:

$$p_i = P(x_i | x_{<i}, s_{\leq i}, a_{\leq i}) \quad (8)$$

Dialogue Act Label	Example	Train (%)	Test (%)
Statement	*And, uh, it's a legal firm office.*	36.9	31.5
Backchannel/Acknowledge	*Yeah, anything could happen.*	18.8	18.2
Opinion	*I think that would be great.*	12.7	17.1
Abandoned/Uninterpretable	*So, -*	7.6	8.6
Agreement/Accept	*Yes, exactly.*	5.5	5.0
Appreciation	*Wow.*	2.3	2.2
Yes−No−Question	*Is that what you do?*	2.3	2.0
Non−Verbal	*[Laughter], [Throat-clearing]*	1.7	1.9
Other labels (34)		12.2	13.5
Total number of utterances		196258	4186
Total number of dialogues		1115	19

Table 1: Most frequent dialogue act labels with examples and frequencies in train and test data.

An RCNN and the unravelling to depth $d = 2$ are depicted respectively in Fig. 2 and Fig. 4. With regards to vector representations of discourse, we take the hidden layer $\mathbf{h}_i$ as the vector representing the discourse up to step i. This concludes the description of the discourse model. Let us now consider the experiment.

4 Predicting Dialogue Acts

We experiment with the prediction of dialogue acts within a conversation. A dialogue act specifies the pragmatic role of an utterance and helps identifying the speaker's intentions (Austin, 1962; Korta and Perry, 2012). The automated recognition of dialogue acts is crucial for dialogue state tracking within spoken dialogue systems (Williams, 2012). We first describe the Switchboard Dialogue Act (SwDA) corpus (Calhoun et al., 2010) that serves as the dataset in the experiment. We report on the training procedure and the results and we make some qualitative observations regarding the discourse representations produced by the model.

4.1 SwDA Corpus

The SwDA corpus contains audio recordings and transcripts of telephone conversations between multiple speakers that do not know each other and are given a topic for discussion. For a given utterance we use the transcript of the utterance, the dialogue act label and the speaker's label; no other annotations are used in the model. Overall there are 42 distinct dialogue act labels such as Statement and Opinion (Tab.1). We adopt the same data split of 1115 train dialogues and 19 test dialogues as used in (Stolcke et al., 2000).

4.2 Objective Function and Training

We minimise the cross-entropy error of the predicted and the true distributions and include an l_2 regularisation parameter. The RCNN is truncated to a depth $d = 2$ so that the prediction of a dialogue act depends on the previous two utterances, speakers and dialogue acts; adopting depths > 2 has not yielded improvements in the experiment. The derivatives are efficiently computed by back-propagation (Rumelhart et al., 1986). The word vectors are initialised to random vectors of length 25 and no pretraining procedure is performed. We minimise the objective using L-BFGS in mini-batch mode; the minimisation converges smoothly.

4.3 Prediction Method and Results

The prediction of a dialogue act is performed in a greedy fashion. Given the two previously predicted acts $\hat{x}_{i-1}, \hat{x}_{i-2}$, one chooses the act $\hat{x}_i$ that has the maximal probability in the predicted distribution $P(x_i)$. The LM-HMM model of (Stolcke et al., 2000) learns a language model for each dialogue act and a Hidden Markov Model for the sequence of dialogue acts and it requires all the utterances in a dialogue in order to predict the dialogue act of any one of the utterances. The RCNN makes the weaker assumption that only the utterances up to utterance i are available to predict the dialogue act $\hat{x}_i$. The accuracy results of the models are compared in Tab. 3.

4.4 Discourse Vector Representations

We inspect the discourse vector representations that the model generates. After a dialogue is processed, the hidden layer $\mathbf{h}$ of the RCNN is taken

Center Dialogue	A: *Do you repair your own car?* B: *I try to, whenever I can.*	A: *– I guess we can start.* B: *Okay.*	A: *Did you use to live around here?* B: *Uh, Redwood City.*
First NN	A: *Do you do it every day?* B: *I try to every day.*	A: *I think for serial murder –* B: *Uh-huh.*	A: *Can you stand up in it?* B: *Uh, in parts.*
Second NN	A: *Well, do you have any children?* B: *I've got one.*	A: *The USSR – wouldn't do it* B: *Uh-huh.*	A: *[Laughter] Do you have any kids that you take fishing?* B: *Uh, got a stepdaughter.*
Third NN	A: *Do you manage the money?* B: *Well, I, we talk about it.*	A: *It seems to me there needs to be some ground, you know, some rules –* B: *Uh-huh.*	A: *Is our five minutes up?* B: *Uh, pretty close to it.*
Fourth NN	A: *Um, do you watch it every Sunday?* B: *[Breathing] Uh, when I can.*	A: *It sounds to me like, uh, you are doing well.* B: *My husband's retired.*	A: *Do you usually go out, uh, with the children or without them?* B: *Well, a variety.*

Table 2: Short dialogues and nearest neighbours (NN).

	Accuracy (%)
RCNN	**73.9**
LM-HMM trigram	71.0
LM-HMM bigram	70.6
LM-HMM unigram	68.2
Majority baseline	31.5
Random baseline	2.4

Table 3: SwDA dialogue act tagging accuracies. The LM-HMM results are from (Stolcke et al., 2000). Inter-annotator agreement and theoretical maximum is 84%.

to be the vector representation for the dialogue (Sect. 3.2). Table 2 includes three randomly chosen dialogues composed of two utterances each; for each dialogue the table reports the four nearest neighbours. As the word vectors and weights are initialised randomly without pretraining, the word vectors and the weights are induced during training only through the dialogue act labels attached to the utterances. The distance between two word, sentence or discourse vectors reflects a notion of pragmatic similarity: two words, sentences or discourses are similar if they contribute in a similar way to the pragmatic role of the utterance signalled by the associated dialogue act. This is suggested by the examples in Tab. 2, where a centre dialogue and a nearest neighbour may have some semantically different components (e.g. "repair your own car" and "manage the money"), but be pragmatically similar and the latter similarity is captured by the representations. In the examples, the meaning of the relevant words in the utterances, the speakers' interactions and the sequence of pragmatic roles are well preserved across the nearest neighbours.

5 Conclusion

Motivated by the compositionality of meaning both in sentences and in general discourse, we have introduced a sentence model based on a novel convolutional architecture and a discourse model based on a novel use of recurrent networks. We have shown that the discourse model together with the sentence model achieves state of the art results in a dialogue act classification experiment without feature engineering or pretraining and with simple greedy decoding of the output sequence. We have also seen that the discourse model produces compelling discourse vector representations that are sensitive to the structure of the discourse and promise to capture subtle aspects of discourse comprehension, especially when coupled to further semantic data and unsupervised pretraining.

Acknowledgments

We thank Ed Grefenstette and Karl Moritz Hermann for great conversations on the matter. The authors gratefully acknowledge the support of the Clarendon Fund and the EPSRC.

References

[Austin1962] John L. Austin. 1962. How to do things with words. *Oxford: Clarendon.*

[Baroni and Zamparelli2010] Marco Baroni and Roberto Zamparelli. 2010. Nouns are vectors, adjectives are matrices: Representing adjective-noun constructions in semantic space. In *EMNLP*, pages 1183–1193.

[Blacoe and Lapata2012] William Blacoe and Mirella Lapata. 2012. A comparison of vector-based representations for semantic composition. In *EMNLP-CoNLL*, pages 546–556.

[Calhoun et al.2010] Sasha Calhoun, Jean Carletta, Jason M. Brenier, Neil Mayo, Dan Jurafsky, Mark Steedman, and David Beaver. 2010. The nxt-format switchboard corpus: a rich resource for investigating the syntax, semantics, pragmatics and prosody of dialogue. *Language Resources and Evaluation*, 44(4):387–419.

[Collobert and Weston2008] R. Collobert and J. Weston. 2008. A unified architecture for natural language processing: Deep neural networks with multitask learning. In *International Conference on Machine Learning, ICML*.

[Frege1892] Gottlob Frege. 1892. Über Sinn und Bedeutung. *Zeitschrift für Philosophie und philosophische Kritik*, 100.

[Grefenstette et al.2011] Edward Grefenstette, Mehrnoosh Sadrzadeh, Stephen Clark, Bob Coecke, and Stephen Pulman. 2011. Concrete sentence spaces for compositional distributional models of meaning. *CoRR*, abs/1101.0309.

[Hermann and Blunsom2013] Karl Moritz Hermann and Phil Blunsom. 2013. The Role of Syntax in Vector Space Models of Compositional Semantics. In *Proceedings of the 51st Annual Meeting of the Association for Computational Linguistics (Volume 1: Long Papers)*, Sofia, Bulgaria, August. Association for Computational Linguistics. Forthcoming.

[Jones et al.2006] Rosie Jones, Benjamin Rey, Omid Madani, and Wiley Greiner. 2006. Generating query substitutions. In *WWW*, pages 387–396.

[Korta and Perry2012] Kepa Korta and John Perry. 2012. Pragmatics. In Edward N. Zalta, editor, *The Stanford Encyclopedia of Philosophy*. Winter 2012 edition.

[LeCun et al.2001] Y. LeCun, L. Bottou, Y. Bengio, and P. Haffner. 2001. Gradient-based learning applied to document recognition. In *Intelligent Signal Processing*, pages 306–351. IEEE Press.

[Mikolov et al.2010] Tomas Mikolov, Martin Karafiát, Lukas Burget, Jan Cernocký, and Sanjeev Khudanpur. 2010. Recurrent neural network based language model. In *INTERSPEECH*, pages 1045–1048.

[Mitchell and Lapata2010] Jeff Mitchell and Mirella Lapata. 2010. Composition in distributional models of semantics. *Cognitive Science*, 34(8):1388–1429.

[Potts2011] Christopher Potts. 2011. Pragmatics. In Ruslan Mitkov, editor, *The Oxford Handbook of Computational Linguistics*. Oxford University Press, 2 edition.

[Rumelhart et al.1986] D. E. Rumelhart, G. E. Hinton, and R. J. Williams. 1986. Learning internal representations by error propagation. *MIT Press Computational Models Of Cognition And Perception Series*, page 318362.

[Scheible and Schütze2013] Christian Scheible and Hinrich Schütze. 2013. Cutting recursive autoencoder trees. *CoRR*, abs/1301.2811.

[Socher et al.2012] Richard Socher, Brody Huval, Christopher D. Manning, and Andrew Y. Ng. 2012. Semantic Compositionality Through Recursive Matrix-Vector Spaces. In *Proceedings of the 2012 Conference on Empirical Methods in Natural Language Processing (EMNLP)*.

[Stolcke et al.2000] Andreas Stolcke, Klaus Ries, Noah Coccaro, Elizabeth Shriberg, Rebecca A. Bates, Daniel Jurafsky, Paul Taylor, Rachel Martin, Carol Van Ess-Dykema, and Marie Meteer. 2000. Dialog act modeling for automatic tagging and recognition of conversational speech. *Computational Linguistics*, 26(3):339–373.

[Sutskever et al.2011] Ilya Sutskever, James Martens, and Geoffrey E. Hinton. 2011. Generating text with recurrent neural networks. In *ICML*, pages 1017–1024.

[Turney and Pantel2010] Peter D. Turney and Patrick Pantel. 2010. From frequency to meaning: Vector space models of semantics. *J. Artif. Intell. Res. (JAIR)*, 37:141–188.

[Wang and Manning2012] Sida Wang and Christopher D. Manning. 2012. Baselines and bigrams: Simple, good sentiment and topic classification. In *ACL (2)*, pages 90–94.

[Williams2012] Jason D. Williams. 2012. A belief tracking challenge task for spoken dialog systems. In *NAACL-HLT Workshop on Future Directions and Needs in the Spoken Dialog Community: Tools and Data*, SDCTD '12, pages 23–24, Stroudsburg, PA, USA. Association for Computational Linguistics.

Author Index

Association for Computational Linguistics
209 N. Eighth Street
Stroudsburg, Pennsylvania 18360

CURRAN ASSOCIATES INC
proceedings.com